THE COMPLETE IDIOT'S GUIDE® TO

The Book of Revelation

by Stan Campbell and James S. Bell Jr.

ALPHA

A member of Penguin Group (USA) Inc.

From James Bell: To my wife Margaret, a "revelation" of what love is all about.

Copyright © 2002 by Stan Campbell and James S. Bell Jr.

International Standard Book Number: 0-02-864238-4
Library of Congress Catalog Card Number: 2001097253

06   05   04   8   7   6   5   4   3

Interpretation of the printing code: The rightmost number of the first series of numbers is the year of the book's printing; the rightmost number of the second series of numbers is the number of the book's printing. For example, a printing code of 02-1 shows that the first printing occurred in 2002.

Printed in the United States of America

Note: This publication contains the opinions and ideas of its authors. It is intended to provide helpful and informative material on the subject matter covered. It is sold with the understanding that the authors and publisher are not engaged in rendering professional services in the book. If the reader requires personal assistance or advice, a competent professional should be consulted.

The authors and publisher specifically disclaim any responsibility for any liability, loss, or risk, personal or otherwise, which is incurred as a consequence, directly or indirectly, of the use and application of any of the contents of this book.

Publisher
Marie Butler-Knight

Product Manager
Phil Kitchel

Managing Editor
Jennifer Chisholm

Senior Acquisitions Editor
Renee Wilmeth

Development Editor
Michael Thomas

Production Editor
Katherin Bidwell

Copy Editor
Susan Aufheimer

Illustrator
Jody Schaeffer

Cover Designers
Mike Freeland
Kevin Spear

Book Designers
Scott Cook and Amy Adams of DesignLab

Indexer
Tonya Heard

Layout/Proofreading
Angela Calvert
Kimberly Tucker
John Etchison

Contents at a Glance

Part 1: The Beginning of the End   **1**

1 Hey, Who's Been Messing with the End of My Bible?   3
Here's what you're getting yourself into as you approach the Book of Revelation: apocalyptic style, biblical references, numerous interpretations, and much more.

2 Future Schlock?   11
A consideration of future things, and what you will and won't learn from this book.

3 A Drear John Letter   21
(Revelation 1) An introduction to the Book of Revelation: the author, the setting, and the circumstances at the time of writing.

4 Seven Churches Get a Performance Review   31
(Revelation 2–3) Putting the message of Revelation into context by focusing on who sent it and who was to receive it.

Part 2: The Storm Clouds Gather   **49**

5 Scrolled, Sealed, Delivered   51
(Revelation 4–5) We shift from earth to heaven, where we see angels, thrones, wondrously unusual beings, and a very important scroll.

6 Sealings, Nothing More Than Sealings   61
(Revelation 6–7) The first six seals on the scroll are opened, unleashing the four horsemen of the apocalypse and other dreadful events, but also introducing a special group of 144,000 "sealed" people.

7 Horns of Plenty (of Trouble)   73
(Revelation 8–9) After a silence in heaven, the seventh seal is opened, revealing seven angels with trumpets who initiate a new series of judgments.

8 Witness for the Persecution   85
(Revelation 10–11:14) John eats a (different) scroll, two amazing witnesses appear, a beast is introduced, and a period of three and a half years begins to be emphasized.

9 A Beauty and Some Beasts   95
(Revelation 11:15–13) The seventh trumpet sounds, and major conflict begins involving a red dragon, two beasts, a pregnant woman, the child she delivers, and an archangel. We're also warned about someone represented by the number 666.

10   Where the Grapes of Wrath Are Stored   111
(Revelation 14) Several more significant angels, a return of the 144,000, and a sobering look at the wrath of God as "the earth is harvested" and blood flows.

11   The Bowled and the Beautiful   123
(Revelation 15–16) Seven more plagues invoked by angels with "bowls of wrath," which include a massive war at Armageddon.

12   The Elaborately Dressed, Blood-Drinking, Scarlet-Beast-Riding Prostitute   135
(Revelation 17–18) "Babylon the Great" is represented by an elegant prostitute as well as a glorious city—both of which are brought to great and final ruin.

Part 3: High Noon at the End Times Corral   **149**

13   All Bad Things Must Come to an End   151
(Revelation 19–20) Jesus returns, evil leaders are sentenced to final justice, the dead are judged, and the righteous people participate in a 1,000-year reign of Christ.

14   Imagine There's a Heaven   165
(Revelation 21–22:6) Many of the glories of heaven are revealed, and are promised to those who overcome the sin and evil that will become so rampant.

15   A Real Page-Turner Comes to a Close   177
(Revelation 22:7-21) The Book of Revelation ends with some warnings, yes, but also several surprisingly optimistic invitations.

Part 4: Theology Meets Optometry   **185**

16   Open to Interpretation?   187
Why everyone doesn't come to the same conclusions as to the significance of Revelation, and a preview of some of the traditional interpretations.

17   It's the End of the World and We Missed It?   197
The "preterist" view of Revelation, which interprets described events as being mostly (if not entirely) in our past.

18   Revelation Interpretations: Some Minority Viewpoints   207
Two more interpretations of Revelation (the "historicist" and "idealist" views), as well as a couple of other ways to approach the book.

19   Back to the Future   217
The "futurist" interpretation of Revelation, which looks to the future for a literal fulfillment of the events described.

20 Putting the Elation Back in Revelation   233
*In spite of the many confusing symbols throughout
the Book of Revelation, here are a few things we can
be sure of.*

21 Epilogue: Biding Your Time, or Timing Your Goodbye?   243
*A few final words and warnings about the temptation
to go overboard in regard to prophecy and end-times
teachings.*

Appendixes

A Interpretation Methods   257

B Additional Reading   267

C A Few Web Links for Exploring   271

Index   277

Contents

Part 1: The Beginning of the End   1

1 Hey, Who's Been Messing with the End of My Bible?   3

Read Any Good Book Lately? 3
Where the Jukebox Plays Apocalyptic Bebop 5
   Apocalyptic Lit 101 5
   Apocalyptic Literature Has Style 6
Apocalyptic *and* Apodictic 8
Death, Despair, and Destruction—So Cheer Up! 9
There's a Reason They Call It "Revelation" 9

2 Future Schlock?   11

It's Only a Day Away 12
Hopeful and Fearless? Or Hopeless and Fearful? 13
   Don't Fence Me Out 13
   Eternal Life Insurance 14
   Hope: What's It Worth to You? 14
The Empire Strikes Back 15
   Open Season on the Apostles 15
   Oh Lord, Please Don't Let Me Be Misunderstood 16
Hearsay and Heresy 17
   A Relevant Revelation 18
   A "Revealing" Book 18

3 A Drear John Letter   21

The Beginning of the End 22
The Revelation Salutation 22
Meet the Author 24
My Lord, How You've Changed! 25
The Times They Have a'Changed 27
Same As It Ever Was 28

4 Seven Churches Get a Performance Review 31

Fresh Churches: U Pick Your Own 32
The Church at Ephesus: I Got Those "Lost My
    First Love" Blues 33
  *How Do You Compete with the Church of the Naked
    Goddess?* 33
  Restoring the Relationship 34
The Church at Smyrna: Down but Never Out 35
The Church at Pergamum: In Need of Some
    Good Bouncers..36
The Church at Thyatira: Guild-Y of Too Much
    Tolerance? 38
The Church at Sardis: Dead Church Walking! 40
The Church at Philadelphia: Weak Enough to
    Be Strong 41
The Church at Laodicea: They Make Jesus Want
    to Puke! 43
Why These Seven Churches?...45
Back to the Future 46

Part 2: The Storm Clouds Gather 49

5 Scrolled, Sealed, Delivered 51

Knock, Knock, Knockin' on Heaven's Door 52
Who *Are* Those Guys? 53
Scroll Call..55
Nothing Sheepish About This Lamb 56
The Heavenly Huddle 57

6 Sealings, Nothing More Than Sealings 61

Our Lids Are Sealed 61
God's Housecleaning Seals of Disapproval 62
Are You Sure You Want to Go Through with This? 64
White Clothes and Dark Skies 65
After Six Terrible Seals, 144,000 Good Ones....................67
Tonight We're Going to Party Like It's When
    We Were Alive 69

7 Horns of Plenty (of Trouble)   **73**

  The Calm Before the Storm 74
   Deafening Silence 74
   Censered 75
  Torched by an Angel 76
  Woe, Woe, Woe, Your Boat Sank at Trumpet #2 78
   A "Star" Is Born 79
   Day of the Locust 80
  If You Thought the Locusts Were Bad, Take a
   Look at These Horses! 81
  Time for an Intermission in the Trumpet Recital 83

8 Witness for the Persecution   **85**

  A Mightier Angel, a Tinier Scroll 86
  Got Any Good Recipes for Scroll? 87
  The Man of a Measure 89
  The Power of Two 90
  The Witness Rejection Program 92
  Still Waiting for the Grand Finale 94

9 A Beauty and Some Beasts   **95**

  Who Plays Seventh Trumpet in Handel's Messiah? 96
  And You Think *You* Had a Hard Labor! 97
  The War Above the Worlds 100
  You Go, Girl! (And Go Quickly!) 101
  A New "King of the Beasts" 102
  Two Beasts Are Far Worse Than One...............................105
   A Dragon in Lamb's Clothing......................................106
   Pleased to Meet You. Won't You Guess My Name? 107
  And the Beast Goes On 108

10 Where the Grapes of Wrath Are Stored   **111**

  That's It! You're Grounded 112
  A Thousand Gross Believers 112
  Just Call Them Angels of the Mourning 114
  It's Enough to Make You Sickle 116
  A Topic We'd Wrath-er Avoid 119
   What the Judge Said: The Judgment 119
   Judgment Requires a Battle Hymn 120

11 The Bowled and the Beautiful   **123**

Just the Blame Old Story 124
Last Is Hardly Least 125
Down to the Last Seven Super Bowls 128
A Call to Armageddon...130
Come Hail and High Richter...132

12 The Elaborately Dressed, Blood-Drinking, Scarlet-Beast-Riding Prostitute   **135**

God May Not Be Quick to Judge—But We Are 135
Ride 'Em, Call Girl 136
No Good to the Last Drop *137*
You've Come a Long Way, Babylon *138*
Here It Is—The Full Explanation! 139
The Bigger They Are … 142
Aye, Captain, Thar She Blows … Up............................144
Is That Angel Doing an End Zone Dance? 146

Part 3: High Noon at the End Times Corral   **149**

13 All Bad Things Must Come to an End   **151**

A Hallelujah Chorus 152
Look … Up in the Sky … It's a Horse!? 155
Carrion, My Wayward Sons 156
Today's Forecast: 1,000 Years of Reign 158
After All These Centuries, the Devil Gets Fired 159
No Place to Run, No Place to Hide 162

14 Imagine There's a Heaven   **165**

Above Us Only Sky? 165
No "New"s Is Bad News...167
Urban Renewal 169
Talk About a Happy Meal!...171
Pie in the Sky When We Die? 173

15 A Real Page-Turner Comes to a Close   177

Revelation: The Epilogue 178
Hold On, I'm Coming 179
Famous Last Words 181

Part 4: Theology Meets Optometry   185

16 Open to Interpretation?   187

Call Me Confused 188
The Book of Revelation: Essential or Optional? 189
Life's a Picnic ... or Should That Be "Panic"? 189
Be Prepared 190
Reviewing the Viewing 190
The "Rapture" 191
Jesus' Predictions About the End of the Age 192
Old Testament Prophecy 193
Other Promises 193
For What It's Worth ... .194
So Many Different Views 194
New Discoveries 195
Multiple Layers 195

17 It's the End of the World and We Missed It?   197

When the Temple Topples ... .198
Revelation Through a Preterist Lens 199
Where's Jesus? 201
Help from the Historians 202
Where Preterists Disagree 203
Going on a Bad Date? 204
Case Closed? 205

**18 Revelation Interpretations: Some Minority
Viewpoints   207**

A Roadmap of Human History? (Historicism) 208
*Pages of History and Pages of Revelation: One and
the Same?* 208
Churchistory: An Intersection of Major Concepts 209
Historicism Loses Ground 210

Can't You Tell Symbolism When You See It?
(Idealism) 211
Other Perspectives 213
The Play's the Thing? (The Dramatic Approach) 213
What You Talkin' About, John? (The Literary-
Analytical Approach) 214
The Final Four 214

19 Back to the Future   217

Anticipation, It's Making Me Wait 218
Revelation: Both Sensational and Dispensational? 220
Here's One Way of Looking at It ... .222
Gone Today, Here Tomorrow 223
Good News, Bad News for Jews (So What's New?) 225
What in the Millennium Is Going On Here? 227
Premillennialism 228
Postmillennialism 228
Amillennialism 229
A Rubik's Cube of Options! 229
One More Issue to Get Crypt Up On 230
Authors' Disclaimers 231

20 Putting the Elation Back in Revelation   233

Why Bother? 234
What Do You Know? 235
The Age-Old Conflict Between Good and Evil Will
Continue to the End 235
No Matter How Grim the Situation Gets, Good
Will Triumph 235
People Have Choices 236
Choices Have Results—Sometimes Eternal Ones 236
God Is More Patient Than We Give Him Credit For 237
We Who Are About to Screw Up Salute You! 237
Revelationmania vs. Revelationphobia 238
Now What? 239

21 Epilogue: Biding Your Time, or Timing Your Goodbye? **243**

When Faith Becomes Fantastic (and Fatal)
Fanaticism 244
Mr. Jones and Me Look into the Future 244
Good Reason to Follow 245
A Shift of Emphasis 245
Misled to Death 245
Gateway to Heaven? 246
The Two and Their Spaceship...................................247
Delusion Goes High-Tech 247
Wrong Gate, but Too Late 248
Predicting the Future on a Date-to-Date Basis 248
*Doug Clark: Jumpin' Jupiter, the World's Gonna
End, Eh!*...249
*Edgar Whisenant: Rapture Report for Year
(Fill in Blank)* 250
Harold Camping: Still Ready After All These Years 251
Jack Van Impe: Pushing Back the Deadline.....................251
Hal Lindsey: In a Class of His Own 252
Some Day My Prince of Peace Will Come 252
A Few Rules of Thumb 253
Check the Source 254
Check the Track Record 254
Check the Doctrine 254
Check the Numbers 255
Remain Open to Truth 255

Appendixes

A Interpretation Methods **257**

B Additional Reading **267**

C A Few Web Links for Exploring **271**

Index **277**

Foreword

Of all biblical texts, prophetic books are the most enigmatic. There are several reasons for this.

First, the literature speaks of future things, and therefore judgments about them are more difficult to confirm. Interpretations cannot be verified with certainty. The complexities to be found in Revelation therefore make the interpreter's work difficult. Interpretation must be done with patience and humility. The rush to judgment is incautious.

Second, the language is often a hybrid of propositions and figurative statements. This is, in part, due to the subject matter. The word *definition* means "of the finite." We define things by their limitations and function. A thing must be small enough to wrap words around it if it is to be defined. But then, how do we define God? If he is infinite, he defies the categories of definition. This necessitates the use of metaphors, similes, figures of speech, parables, and the like. Prophetic texts revealing God's future plans and actions would necessarily have to accommodate themselves to this kind of figurative language.

Third, it is important to note that biblical writers recording the future are describing things and events for which words, at the time of writing, may not have existed. How might a person living in biblical times write about unimaginable things like an airplane or a television? This multiplies the difficulty of the writer's task and the need to use figurative language. It also compounds the task of the interpreter.

Nevertheless, since Revelation has been written it would appear that the writer believed his readers could understand something of these future events and therefore considered that what he wrote was, at least in part, accessible to them.

At a time in history when there is much interest in the future, as evidenced by popular culture and the best-selling *Left Behind* series, *The Complete Idiot's Guide to the Book of Revelation* clarifies as much as possible one of the most fascinating books of the Bible. The approach given is to develop a clear outline for the book by following the obvious clues that the Book of Revelation itself provides. The authors also consider the various interpretations and schools of thought about the book, realistically guiding the reader in considering how to make the most sense of the text.

Throughout history people have often thought that they lived in "the last days." We can claim with confidence that no one was saying a thousand years ago that he was living in the Middle Ages. Certainly some people from every age have believed that theirs was the final hour of history. And though the climax of the ages has eluded all who have preceded this hour, eventually one generation will live at that unique moment. Perhaps it will come in the lifetime of the readers of this book. But whether it should come for us to see or not, *The Complete Idiot's Guide to the Book of Revelation* makes it clear that there is still much in prophetic literature that is relevant for us today.

—Jerry Root

Jerry Root is a professor of Christian Education at Wheaton College.

Introduction

When Jesus was asked about the signs of the end times, he warned of things such as spiritual imposters, earthquakes, famines, wars and rumors of wars, and other grim things. One thing not on his list, however, was the glut of books and movies loosely based on the biblical forecast of what was supposed to happen in the future.

You've probably seen a lot of these titles. Jerry Jenkins's and Tim LaHaye's *Left Behind* series is perennially on the bestsellers lists. *The Chronicles of Narnia* series by C.S. Lewis (which concludes with *The Last Battle*) has been a favorite of children for decades. Movies such as *The Seventh Seal, The Seventh Sign, End of Days, The Omen,* and others make ample references to the end of the world, Satan, death personified, and other apocalyptic images from the Bible—particularly from the Book of Revelation.

But as you watch Arnold Schwarzenegger doing battle with Satan to keep him from taking a bride before the turn of the century, you may be left pondering, "I wonder where *this* is in the Bible?" Hollywood, famous for rewriting endings, has taken quite a few liberties in presenting last-days/end-times amusements. Some of us enjoy the show and go home; others have our curiosity piqued and begin to wonder just what the Book of Revelation *does* say about the future.

And that's where this book comes in. Whether you're merely a little curious as to biblical prophecy and predictions, or whether you're looking for source material to help you better understand the fiction you've been reading, this book is for you. Even without the plethora of modern books and movies it inspires, the Book of Revelation is a wonderfully intriguing and rewarding work in itself.

What You Will Find in This Book

Part 1: "The Beginning of the End." The Book of Revelation may be at the end of the Bible, and it may be about the end of the world, but we have to begin somewhere. This section starts you off with some background and relevant context, and then starts you through the Book of Revelation itself.

Part 2: "The Storm Clouds Gather." You won't get far in the Book of Revelation before you encounter a lot of dark and foreboding content. Prepare yourself. It will last a while.

Part 3: "High Noon at the End Times Corral." As the Book of Revelation continues, the scene it describes just keeps getting worse and worse. Then suddenly it takes a turn and you discover a big finish that makes you glad you made it all the way to the end.

Part 4: "Theology Meets Optometry." When interpreting the Book of Revelation, people use several different "lenses" by which to view the material. We'll examine several basic interpretations and then you can begin to ask yourself, "Which is clearer, #1 or #2? This one or that one?"

The authors are not promising you'll understand all the intricacies of Revelation after a cursory reading of this *Complete Idiot's Guide*. We're not even suggesting you'll *ever* understand it fully. Rather, what we hope to accomplish is to make you more aware of what is actual biblical prophecy, and what is clearly fiction. Rather than being dependent on others for your information (and wondering how much they really know), *you* will become an authoritative source.

What you *won't* find in this book is a clear outline and timetable of what is going to happen in your future. The end times are described in great detail, though the presentation is largely symbolic. Consequently, there are various interpretations. We will deal with a lot of the symbols and options, but you will probably be disappointed if you're looking for black-and-white answers to all your questions.

Is slogging through the Book of Revelation worth your time? We think so. You'll find a lot of things that have become literary cornerstones: the four horsemen of the apocalypse, the seven seals, figures playing harps in heaven, the antichrist (though not by this title), that mysterious number 666, the pearly gates of heaven, streets of gold, and much more. Whether or not you're searching from a spiritual perspective, the contents of Revelation are still very much relevant from a cultural/literary perspective.

A Few Things You Need to Know

Before we begin, we need to make a few things clear. For example …

> ➤ **The Book of Revelation is apocalyptic and symbolic.** We will explain these terms and their significance in Chapter 1. Just don't expect an "easy read" as you peruse its pages. After a couple of chapters preparing you for what to expect, we will go straight through Revelation, examining the action and the symbols used, as if you've never read it before. To the best of our abilities, we will stay focused on what we're being told and will resist making bold speculations about what *might* be. (At times, however, a bit of speculation is necessary.)

> ➤ **The Book of Revelation is biblical.** Not only is Revelation in the Bible, but it also contains numerous references to *other* Bible stories, themes, and prophecies. Consequently, in order to understand Revelation, we will at times need to explore those references.

> ➤ **The Book of Revelation is not necessarily chronological.** Many portions are, but we will get to sections that are parenthetical to the ongoing action, or that go back and overlap events we've already seen. For example, the text might follow the action of what's going on in heaven, and then rewind a bit to reveal what has been happening on earth in the meantime.

> ➤ **The Book of Revelation tells a story.** Whether the story is primarily literal or symbolic is a matter of interpretation. However, for editorial purposes, the authors will comment on the biblical text as if the action described is literally

taking place. We will offer occasional reminders that some people see the entire Book of Revelation as symbolic, but it will certainly get tiring if we bring up the point at every shift of the action. That's why we're telling you now.

➤ **The Book of Revelation has numerous traditional interpretations.** For example, when the text says that Satan will be bound for 1,000 years, does that mean the devil will be literally imprisoned, or merely that his influence is not so strong for a period of time? Is the thousand years a literal millennium as we know it, or a symbolic length of time? These (and thousands of other) questions lead to the various interpretations. Only after going through the entire Book of Revelation will we begin to examine these interpretations, ordering the events in a number of different ways to let you determine what makes the most sense to *you*.

Sidebar Support

The running text of this book will generally follow the flow of the Book of Revelation with observations about the contents. But to bring a bit more clarity to our pursuit of information are the following sidebars that will pop up with regularity throughout the book.

A Bright Spot

As we get deeper into the Book of Revelation, it's easy to get bogged down in the violence and terror it portrays. But if we look closely, we're never very far from a bright and shining source of hope and optimism. We will attempt to highlight a number of these "encouragements" tucked away in the darkness of the running text.

Flashback

The Book of Revelation is not a stand-alone work. It is in the Bible for a reason. And *if* we want to have any hope of understanding it and interpreting it properly, we need some context and insight from other biblical sources. These Flashback sidebars will contain helpful clues from other portions of the Bible—both Old Testament and New Testament.

Apoca-Lips Now

Lots of people have comments and opinions concerning the end times and other themes found in the Book of Revelation. We will spotlight a number of their quotes throughout this book. The authors don't necessarily endorse all these opinions, but offer them for variety.

Clanging Symbols

Revelation is marked by symbolism. As we come across various symbols, many will be clear while others are much more obscure. This sidebar will dwell on the importance of the symbol and help clarify its significance.

We Couldn't Have Done It Without ...

The authors would like to thank everyone at Alpha Books who made this a better book than it started out to be:

Renee Wilmeth, acquisitions editor, who saw a need for a subject like this one in the often uncertain times we live in;

Michael Thomas, development editor, who tactfully let us know whenever our original efforts became a bit too obscure, irrelevant, or unclear;

Katherin Bidwell, production editor, who valiantly attempted to keep us on schedule;

Susan Aufheimer, copy editor, who literally read between the lines to catch our mistakes (and whom we kept quite busy);

The dozens of other unseen and usually unattributed contributors at every publishing house: artists, designers, warehouse employees (where Stan got his start in publishing), and all the rest;

And finally, to every author's favorite employee (the individual in accounting who cuts the checks), may your health increase and your house be blessed.

In addition, if you enjoy the quotations we use throughout the book, we would like to recommend a spunky little book titled *A Portable Apocalypse: A Quotable Companion to the End of the World* (compiled and edited by Allan Appel, Riverhead Books, New York, 1999). In addition to our usual resources (*Bartlett's Familiar Quotations* and numerous others), we borrowed several quotations from *A Portable Apocalypse* and think you might also enjoy many we didn't use.

What's in It for You?

In this trip through the remarkable Book of Revelation, the authors are not trying to come up with any strange new interpretations or secret insights. (The Book of Revelation ends with a curse on those who indiscriminately add to what's there, or who leave out portions!) Rather, we want to work as reporters to strip away the myths connected with Revelation and to help you understand some of the more common interpretations that have made the most sense to Bible scholars throughout the ages. We're going to attempt to stick closely to what was written late in the first century and has been passed along since then.

A reading of Revelation might not reveal the day you're going to die or the name of the person you're going to marry, but it won't be a waste of time. While it may not be as precise as you might want it to be, neither is it as complicated as a lot of people suppose. By the time you get through this book, we feel fairly certain that you will have gleaned a lot of useful information—both spiritual and practical.

If not, well, it's not the end of the world ... or *is* it?

Special Thanks to the Technical Reviewer

The Complete Idiot's Guide to the Book of Revelation was reviewed by an expert who double-checked the accuracy of what you'll learn here, to help us ensure that this book gives you everything you need to know about Revelation. Special thanks are extended to Joris Heise.

Currently a special education teacher of retarded adolescents in the Dayton Public Schools and a part-time instructor of Classical Literature and Great Books in the Dayton, Ohio, area, Joris John Heise has been a professor of Biblical Theology in a seminary.

Trademarks

All terms mentioned in this book that are known to be or are suspected of being trademarks or service marks have been appropriately capitalized. Alpha Books and Penguin Group (USA) Inc., cannot attest to the accuracy of this information. Use of a term in this book should not be regarded as affecting the validity of any trademark or service mark.

Part 1

The Beginning of the End

You've probably heard at least a dozen versions of how the world will end, all of which include death, destruction, fire from heaven, and more. You've seen the Hollywood accounts of the earth being destroyed by aliens, smashed by asteroids, or erupting to bury everything in molten lava and ash. And then there are all those people droning on about how the end is near and everyone better get ready. If you aren't jittery enough already, those guys can give you a major case of the heebie-jeebies.

We've developed this book to help guide you through the wonders and warnings that are recorded in the biblical Book of Revelation. Our first two chapters provide some history and background about the author and the times he lived in. Then we'll jump right into the opening portion of Revelation, which consists of seven letters to seven churches.

We hope you'll stop quivering long enough to have some fun as you journey through this amazing and unique book from the Bible!

Chapter 1

Hey, Who's Been Messing with the End of My Bible?

In This Chapter

➤ How the Book of Revelation is unique among the Bible's books

➤ The distinctive nature and characteristics of apocalyptic literature

➤ Various ways to approach the Book of Revelation

➤ How to enjoy the search when truth appears to be hidden

When you get a new car, it's natural to want to toss the owner's manual into the glove compartment and hit the road right away. If you don't bother reading the basic information, however, you risk flashing your bright lights in someone's eyes while attempting to turn on your windshield wipers, not knowing how to change a tire in an emergency, or getting into other potentially hazardous situations that might have been avoided.

Similarly, the authors realize you bought this book because you're ready to delve into the complex Book of Revelation. But instead of rushing headlong into the text, we want to give you a little advance notice of what you can expect.

Read Any Good Book Lately?

Let's suppose that in the world's strangest twist of fate, you find yourself locked in a room in a secluded hotel for a week. The owner has been called away for an emergency, your family is elsewhere, and no one else appears to be staying there. You have a well-stocked minibar and a working bathroom, so you won't starve or explode, even though you have to drink the Diet Pepsi warm. (Did we mention a storm has knocked out the phone lines and electricity as well?) With no radio or TV, and nothing else to do, you pick up the apparently never-opened Gideon's Bible and begin to read.

To be honest, you've always wanted to know more about the Bible, but the time was never right. Now you have no other options. And to your surprise, it's actually a pretty good book. Genesis and Exodus start out with a lot of interesting stories. Leviticus, Numbers, and Deuteronomy are a bit long for your taste, but contain some intriguing laws about diet, mildew, skin disease, sexual taboos, and such. Joshua picks up the action again, and in Judges you finally figure out who that Gideon guy is who keeps leaving Bibles lying around.

The poetry of Psalms and practicality of Proverbs have a different and refreshing tone. The prophetic books—Isaiah to Malachi—while containing more than a few potent warnings and promises, are quite lengthy, and because no one's looking you decide to skim quickly to the New Testament.

The gospels (Matthew, Mark, Luke, and John) are like a breath of fresh air—parables, conversations, miracles, love and betrayal, and everything you want in good reading material. The Book of Acts is a concise history of the early church, without being at all dry. The letters that follow—Romans to Jude—contain a lot of good advice for daily living (and besides, most are short enough to keep you motivated as you approach the end).

After all your reading and determination to be able to say you've read the entire Bible, you can hardly wait to see how everything turns out. But what you find in the Book of Revelation is so freakishly odd that you can hardly believe it belongs in the Bible—much less as the culmination of everything else. It seems as if some kids have gotten hold of the original Bible and replaced holy Scripture with something out of Dungeons and Dragons!

Indeed, Revelation does speak of dragons, as well as multiheaded beings, figures who resemble previously killed sheep, prostitutes riding beasts while drinking blood, strange horsemen, super locusts that can't be stopped with any amount of pesticide, angels pouring out bowls of destruction on the earth, and much, much more. Gone is the clear story line of the Bible, replaced with some cryptic, mysterious language that seemingly requires a heavenly translator, if not a magic decoder ring as well.

Apoca-Lips Now

"If the world has not approached its end, it has reached a major watershed in history, equal in history to the turn from the Middle Ages to the Renaissance. It will demand from us a spiritual blaze .... No one on earth has any other way left but—upward."

—Aleksandr Solzhenitsyn

Where the Jukebox Plays Apocalyptic Bebop

Welcome to the wonderful world of apocalyptic literature. Many people have had similar experiences upon confronting the Book of Revelation for the first time. Nobody "gets it" on the first reading—or the 500th, for that matter. What you can learn about Revelation depends on how much you want to work at figuring it out. Some people, upon finally being freed from their hotel-room cell, would return the Bible to the drawer, never to deal with the confusion of Revelation again. Others would drop the Bible into their luggage and take it home for future reading—or better yet, would seek out a good study Bible and/or commentaries to get help from people who may have spent their lifetimes struggling with the myriad mysteries contained in the Bible's final book.

And without a doubt, those who approach the Book of Revelation *after* reading the rest of the Bible have a distinct advantage over someone who wants to *start* with Revelation. There's a reason it's last in the Bible. You will see as we go through this book that we'll keep bouncing back to many, many references in both the Old and New Testaments to provide key clues to better understanding the Book of Revelation.

Apoca-Lips Now

"Had the Bible been in clear straightforward language, had the ambiguities and contradictions been edited out, and had the language been constantly modernised to accord with contemporary taste it would almost certainly have been a work of lesser influence."

—John Kenneth Galbraith

Apocalyptic Lit 101

As it turns out, the biblical Book of Revelation isn't the only place you'll find what's called apocalyptic literature. Like poetry, apocalyptic is a specific writing style. The word itself derives from the Greek *apokalypsis,* meaning unveiling or revelation. However, the writing style is marked by so much symbolism that in a lot of cases you probably won't feel much is being revealed.

Numerous Jewish and Christian writings have been found written in this apocalyptic style that dates back to the period between about 200 B.C.E. and 200 C.E. Much of the Bible was written during this period, but Revelation contains essentially all of the portions considered apocalyptic. (The other significant section is Daniel 7–12 in the Old Testament, but that's where you started skimming.)

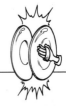

Clanging Symbols

In the last half of his book (chapters 7–12), Daniel writes about visions of beasts, a figure known as the Ancient of Days, 70 "sevens" of time, resurrection, and other symbols that will later be important in helping us understand the events described in the Book of Revelation.

Some Bible scholars have more respect for the apocalyptic style than others, believing that it arises out of biblical prophecy. In fact, many writers of apocalyptic literature used pen names of prominent Old Testament figures (such as Adam, Moses, Daniel, Ezra, and others). Since these works were being written at a time when respect for God's prophets was at an all-time low, the apocalyptic authors probably were attempting to achieve a better degree of credibility by latching onto the reputations of those who were already revered by the people.

Flashback

Even though prophets may seldom have received the credit they were due, biblical prophecy was *supposed* to be respected as a clear message from God. Here's how the prophet Amos explained it: "When a trumpet sounds in a city, do not the people tremble? When disaster comes to a city, has not the Lord caused it? Surely the Sovereign Lord does nothing without revealing his plan to his servants the prophets. The lion has roared—who will not fear? The Sovereign Lord has spoken—who can but prophesy?" (Amos 3:6–8).

Just as people startle at the sound of a lion roaring nearby or a trumpet blast warning of danger, they were expected to respond to what the prophets had to say.

The differences between prophetic and apocalyptic writings are subtle, but significant. The prophets were like master chefs, weaving current ingredients of sin and salvation into God's message for the future. Their perception was that while things would be imperfect and difficult for a while, the future was assured to rise up and be rosy for those who placed their faith in God.

Apocalyptic writers, in contrast, dealt with the future in much more brash and abrupt terms—more in the style of energetic Creole chef Emeril Lagasse than the more subdued French chef Julia Child: "*Bam!* The future will unexpectedly come slamming into the present, and it's not going to be pretty!"

Apocalyptic Literature Has Style

When you begin to get into details of philosophy, accuracy, and interpretation of much apocalyptic literature, you get a lot of different opinions. You could lock a bunch of scholars in a room and the end of the world would probably come and go before they agreed on any of the specifics of what would take place at the end of the world.

But in general, apocalyptic literature has a unique style that incorporates the following characteristics:

➤ **What to expect in the future.** The writers discuss their alleged revelations of what God has told them will happen. Such insight frequently comes through dreams, visions, or journeys to heaven where incredible things are witnessed first-hand. Predictions are made, which many times were simply a rewriting of history as the present-day writer projected himself into the past and wrote about what would happen (much of which had already taken place). Then, to keep things juicy, he would usually include a section about the end of the world.

➤ **Pseudonyms of the authors.** As we have said, many writers assumed names of long-ago religious figures, even though the writing was done much nearer to New Testament times. Some people believed God had already said everything he had to say through the Old Testament prophets, and few people were willing to go "on record" with a newer prophecy using their own names.

➤ **Symbolism.** Another way to keep from getting nailed on something that didn't come true was the heavy use of symbols that could be interpreted in more than one way.

➤ **Historical "chapters."** Apocalyptic literature typically divides history into periods, giving rise to the concept that it follows a pre-established plan.

➤ **Expectation of better things.** In spite of the gloom and doom of apocalyptic literature, at the end is usually the establishment of the reign of God, a reward for those who have been faithful.

Apoca-Lips Now

"God gave ... the Prophecies of the Old Testament, not to gratify men's curiosities by enabling them to foreknow things, but that after they were fulfilled they might be interpreted by the event, and his own Providence, not the Interpreters, be then manifested thereby to the world."

—Isaac Newton

Apoca-Lips Now

"The vast bulk of the population believe that morality depends entirely on revelation; and if a doubt could be raised ... men would think they were at liberty to steal, and women would consider themselves absolved from the restraints of chastity."

—John Campbell

Some people list other characteristics of apocalyptic literature, but these are the widespread traits that will provide a basis of what to expect.

Apocalyptic *and* Apodictic

With all the apocalyptic and apocryphal (questionable) literature written during the same period, why is it that only a portion of Daniel and the Book of Revelation are included in official Scripture? Among other reasons, both Daniel and John (the author of Revelation) went on record with their real names. They claimed to be communicating genuine interactions with God, and weren't trying to hide behind pseudonyms or anonymity. So according to these biblical authors, as well as the committees that, over the centuries, verified their writings as inspired, their works were not only apocalyptic, but apodictic (incontrovertible) as well.

In fact, we'll see that the whole of the Book of Revelation was intended to be circulated to lots of people with John's credentials as someone who had known Jesus as a disciple and therefore could be trusted. In contrast, many other apocalyptic writings were literary works that simulated prophecy, but clearly weren't genuine looks into the future.

Yet because the Book of Revelation was written in this unusual style (at least, in comparison to most of the rest of the Bible), it has always been controversial. Many people resisted having it included in the official canon of Scripture, but it eventually was accepted. Still, it continues to provoke controversy and debate, and we may not be much closer to understanding it in the twenty-first century than its original readers were.

Whatever else we might think about Revelation and other apocalyptic works, they offered new possibilities to their readers. Most of the prior religious works had done little to expand the thinking of people beyond this earthly life. The "biggie" blessings of God were perceived to be long life, comfort, children to care for us in our old age, and a minimum of crop failures. And to be sure, those things were highly prized by most people.

But with the tele-future lens of apocalyptic literature, people started envisioning a future world with a greater degree of certainty. They were shown the potential of hanging around with angels and even living within proximity of God's throne. As good as the blessings of *this* world can be, they were intrigued that the future promised even better things.

A Bright Spot

Apocalyptic literature in general, and the Book of Revelation specifically, presents a spectacular quality of life (ultimately) in the future. If faced with terrible suffering in this world—even the worst that might happen—we are never without hope if we believe that one blow of a sword or fatal defeat in the arena takes us from the pain of the here and now to the sheer glory of forever.

Death, Despair, and Destruction—So Cheer Up!

So in spite of the harsh and foreboding tone of much apocalyptic literature, its purpose was to provide a degree of consolation for its readers. This is true of Revelation as well as other noncanonical religious works, yet Revelation is distinct in many ways.

While the author of Revelation is the apostle John, he makes it clear that his role is merely that of scribe. He never purports to be the source of the wisdom and warnings he writes about. Indeed, the first five words of his book are, "The revelation of Jesus Christ." John merely takes dictation for a brilliant and intimidating manifestation of Jesus, and he passes along the things he sees and hears (except in a few cases where he is forbidden to do so).

He records an account of times to come that from all appearances seem to be God-forsaken. Yet the point of the writing, as we will see, is to show exactly the opposite—to clue the readers to the fact that God is behind everything that is taking place.

If any comfort is to be derived from Revelation at all, it will come from acknowledging that the chaos taking place all around us is not the result of futile and random events. The things that are good and beautiful have a source. The things that are ugly and evil have a source as well. The good and evil are in perpetual conflict, and we are caught in the middle.

If we perceive good and evil to be fatalistic (predetermined and inevitable), we are led to certain perceptions and expectations from life. If we perceive good and evil to be merely random occurrences, we are led to another perspective. But if we believe those events to be intentional, whether from the God of love or the father of lies, we tend to find ourselves choosing sides and supporting one source or the other. And while we might not understand or endorse everything going on, we find that our lives make more sense than before. Perhaps, then, we can continue our search for answers without giving up.

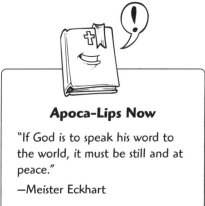

Apoca-Lips Now

"If God is to speak his word to the world, it must be still and at peace."

—Meister Eckhart

There's a Reason They Call It "Revelation"

As we turn our attention to Revelation, we must always remember that we are now dealing with apocalyptic literature. Many truths in Scripture are clear and plain, nicely wrapped up in shiny paper and a bow. They are dropped in our laps, and like kids at Christmas we joyfully receive what we have been given. Revelation won't be that way—at least, not most of the time. While the book contains much truth, hope, and insight for people—especially believers—those truths aren't always clear.

Apoca-Lips Now

"Instead of complaining that God had hidden himself, you will give him thanks for having re-vealed so much of himself."

—Blaise Pascal

When reading Revelation, discovering truth is less like opening a Christmas present and more like going on an Easter egg hunt. Many of its secrets are well-hidden, and we will probably leave more undiscovered than we find. Yet uncovering concealed truths can be very rewarding if you're prepared to enjoy the search.

As a final optimistic note, we need to remember that as confused as we might get from time to time, the book is called "Revelation" because it is a revealing of things previously hidden or kept secret. It is the hope of the authors that much is revealed to you as you turn your attention to the Book of Revelation. And if it's not too much to wish for, we hope that in the midst of the revealing that you'll do a bit of reveling as well.

The Least You Need to Know

➤ Apocalyptic literature is highly symbolic, and therefore the Book of Revelation must be treated differently than most other parts of Scripture.

➤ The Book of Revelation is not a stand-alone work, and it benefits by being viewed in context with other biblical prophecies and passages.

➤ In spite of all the doom and gloom associated with apocalyptic literature, the result is usually insight into eternal rewards and God's ultimate triumph over evil.

➤ If you're willing, your perusal of the Book of Revelation can be a lot of fun.

Chapter 2

Future Schlock?

> **In This Chapter**
>
> ➤ A few explanations for the widespread desire to know the future
>
> ➤ The value of learning what we can about things to come
>
> ➤ Setting the scene for the world and the church when Revelation was written
>
> ➤ A few cautions about attempting to use the Book of Revelation as a window to the future

As a society, we seem to be quickly losing touch with the past ... and even the present. Just watch Jay Leno walk around interviewing people on the street. They can't come up with the current secretary of state, the capital of Missouri, or who's buried in Grant's tomb. Even many game-show contestants—the very ones who consider themselves smarter than the average citizen—don't seem to do much better.

We know woefully little about people who should be our closest relatives. We don't know much, if anything, about our neighbors. If something happened further back than yesterday, we consider it old news and write it off as ancient history. Wars, floods, earthquakes, and such are rattling our world every day, but we hardly notice if it's not on our street. The scenes on the evening news look pretty much the same, day to day, week to week. Why pay attention? After all, another disaster will just come along tomorrow.

Yet our fascination with the *future* seems unquenchable, and each year we spend billions of dollars seeking hints (or even empty promises) about what to expect. What's all the fuss about, anyway? Let's find out.

It's Only a Day Away

Lack of clarity doesn't seem to be a problem. If it's precise facts about the future people seek, then how do we explain the popularity of horoscopes? Some people read their horoscopes faithfully, and many put significant stock in those predictions. Yet you never seem to find a horoscope that says, "Tomorrow at 3:37 P.M. you will meet a brown-haired, blue-eyed man who, while asking you the time, will step on your toe and then ask you to dinner." Instead, we read things more like, "Meeting a stranger leads to unexpected developments." That same horoscope supposedly applies to every single person born within a 30-day period, yet that's good enough for a lot of us. Maybe, just maybe, we can capture a glimpse of what will happen tomorrow.

And besides horoscopes we have other options: tarot cards, crystal balls, palm readers, tea leaves, and even fortune cookies. Or we can go back to the old ways of oracles and examining sheep intestines. As we consider society's fascination with the future, it should come as no surprise that perennially best-selling "toys" are Ouija Boards and Magic 8-Balls.

But why? After all these options and the pursuit of what may or may not happen, we are rarely if ever *promised* anything. More often than not, we get a response along the lines of, "Reply hazy. Please try again later." Yet lots of us keep going back again and again.

Even many of us who don't take such fortune-telling diversions seriously still enjoy speculating about what *might* happen. Maybe we have Jules Verne to blame. In the mid- to late-1800s, he wrote about journeying to the center of the earth, going 20,000 leagues under the sea, and trekking from the earth to the moon. In doing so, he foresaw the invention of the submarine, the television, and the Aqua-lung—and he planted the concept of space travel in people's minds. Since then, many others have carried on the grand tradition of peering into the future, not to declare what *will* be, but rather what *might* be. And the fascination continues to grow about all things future.

Apoca-Lips Now

"*Future,* n. That period of time in which our affairs prosper, our friends are true and our happiness is assured."

—Ambrose Bierce

Apoca-Lips Now

"Those who cannot remember the past are condemned to repeat it."

—George Santayana

Flashback

From a biblical perspective, people are supposed to be picky about where they get their predictions. Prophets whose predictions didn't come true were to be considered phonies and put to death (Deuteronomy 18:17–22). And occult practices were big no-nos: "Let no one be found among you who sacrifices his son or daughter in the fire, who practices divination or sorcery, interprets omens, engages in witchcraft, or casts spells, or who is a medium or spiritist or who consults the dead. Anyone who does these things is detestable to the Lord" (Deuteronomy 18:10–12).

Hopeful and Fearless? Or Hopeless and Fearful?

After reading Chapter 1, "Hey, Who's Been Messing with the End of My Bible?" and our discussion of apocalyptic literature, you might wonder why anyone would ever put stock in something so strange and nonspecific. Why do so many people attempt to read between the lines in Revelation seeking clues for what lies ahead? After all, if we aren't getting any "for sure" insights into future events, why bother?

Don't Fence Me Out

One reason may be that we can hardly stand to think that someone knows something we don't. From the time we are children, we learn to detest when someone whispers secrets to someone else, and we're left out of the loop. Even adults in the business world desire to be among the first to know what rolls off the grapevine. It may only be gossip, but there's value in being the source rather than one of the last to hear of it.

Yet even the best-informed know-it-alls are hard-pressed to know the future. Stories abound of stock-market wizards who are millionaires one day and destitute the next, due to an unexpected turn of the future. It is sometimes hypothesized that the CEO of Buggy Whip Industries might have been planning a major expansion when Henry Ford rolled out his first Model T's.

More recently, you might recall the hubbub around the Y2K scare at the turn of the century. The facts were sketchy: Some of the existing computer chips would not register the correct date, and might respond peculiarly. No one knew for sure. Yet out of those uncertain facts came a tremendous worldwide fear that planes would fall from the sky, nuclear weapons would arm themselves and launch like Fourth-of-July fireworks, banks would fail, and worse. In response, some people stocked up on food and water (weapons optional), and headed for remote shelters. Even many levelheaded people who witnessed such panicked behavior were rattled by the mass fear and uncertainty. Many others seemed so sure of a coming catastrophe, and the rest of us didn't want to be caught unawares.

Eternal Life Insurance

When you add a spiritual level on top of the usual confusion about the future, the situation intensifies. If, for example, someone comes along and says that Jesus is supposed to return on a particular date, we tend to scoff at first. But if that person develops a large following who all declare that one's eternal destination depends on making the proper choice, the pressure may become too intense for many people. Better safe than sorry, right?

Apoca-Lips Now

"Our faith in the present dies out long before our faith in the future."

—Ruth Benedict, quoted by Margaret Mead

When it comes to future events, we are taught to hedge our bets. We buy life insurance because we know we won't live forever. But we also buy business insurance, home insurance, fire insurance, car insurance, and other things "just in case." We don't expect the worst, yet we can't ignore the possibility. When religion becomes a priority, we then tend to think in terms of eternal-life insurance. Many people are "just in case" believers. Deep in their hearts they think most religious doctrines are just a lot of hokum, yet on the off chance that they hear a trumpet sound in the heavens tomorrow, they want to be able to provide official certification of their "faith."

Hope: What's It Worth to You?

So *fear* is one big motivation for wanting to know about the future. But a second reason for the intense desire is probably even more common: We want *hope*. Most of us have lived through some pretty wonderful times, and many of us have faced some awful times as well. Our current situation is seldom as perfect as we might like, yet we fear changes. We can hope and pray for better days, yet we simultaneously fear that the good times will tank and we'll find ourselves worse off than before.

Apoca-Lips Now

"Look not mournfully into the Past. It comes not back again. Wisely improve the Present. It is thine. Go forth to meet the shadowy Future, without fear, and with a manly heart."

—Henry Wadsworth Longfellow

So we pursue clues that offer hope. We no longer need to leave home to find it, either. Our psychic friends are only a phone call away, and are glad to hold out hope for us at $4.99 a minute, or we can turn to the Internet to find equivalent services. Some TV evangelists have caught on as well, and offer certain blessings in direct proportion to your "gifts" to their ministries. Some call it God, some call it special knowledge, and others call it by other names—but in many cases they have discovered that the product that brings in the profits is *hope*. When the past has been less than desirable and the present is a bit shaky, we will pay good money to hear someone tell us the future holds better things.

The Empire Strikes Back

We may think *we* have it bad, but if anyone needed hope, it was the believers of the first century. The good news was that Jesus had come, claiming to be God and backing his claims with bold new truths, powerful miracles, and unprecedented love for those who were not among the rich and influential of their day. The bad news, or so it would seem, was that Jesus had been crucified by the Romans. He was gone, but the Roman Empire was still there.

Since Jesus hadn't done anything about Roman dominance, a group of activist Jews stepped up their opposition. Bad move. They were no match for the Romans, and an ongoing skirmish sent many Jews into hiding and resulted in the destruction of their Temple in 70 C.E. Meanwhile, Christians weren't faring much better under the reign of Nero (54–68 C.E.).

As a result, many believers scattered from Jerusalem, where they had been assembled, to remote areas. The church quickly went from being a large, collective body to a number of smaller groups, yet continued to do surprisingly well. The apostles remained in Jerusalem and began to send out teams to support the various churches.

Apoca-Lips Now

"Their death was made a matter of sport; they were covered in wild beasts' skins and torn to pieces by dogs; or were fastened to crosses and set on fire in order to serve as torches by night .... It was felt that they were being sacrificed not for the common good, but to gratify the savagery of one man [Nero]."

—Tacitus, a first-century historian writing about the fate of the Christians

Open Season on the Apostles

But the apostles weren't immune to persecution—far from it. The Apostle John saw his peer group decrease with a depressing regularity. His flesh-and-blood brother, James, had been the first of the group to go—killed by the sword of Herod's henchmen. Tradition holds that Peter had been crucified upside down at his own request, feeling that he didn't deserve to die in the same manner as his Lord. And it is believed that eventually, all of the 12 apostles had died martyrs' deaths—all, that is, except Judas (who offed himself) and John.

While John had managed to avoid the swords and crosses that were killing off his friends, he was just as outspoken as they were about what he believed. John's punishment, however, was banishment. While martyrs sometimes were more trouble after death than they had been while alive, perhaps the intention of exiling John was "out of sight, out of mind."

John was sentenced to a rocky island in the Aegean Sea called Patmos, which wasn't exactly high on the list of Club Mediterranean sites for a vacation. It was about 25 square miles of volcanic, essentially treeless, rocky hills. Today it is known as Patino, and contains a tourist-stop grotto near the city of Scala where John supposedly lived during his year and a half (or so) on the island.

Some scholars disagree, but many believe John's exile took place in 95 C.E. under the leadership of Domitian. The reign of Domitian was one of the peak periods of persecution for Christians. Nero had been bad news, but things had gotten a little better for a while. Then Domitian took over in 81 C.E., and you have to expect a bit of trouble from someone who insisted on being addressed as *dominus et deus* (master and god). He had that sadistic wackiness associated with many of the Roman emperors, and displayed it in ways such as burning the sexual organs of his enemies and catching flies to stab them and rip off their wings.

Jews as well as Christians were targets of Roman hostility. Anyone claiming King David as an ancestor was hunted and killed. Domitian even killed some of his own relatives whom he thought were sympathizing with the Christians and Jews.

Flashback

"It was about this time that King Herod arrested some who belonged to the church, intending to persecute them. He had James, the brother of John, put to death with the sword. When he saw that this pleased the Jews, he proceeded to seize Peter also" (Acts 12:1–3).

A Bright Spot

John's exile is one of those good news/bad news stories in the Bible. The bad news was he had been busted and sent to the first-century equivalent of Alcatraz. But the good news was he had lots of time to write. If the Romans hoped to keep John quiet about his faith, they failed miserably. His record of Revelation, which he wrote while on the rocky island, continues to influence believers and others today.

Oh Lord, Please Don't Let Me Be Misunderstood

So enough time had passed since the death of Jesus for churches to rise up and boldly carry on what he had begun. Yet enough additional time had passed for them to draw attention to themselves and become targets for persecution. And it wasn't just the Romans who made things tough on believers. It is said that in the first couple of centuries of Christianity, far more believers died at the hands of their neighbors than from any kind of organized governmental attempt to stamp them out.

This new "cult" of Christianity was frequently misunderstood. As believers began to flourish and promote a message of unconditional love, rumors spread that they were sponsoring orgies. Their partaking of "the body and blood of Christ" created accusations of a sick and disgusting form of cannibalism. And rather than check out the facts, it was frequently easier simply to beat or kill anyone who might be involved in such awful things.

Clanging Symbols

"The body and blood of Christ" is a good example of how groups—all Christian—reach vastly different conclusions based on whether they interpret a biblical passage to be literal or symbolic. At the Last Supper, Jesus passed around bread and told his disciples, "Take and eat; this is my body." Then he passed around a cup of wine and said, "Drink from it, all of you. This is my blood of the covenant, which is poured out for many for the forgiveness of sins" (Matthew 26:26–28).

When partaking of the Lord's Supper, or Eucharist, most Catholics believe the bread and wine is literally changed by the power of the Holy Spirit into the substance of the body and blood of Jesus Christ. Most Protestants feel the bread and wine are only symbols of Jesus' body and blood to be consumed as reminders of his bodily sacrifice.

The Book of Revelation is filled with symbols, many of which have similar polarized interpretations based on literal vs. symbolic leanings.

Hearsay and Heresy

But just as dangerous (from a spiritual perspective) as outside persecution was heresy that was drifting into the church from within. With no written creeds yet, and with the basics of theology still to be formalized, various and competing teachings about Jesus were being promoted. Some were subtle twists of the words of Christ, and others were outright lies. Both threatened to deceive the early believers.

Churches responded to persecution and heresy in different ways. Some were quick to compromise in order not to stand out as a threat to the Romans or to make waves for those with different viewpoints. Others dug in and became quite firm in their policies and practices. Consequently, some churches faced terrible persecution while others seemed to breeze by with little if any outside interference. (We'll look at some specific examples in Chapter 4, "Seven Churches Get a Performance Review.")

A Relevant Revelation

You might imagine what would happen if, out of the blue, the government decided to sanction one religion while outlawing all others. Those who didn't happen to agree with the official religion would probably respond in ways that reflected various degrees of commitment to their chosen religions. If initial protests resulted in loss of privileges to buy or sell, social ostracism, or worse forms of persecution, some people might quickly change their religion—outwardly, if not from a genuine heartfelt conviction. Others might cling to what they believed no matter what, leading to even worse treatment.

Such was Christian life late in the first century. Things had gone from good to bad to worse—from Jesus to Nero to Domitian. And then along came John. Elderly by now, the spunky disciple still endured his Roman punishment and came out of it with a message for believers everywhere. Those who had quickly swung their religious loyalties over to the secular government would likely feel some degree of shame upon reading the words of Revelation. In contrast, the faithful who were losing the battle of strength and power would be invigorated to discover that God was aware of their plight. To them, Revelation with all its dragons, demons, and devastation, was ultimately a message of hope.

Apoca-Lips Now

"We should all be concerned about the future because we will have to spend the rest of our lives there."

—Charles Franklin Kettering

A "Revealing" Book

Some people think the Bible as a whole—and particularly the Book of Revelation—is a bunch of schlock. They put biblical prophecy in the same category as unicorns and fairy dust. Perhaps you're leaning in that direction. But many other people are seriously intrigued by the Book of Revelation.

From a biblical perspective, Revelation is a book of "revealing," a book of the future. And whether you're hoping to glimpse into the future out of fear of what might happen, to establish a greater degree of hope for what is to come, or both, your personal examination of Revelation should be helpful and lead to some positive results. Millions of people before you have sought answers and/or solace from the same pages, and can testify to a sense of confidence in spite of occasional confusion and head-scratching.

The next several chapters will take you straight through the Book of Revelation. As you read, file away your questions and comments. When we finish, we'll try to make sense of John's cryptic message by examining some popular interpretations. Many of your questions should be answered at that point.

Yet it is not our primary purpose to examine the writings in search of specific events or even definite chronology. We will not speculate on, for example, who the antichrist might be or whether he might be living today. (Other books on Revelation will help you speculate to your heart's desire.)

Our goal is to present the biblical Book of Revelation for your consideration, providing adequate commentary to help you understand its clear teachings—of which there are many. Any speculation to be done will be in regard to what certain symbols most likely represent. Where there are diverse viewpoints, we will attempt to make you aware of them.

Much can be gleaned from Revelation simply by knowing what it does say and what it doesn't. You will soon discover that almost any interpretation includes a number of additional events that aren't specifically mentioned in the book itself.

We'll get to the future soon enough. But before we do, we need to make a brief stop in the past.

Apoca-Lips Now

"Whoso neglects learning in his youth loses the past and is dead for the future."

—Euripides

The Least You Need to Know

➤ People want to know the future out of hope as well as fear, and Revelation addresses both motivations.

➤ The Book of Revelation was written during a period of Roman dominance and strong persecution of the Christian church.

➤ In addition to persecution, heresy was also having a destructive influence on the church.

➤ We will have a better context for understanding the future if we first get a better grip on the past and present.

Chapter 3

A Drear John Letter

In This Chapter

➤ A look at Revelation 1

➤ The intended recipients of the Book of Revelation

➤ The identity and background of John, the writer

➤ Why John wrote Revelation

Society in general tends to scoff at people who make a big deal about Jesus coming back to earth. That kind of talk may be okay while inside church walls, but out in the "real world" it doesn't set well. How many cartoons have you seen poking fun at "prophets" with a sign around their necks reading, "The end is near"?

Perhaps your complaint is more personal. Maybe you know someone who attempts to evangelize by reminding you again and again of the ticking clock of time that won't go on forever. Hurry and commit yourself to Jesus, for tomorrow might be too late! Don't "those people" just drive you nuts?

If so, the Book of Revelation may drive you nuts as well because it opens with a similar message.

The Beginning of the End

A Bright Spot

Before the close of the first paragraph of Revelation, we find a promise: "Blessed is the one who reads the words of this prophecy, and blessed are those who hear it and take to heart what is written in it." Whether or not you take to heart what you discover in Revelation, may you benefit even from a complete idiot's–level approach to this fascinating book.

The revelation of Jesus Christ, which God gave him to show his servants what must soon take place. He made it known by sending his angel to his servant John, who testifies to everything he saw—that is, the word of God and the testimony of Jesus Christ.

Blessed is the one who reads the words of this prophecy, and blessed are those who hear it and take to heart what is written in it, because the time is near (Revelation 1:1–3).

The Book of Revelation deals with two interwoven themes. One theme dwells on the "testimony of Jesus Christ" that provides blessings for those who respond. As we'll see in verse 4, the offer of "grace and peace" is extended for believers. So far, so good.

Yet in addition we find a second, recurring emphasis that time is indeed winding down. The very first verse refers to the things that must soon take place. Verse 3 echoes that the time is near. And as we go through the book, this theme will be repeated with an even greater sense of urgency because (here it comes) Jesus is returning soon.

The Revelation Salutation

Yet we need to note the salutation of this message from John. Think how disappointed you would be to get a letter informing you that you've just won the Publishers Clearinghouse Sweepstakes, only to discover you had your neighbor's mail by mistake. However, your disappointment might turn to elation when you discover that the notice of the IRS audit was your neighbor's as well. Whether the news is good or bad, you need to know if it applies to *you*. So let's check the address on the Book of Revelation before we work up too much emotion.

John, to the seven churches in the province of Asia: Grace and peace to you from him who is, and who was, and who is to come, and from the seven spirits before his throne, and from Jesus Christ, who is the faithful witness, the firstborn from the dead, and the ruler of the kings of the earth. To him who loves us and has freed us from our sins by his blood, and has made us to be a kingdom and priests to serve his God and Father— to him be glory and power for ever and ever! Amen.

Look, he is coming with the clouds, and every eye will see him, even those who pierced him; and all the peoples of the earth will mourn because of him. So shall it be! Amen.

"I am the Alpha and the Omega," says the Lord God, "who is, and who was, and who is to come, the Almighty" (Revelation 1:4–8).

The entirety of the book is written "to the seven churches in the province of Asia" (1:4). There were certainly more than seven churches in Asia at the time, and we will consider in Chapter 4, "Seven Churches Get a Performance Review," why seven specific ones were selected. For now, however, it's important to understand that the contents of Revelation were originally intended to go to people who had a basic understanding of Christianity and had professed belief in God and his Son, Jesus. Anything that appears scary or threatening should not have alarmed those who were being faithful. To them, John's message would have been a message of hope, even though the same words might have quite a different effect on someone unfamiliar with the whole Christianity thing.

Revelation, therefore, is not primarily intended to be evangelistic. Its purpose is not to scare the be-jesus out of people, but to console those who already claim to have Jesus in them. Many people who use the gloom and doom of this book to motivate loved ones to "get religion" are sincere in their efforts. It's frustrating when someone they love continually stalls or postpones any kind of spiritual commitment. They have come to the conclusion, perhaps based on the words of this book, that if time doesn't run out for the world during their lifetime, it will certainly run out for *their loved one* before too long. And in an effort to emphasize their point, they may resort to the high-pressure marketing techniques of "Limited time offer!" or "Hurry before it's too late!"

Apoca-Lips Now

"If Christianity goes, the whole of our culture goes. Then you must start painfully again, and you cannot put on a new culture ready made. You must wait for the grass to grow and feed the sheep to give the wool out of which your new coat will be made. You must pass through many centuries of barbarism."

—T.S. Eliot

The Bible is filled with examples of God's unconditional love, and his infinite mercy, grace, and patience. And surely God would rather have spiritual seekers *think* about what they're doing instead of hastily agreeing to something they don't really understand. But many Christians are frequently guilty of getting the spiritual cart before the horse. If people don't respond immediately to those positive aspects of Christianity, some Christians are quick to pull out the Book of Revelation and start quoting passages about judgment and apocalypse.

No matter what we might think about those believers who dwell more on the dwindling sand in the hourglass of time than on Jesus' eternal love and mercy, it is clear from the opening verses of Revelation that John feels both truths are important. But his target audience is the group of believers who comprise the church.

Meet the Author

The writer identifies himself three times in the first nine verses as "John," and lest there be any doubt, he confirms it again as he closes the book (Revelation 22:8). Writings dating back to the early second century identify this John as the disciple of Jesus. Tradition and much other evidence support John the apostle as the author. However, a bishop in the third century speculated that the writer might have been someone else, and since that time people haven't been in total agreement.

Clanging Symbols

You may have noticed the various symbolism used to describe Jesus in these opening verses of Revelation. He is called "the faithful witness," "the firstborn from the dead," and "the ruler of the kings of the earth" (v. 5). Such titles establish his credibility and authority as he begins to dictate what he wants John to write. But in addition, he includes titles of divinity on par with God the Father: "the Alpha and the Omega," and "the Almighty" (v. 8).

Apoca-Lips Now

"Things that are holy are revealed only to men who are holy."

—Hippocrates

As the disciples went, John was a cut above most of the others. While the 12 were a rather tight-knit group, three (including John) were present on certain important occasions when the others weren't. For example, Jesus took Peter, James, and John with him to witness his transfiguration. Secluded high on a hill, John saw Jesus temporarily transformed into a glorious, supernatural figure whose "face shone like the sun, and his clothes became as white as the light." John also witnessed Jesus speaking to Moses and Elijah, both of whom had died centuries before (Matthew 17:1–3).

Peter, James, and John were also selected to pray with Jesus on the night of his arrest in the Garden of

Flashback

A crucial doctrine of the Christian Church is that Jesus, like God the Father, is eternal, omnipotent, and "God" in every sense of the word. The Bible tells us he was involved in creation (John 1:1–3; Colossians 1:16). So from a biblical standpoint, "the Alpha and the Omega" not only was around to see time (as we know it) begin, but also will oversee the conclusion of all earthly activity. We are told that "Jesus Christ is the same yesterday and today and forever" (Hebrews 13:8). Planets come and go, but God lives on.

Gethsemane (although they kept falling asleep). John is likely the disciple mentioned who sneaked Peter into the high priest's courtyard later that night to await word on what would happen to Jesus (John 18:15–16). It was John to whom Jesus, while on the cross, entrusted care of his mother (John 19:26–27). And it was John who first seemed to recognize the resurrected Jesus on shore after a long night of fishing (John 21:7). In fact, John so associated himself with Jesus that in his gospel he referred to himself not by name, but only as "the disciple whom Jesus loved."

But although John is the author, he makes it clear that this book is "the revelation of Jesus Christ" (v. 1). Several decades had passed since Jesus had died, been resurrected, and ascended into heaven. But Jesus and John were about to be reunited on a lonely island in the Aegean Sea, and both had changed considerably. John was quite a bit older, though his outspokenness for Jesus was still consistent. And as we are about to see, Jesus looked a lot different on Patmos than he had walking the streets of Nazareth and Jerusalem.

My Lord, How You've Changed!

I, John, your brother and companion in the suffering and kingdom and patient endurance that are ours in Jesus, was on the island of Patmos because of the word of God and the testimony of Jesus. On the Lord's Day I was in the Spirit, and I heard behind me a loud voice like a trumpet, which said: "Write on a scroll what you see and send it to the seven churches: to Ephesus, Smyrna, Pergamum, Thyatira, Sardis, Philadelphia and Laodicea."

I turned around to see the voice that was speaking to me. And when I turned I saw seven golden lampstands, and among the lampstands was someone "like a son of man," dressed in a robe reaching down to his feet and with a golden sash around his chest. His head and hair were white like wool, as white as snow, and his eyes were like blazing fire. His feet were like bronze glowing in a furnace, and his voice was like the sound of rushing waters. In his right hand he held seven stars, and out of his mouth came a sharp double-edged sword. His face was like the sun shining in all its brilliance.

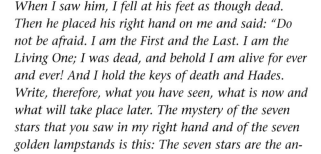

When I saw him, I fell at his feet as though dead. Then he placed his right hand on me and said: "Do not be afraid. I am the First and the Last. I am the Living One; I was dead, and behold I am alive for ever and ever! And I hold the keys of death and Hades. Write, therefore, what you have seen, what is now and what will take place later. The mystery of the seven stars that you saw in my right hand and of the seven golden lampstands is this: The seven stars are the angels of the seven churches, and the seven lampstands are the seven churches (Revelation 1:9–20).

Apoca-Lips Now

"Who, doomed to go in
  company with pain,
And fear, and bloodshed,
  miserable train!
Turns his necessity to glorious
  gain."

—William Wordsworth

Before we get to the juicy parts of the action, we need to remember that John was suffering just as all of us do. He could relate to the persecution being felt by the people who would eventually read his words. Yet his "patient endurance" on the island of Patmos was about to be rewarded.

John heard Jesus before he saw him. A voice behind John designated seven churches to receive John's eyewitness account. (More on these churches in Chapter 4.) When John whirled around to see what was going on, he saw a magnificent figure standing amid seven golden lampstands and holding seven stars.

Flashback

Even though Jesus certainly looked different in this vision, perhaps John was expecting him. John had already recorded a promise of Jesus in his gospel: "In my Father's house are many rooms; if it were not so, I would have told you. I am going there to prepare a place for you. And if I go and prepare a place for you, I will come back and take you to be with me that you also may be where I am" (John 14:2–3).

This figure could be none other than Jesus, because he identified himself as "the First and the Last," "the Living One," the one who "holds the keys of death and Hades," and someone who "was dead, and behold I am alive for ever and ever." John had been as close to Jesus as anyone, yet upon seeing this particular manifestation, he just about passed out at first.

Still, John got much more than a glimpse of this figure. Note the detail he provides. His dress: a robe and golden sash. Hair: like wool, and as white as snow.

Eyes: like blazing fire. Feet: like superheated bronze. Voice: like rushing waters. Face: a brilliance that could be compared only to the sun.

Apparently John didn't panic. His description is much better than we might expect from the average eyewitness on the scene of a crime or catastrophe. Besides, the figure (Jesus) encouraged John and gave him a job to do. John was instructed to write down the things he was about to see and hear.

Clanging Symbols

Get ready to find a lot of "sevens" in Revelation. The number seven symbolized completeness throughout the Bible (as in the days of creation, or the statements of Jesus from the cross). Here we have seven churches, seven lampstands, and seven stars—and we're only getting started. But also notice that these particular symbols are clearly explained in the text itself: the lampstands represent churches and the stars represent "angels," which may be a reference to the pastors of the churches (as we will see in Chapter 4).

The Times They Have a'Changed

Let's assume for a moment that John is about to see some things that are still in *our* future. Not everyone agrees with such an interpretation, but many do. Send yourself 2,000 years backward in time and try to understand what your life would be like.

The best guess for the date of the writing of Revelation is 95 or 96 C.E. (Again, some people disagree.) But insert yourself late in the first century. This was still almost a century before the oldest known Maya monuments. Silkworms hadn't been introduced to China yet. The cutting edge of technology was alloyed metals, although many people were thankful for the recent Roman adaptation of an invention they got from the Gauls—soap.

While the Romans were highly civilized for the time, with great roads, aqueducts, and such, it would still be centuries before anyone would conceive of electricity. Cities were large enough, but

Apoca-Lips Now

"God, when he makes the prophet, does not unmake the man."

—John Locke

the most impressive "skyscrapers" of the time would pale in comparison to today's. Weaponry had hardly gone beyond pointy things on the end of long sticks.

Place yourself in that era and then suppose you got a good look at today's world. Using your first-century comprehension and vocabulary, how would you describe television, flush toilets, cell phones, nuclear explosions, cars, tanks, missiles, helicopters, and all the rest? It would be hard enough to explain corndogs and cotton candy to someone else, much less the complicated technology of our time.

Apoca-Lips Now

"Great men are the inspired (speaking and acting) texts of that divine Book of Revelations, whereof a chapter is completed from epoch to epoch, and by some named History."

—Thomas Carlyle

Apoca-Lips Now

"If we do not now dare everything, the fulfillment of that prophecy, re-created from the Bible in song by a slave, is upon us: *God gave Noah the rainbow sign, No more water, the fire next time!*"

—James Baldwin

So as we go through this book, let's cut John some slack. We can tell he is a conscientious witness and reporter to what is going on. So later, if his descriptions take on a weird and flaky-sounding tone, perhaps it's a result of 2,000 years or more of time lag. The task he is being assigned on the island of Patmos is no small gig. It's an enormous job, but he's up to it.

To begin with, John is asked to take dictation for letters to go to seven specific churches. That will be the focus of Chapter 4. If you're in a hurry to get to the four horsemen of the apocalypse, the beasts, and the blood that comes later in Revelation, it may be tempting to skip ahead. This is your book and you can ignore as much of it as you like. But if you're willing to take a quick look at the churches described in Revelation 2–3, you will be much better prepared for the later, future things to come. Besides, you might just find a church you recognize among the group.

Same As It Ever Was

It has been over 1,900 years since John's island encounter, leading to the Book of Revelation and much of the fuss about Jesus returning to earth. After so much time, many people scoff all the more loudly at the prospect of Jesus ever coming back. Others, however, are convinced that we're simply a few centuries closer to the event than were those people of the first century. The chance remains, they say, that it *could* be today.

Whichever of these groups you happen to be in, most people agree that it's not a bad philosophy to live each day as if it might be your last. Overzealous believers have looked quite foolish in the past, migrating to hilltops for anticipated mass reunions with

Jesus that, uh, never happened. But just as foolish are those who never give the future *any* consideration—expecting perhaps to live forever?

Somewhere is a sensible middle way that allows faithful and hopeful believers to keep their feet on the ground, even if their heads are in the clouds, and that will allow the most skeptical of agnostics to consider that they may not be in *total* control of every aspect of their lives. The message of Revelation is not to leap to one extreme or the other. Whatever we are or aren't anticipating for the future, let's agree to try to make the most of the time we have now.

The Least You Need to Know

➤ The Book of Revelation was originally intended for churches, not the general public.

➤ The traditional author of Revelation was John, the disciple of Jesus.

➤ A powerful figure (most likely Jesus) appeared to John, instructing him to record what he saw and heard.

➤ Both Christians and non-Christians can benefit from a reading of the Book of Revelation.

Chapter 4

Seven Churches Get a Performance Review

In This Chapter

➤ A look at Revelation 2–3

➤ Letters to seven churches

➤ Assorted promises to "overcomers," images of Jesus, and other key observations

➤ A few opinions as to the significance of the seven churches

The next time you and your cronies have nothing better to do than start a game of word association, try a couple of warm-up words and then see what kind of response you get to the word *church*. Some people can gush for hours about how much church means to them. For others, however, the very word is a source of consternation, avoidance, memories of childhood trauma, or worse.

Some people passionately avoid church and have good stories to explain why. Others feel they ought to attend, but haven't been within a hundred feet of stained glass in decades. For any number of reasons—good and bad—the word *church* is likely to evoke a strong response. In this chapter we'll take a look at several churches that were graded by Jesus himself. They run the gamut from gold-star excellence to "vastly needs improvement."

Fresh Churches: U Pick Your Own

Perhaps never before in the history of the world has it been so easy to find a church that suits your personal tastes. Not only have the Scriptures been translated into more languages worldwide than ever before, but also many of the literal translations have been further simplified into a number of contemporary and easy-to-read para-phrases. If you enjoy a traditional church service with hymns and solemn prayers, you can find it. If you prefer a more active service with rock bands instead of pipe organs and more drama than lecture, you can find that as well. Active or passive, loud or soft, con-servative or liberal, all-encompassing or restrictive—churches exist to accommodate almost any preference.

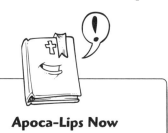

Apoca-Lips Now

"Some to church repair
Not for the doctrine, but the music there."

—Alexander Pope

Indeed, many churches today seem to operate under the motto of "Keep the customer satisfied." They will go to almost any lengths to attract seekers and keep adding names to the rolls. And as you visit some churches, you might wonder if they have any stan-dards at all that would exclude your (or anyone else's) full participation.

The first-century churches also provided a bit of variety, and not all of it was good. Each had its own challenges to contend with, and some churches did a better job of handling problems than others. Yet as we're about to see, whether or not the church leadership was aware of it, the performance of each church was being evaluated ac-cording to a high standard. The initial portion of the Book of Revelation is a frank and enlightening performance review—by Jesus himself—of seven churches. Many of the church names aren't likely to be familiar to you, and some of the comments con-cerning the churches will seem peculiar at first, but we'll take a quick close-up look at each congregation to see what we can find out.

Jesus' comments directed to each of the seven churches follow the same general out-line:

1. Identification of the church to which the comments are to be sent

2. A description of Jesus that more often than not was relevant to the specific church being addressed

3. A review of the strengths of the church

4. A review of the "needs improvement" aspects of the church

5. A challenge to hear and respond

6. A promise to those who are faithful

The Church at Ephesus: I Got Those "Lost My First Love" Blues

To the angel of the church in Ephesus write:

These are the words of him who holds the seven stars in his right hand and walks among the seven golden lampstands: I know your deeds, your hard work and your perseverance. I know that you cannot tolerate wicked men, that you have tested those who claim to be apostles but are not, and have found them false.

You have persevered and have endured hardships for my name, and have not grown weary. Yet I hold this against you: You have forsaken your first love. Remember the height from which you have fallen! Repent and do the things you did at first. If you do not repent, I will come to you and remove your lampstand from its place. But you have this in your favor: You hate the practices of the Nicolaitans, which I also hate.

He who has an ear, let him hear what the Spirit says to the churches. To him who overcomes, I will give the right to eat from the tree of life, which is in the paradise of God (Revelation 2:1–7).

Clanging Symbols

You will notice that each letter is addressed to the "angel" of the particular church. In addition to referring to heavenly beings, sometimes the Bible uses the word *angel* to indicate a human messenger. In this case, it seems likely that the "angel" is the pastor or overseer primarily responsible for communicating the message of God to the people of the church.

The first of the seven churches addressed is the one in Ephesus, which was probably the one with the highest profile. Ephesus was a major seaport and a place where the Apostle Paul had spent some years of personal ministry (about four decades earlier), following up with his letter to the Ephesians found in the New Testament.

How Do You Compete with the Church of the Naked Goddess?

Yet most of the tourists to Ephesus came not to attend the church, but rather to visit the temple of the Greek goddess Artemis (or Diana, to the Romans). Years before, a meteorite had fallen in Ephesus which was said to be in the image of Artemis. So in addition to having a major temple erected in her honor, numerous silversmiths made a good living making and selling souvenir statues of the goddess. (In a nod to the marketing savvy of such craftsmen, Artemis was traditionally portrayed as a nude woman with many, many breasts.) A strong cult had developed around her worship in Ephesus, and the church stood in bold contrast.

Jesus opened his letter to this church by reminding them that he "holds the seven stars"—that is, that he is in control of the churches. And he praises their perseverance and hard work in standing for the truth, even after confronting several people who claimed to be holy, but weren't.

Jesus also had good things to say about Ephesian resistance to a cult called the Nicolaitans. Not a lot of specifics are known about this group, though it is believed they tended to compromise their religious convictions with social idolatry and immorality.

Jesus' only criticism of this church was that it had lost its first love. This may seem like nitpicking since the church was still working hard and doing lots of good things. Yet as soon as we lose the proper motivation for doing the right things, we have already begun a slide toward doing the wrong things.

Flashback

Acts 19 provides good insight into the challenges and triumphs Paul had previously experienced in Ephesus. It was there where handkerchiefs touched by Paul were carried to sick people, who then were miraculously healed. The same chapter also details an uprising of the silversmiths in the city who took offense that Paul's preaching was beginning to affect their business significantly. Their chant was, "Great is Artemis of the Ephesians!" (v. 28).

Apoca-Lips Now

"One can be coerced to church, but not to worship."

—Georgia Harkness

Restoring the Relationship

From a biblical/Christian perspective, the relationship between Jesus and the church is paramount. In terms that we tend to better understand, Jesus is not only the "head" of the body known as the church (Colossians 1:18), but is also frequently portrayed as a "bridegroom." If believers represent the bride, but then lose their first love, it's a serious breach of a relationship indeed.

So Jesus challenged the Ephesian church to repent and get back to basics. Upon closer examination, they would see they had fallen from a great height, and they needed to recover the ground they had lost.

Enough time had passed for many of the founding members to have been replaced by a new generation. Many contemporary churches know what a challenge it is to generate genuine faith from its second-generation members without their leaning too much on the beliefs of their parents. It's still easy to get into a rut, as the Ephesians did, of performance without passion.

So after laying out a challenge, Jesus then closed with the promise that those who overcame would eat from the tree of life in the paradise of God—not a bad deal for someone willing to rekindle devotion to his or her first love.

The Church at Smyrna: Down but Never Out

To the angel of the church in Smyrna write:

These are the words of him who is the First and the Last, who died and came to life again. I know your afflictions and your poverty—yet you are rich! I know the slander of those who say they are Jews and are not, but are a synagogue of Satan. Do not be afraid of what you are about to suffer. I tell you, the devil will put some of you in prison to test you, and you will suffer persecution for ten days. Be faithful, even to the point of death, and I will give you the crown of life.

He who has an ear, let him hear what the Spirit says to the churches. He who overcomes will not be hurt at all by the second death (Revelation 2:8–11).

Clanging Symbols

The tree of life was found in the Garden of Eden (Genesis 2:9) and symbolizes eternal life. Those who eat its fruit do not die (Genesis 3:22). We will see the tree of life again before we finish Revelation, and its location will be significant.

Smyrna was another seaport. As the harbor at Ephesus was on the decline due to increasing silt that was making boat passage too difficult, Smyrna was growing in popularity as a favorite trade route. The city was known for its prominence in science, medicine, and majestic architecture. It was also a politically motivated society, eager to establish ties with Rome, and had erected a temple to the emperor Tiberius in 26 C.E.

Apoca-Lips Now

"The poorer the church, the purer the church."

—W.C. Hazlitt

In contrast, the church members there were both poor and persecuted. The Greek word used to describe their financial condition (*ptocheia*) indicated *extreme* poverty. In light of the grandeur of the city around them, they must have seemed (and perhaps felt) like losers. Yet Jesus' message to them was one of confidence and tremendous hope. He didn't have a single negative thing to say about them.In this case, Jesus identified himself as, "him who is the First and the Last, who died and came to life again." This would have been an extremely significant reminder for a group of people who might have been feeling half-dead themselves. Just as Jesus had suffered persecution from Satan, from those outside the religious community, and even from some of those who called themselves religious leaders, so would the fine folk in the Smyrna church.

But if the church was hoping to hear that things were going to get better, they may have been disappointed. In spite of all they had already endured, their letter was a forewarning to prepare for their situation to get even worse. Some would be imprisoned. Some would face other forms of persecution. And they were challenged to "be faithful, even to the point of death."

It wasn't going to be pretty for the church at Smyrna. Simply for believing something different from the rest of the people around them, they were going to go through some awful times in terms of money, success, and security. Yet their reward would be "the crown of life"—not a reference to a clunky royal crown, but rather to the laurel wreaths placed on the heads of marathon winners and other outstanding athletes. Theirs would be a long and hard test of endurance, yet a sure and certain reward was waiting at the finish line.

History bears out the warning sent to the church at Smyrna. An early bishop of the church was an outspoken Christian named Polycarp. He had been a disciple of John and bishop of the church at Smyrna. An angry mob accused him of "destroying our gods" because he taught Christians not to sacrifice to or worship Roman deities. Because he was an old man, he was given an opportunity to "revile Christ" and be released. When he refused to do so, he was burned at the stake in 155 or 156 C.E.

Clanging Symbols

When the people in the church at Smyrna were told some would suffer "for ten days," this period of time is thought to be symbolic. Their persecution most likely lasted much longer than a week and a half. Some have speculated that it might have referred to a series of 10 Roman rulers, or was simply a poetic way to say, "for a lengthy period of time, but not forever."

Apoca-Lips Now

"For 86 years I have been his servant, and he has done me no wrong. How can I blaspheme my King who saved me?"

—Polycarp, at his trial shortly before being put to death

The Church at Pergamum: In Need of Some Good Bouncers

To the angel of the church in Pergamum write:

These are the words of him who has the sharp, double-edged sword. I know where you live—where Satan has his throne. Yet you remain true to my name. You did not renounce your faith in me, even in the days of Antipas, my faithful witness, who was put to death in your city—where Satan lives.

Nevertheless, I have a few things against you: You have people there who hold to the teaching of Balaam, who taught Balak to entice the Israelites to sin by eating food sacrificed to idols and by committing sexual immorality. Likewise you also have those who hold to the teaching of the Nicolaitans. Repent therefore! Otherwise, I will soon come to you and will fight against them with the sword of my mouth.

He who has an ear, let him hear what the Spirit says to the churches. To him who overcomes, I will give some of the hidden manna. I will also give him a white stone with a new name written on it, known only to him who receives it (Revelation 2:12–17).

Pergamum, or Pergamos (meaning citadel), was a city on a hill with a commanding view of the surrounding area. It was known for a library almost as extensive as the one in Alexandria, and for the invention of parchment (*charta Pergamena*). The city had been a capital of Asia until the Romans hit town, and then it was quick to shift loyalties. Citizens of the city were the first to construct a temple devoted to Caesar worship. The original one was dedicated to Augustus in 29 B.C.E., and a second was dedicated to Trajan years later. Worship of Zeus and other gods and goddesses was also popular.

Flashback

The story of Balaam is a fascinating one. Hired by a local king (Balak) to curse the Israelites on their way from Egypt to the Promised Land, Balaam tried to do so. He just couldn't get his donkey to go where he wanted it to go. As it turned out, his donkey saw an armed angel standing in the middle of the road. After several beatings, the donkey finally turned around and spoke to Balaam (Numbers 22). Balaam ended up blessing the Israelites a number of times rather than cursing them. But later, he took a more devious approach and suggested that Moabite women seduce Israelite men sexually, and follow that up with spiritual idolatry. The plan worked like a charm—until God sent a plague through the camp that killed 24,000 people (Numbers 25). Balaam was later put to death because he had instigated this plan (Numbers 31:8, 16). Since this story is used in connection with the church in Pergamum, their spiritual condition must have been quite in need of attention.

Evidently, some of these other forms of worship had found their way into the church. Although the church had not renounced Jesus, even under strong waves of persecution, neither had they been conscientious in preventing false religions from infiltrating the church *in addition to* what they believed about Jesus.

Antipas, the first known martyr of Asia, was from this church. It is believed by some that the emperor Domitian had him slow roasted in a bronze kettle. Yet while Antipas and some of his peers were clearly faithful, others weren't. The Nicolaitans, who plagued the church at Ephesus, were found here as well. And the "teaching of Balaam" was a reference to not only spiritual corruption, but sexual immorality as well.

Jesus described himself to this church as "him who has the sharp, double-edged sword." In other places in Scripture, a sword represents the word of God and is called a tool that "penetrates even to dividing soul and spirit, joints and marrow; it judges the thoughts and intentions of the heart" (Ephesians 6:17; Hebrews 4:12). If the church didn't take the initiative in separating the heretical teachers from the faithful of the church, Jesus would get the job done. When it came to clearly false teachings, compromise was not the answer.

The closing reference to "hidden manna" and "a white stone with a new name written on it" are clearly positive promises, yet it's difficult to interpret exactly what is being referred to. Manna was the miraculous bread from heaven that sustained the Israelites for 40 years in the wilderness. It also symbolizes Jesus himself (John 6:48–51). Possession of the white stone might have been a jab at the tendency of others to value precious stones, or sometimes such a stone might serve as an admission ticket to a special occasion.

The Church at Thyatira: Guild-Y of Too Much Tolerance?

To the angel of the church in Thyatira write:

These are the words of the Son of God, whose eyes are like blazing fire and whose feet are like burnished bronze. I know your deeds, your love and faith, your service and perseverance, and that you are now doing more than you did at first.

Nevertheless, I have this against you: You tolerate that woman Jezebel, who calls herself a prophetess. By her teaching she misleads my servants into sexual immorality and the eating of food sacrificed to idols. I have given her time to repent of her immorality, but she is unwilling. So I will cast her on a bed of suffering, and I will make those who commit adultery with her suffer intensely, unless they repent of her ways. I will strike her children dead. Then all the churches will know that I am he who searches hearts and minds, and I will repay each of you according to your deeds. Now I say to the rest of you in Thyatira, to you who do not hold to her teaching and have not learned Satan's so-called deep secrets (I will not impose any other burden on you): Only hold on to what you have until I come.

To him who overcomes and does my will to the end, I will give authority over the nations—"He will rule them with an iron scepter; he will dash them to pieces like pottery"—just as I have received authority from my Father. I will also give him the morning star. He who has an ear, let him hear what the Spirit says to the churches (Revelation 2:18–29).

In contrast to the other church locations so far, Thyatira was a Podunk town. Although considerably smaller, it was known for its trade guilds, many of which sold cloth colored from a special purple dye manufactured there. One prominent tradeswoman pops up in the Book of Acts (16:14–15). But from a historical perspective, Thyatira was no big whoop.

It is interesting, therefore, that the Thyatiran church was not only one of the seven singled out in Revelation, but also received the longest letter. Jesus praised its deeds, love, faith, service, and perseverance, yet these attributes don't seem to be the focal point of the letter. Much more was said about the church's faults than its strong points.

Flashback

The Bible doesn't have a lot of cliffhanger endings. While Jezebel seems to get away with a lot of her wicked shenanigans, her inglorious end is recorded in 2 Kings 9:30–37. When she heard someone was coming to kill her, she did her face and hair, and then waited. She was soon pushed out of a high window to her death and then ignored while everyone else had a good meal. When they went to attend to the body, dogs had eaten her except for her skull, feet, and hands.

The mention of Jezebel who was misleading the church was a reference to an infamous Old Testament queen who is commonly associated with evil (1 Kings 16:29–33; 19:1–2; 21; etc.). Like Balaam, she was a corrupting influence on the Israelites. But unlike Balaam, who was an outsider paid to oppose Israel, Jezebel was queen over the nation. She and her equally devious husband, King Ahab, were supposed to be responsible for the welfare of the nation—including accountability before God and pursuit of religious purity. Yet this couple was as self-centered as they come. And apparently, a woman much like Jezebel had risen to prominence within the church at Thyatira, and was corrupting those in the congregation by promoting sexual immorality and idol worship.

Another spiritual concern was the church's involvement in "Satan's so-called deep secrets." A non-Christian religion of the time called Gnosticism promised its followers "secret knowledge." And although it also promoted resistance to Satan, its strategy was to get deeply involved in evil to better understand him. Some of the proponents of this religion had apparently infiltrated the church as well.

The message of Jesus to the church in Thyatira was to quit tolerating such blatantly false teaching. The church needed to disassociate itself from Jezebel, Gnosticism, and other influences that led people away from the truth. Just as the Old Testament Jezebel had been brought to justice, anyone else who pursued deceptive religions would suffer as well—if they didn't repent.

In contrast, those who resisted the false teachers and remained faithful were promised both authority from God and "the morning star." Again, these promises aren't as specific as we might like. Many people associate them with future events we will see later in Revelation. The "authority," for example, might take place during a possible kingdom of Jesus on earth, and the "morning star" (which is the first bright light in the darkness of night) is hoped by some to be the "rapture" of believers prior to the terrible tribulation that precedes Jesus' ultimate kingdom.

> **Apoca-Lips Now**
>
> "Wherever God erects a house of prayer,
> The Devil always builds a chapel there;
> And 'twill be found, upon examination,
> The latter has the largest congregation."
>
> —Daniel Defoe

The Church at Sardis: Dead Church Walking!

To the angel of the church in Sardis write:

These are the words of him who holds the seven spirits of God and the seven stars. I know your deeds; you have a reputation of being alive, but you are dead. Wake up! Strengthen what remains and is about to die, for I have not found your deeds complete in the sight of my God. Remember, therefore, what you have received and heard; obey it, and repent. But if you do not wake up, I will come like a thief, and you will not know at what time I will come to you.

Yet you have a few people in Sardis who have not soiled their clothes. They will walk with me, dressed in white, for they are worthy. He who overcomes will, like them, be dressed in white. I will never blot out his name from the book of life, but will acknowledge his name before my Father and his angels. He who has an ear, let him hear what the Spirit says to the churches (Revelation 3:1–6).

Sardis is another city many of us have never heard of. It now lies in ruins and exists only as a small village called Sart. Yet in its day, it was a capital of the area of Lydia with a king (Croesus) known for vast riches. Aesop told his fables in this area, and it was among the first places where gold and silver coins were minted.

Unfortunately, King Croesus was not known for tact or humility. Feeling that his city was so well positioned that it could not be taken, he attacked the Persian empire at the height of its power. Before long the Persians had raided and captured the city. Later the Greeks did the same ... then the Romans ... then the Turks. And if that weren't bad enough, a big earthquake leveled the city in 17 C.E. The Romans provided a lot of money for rebuilding and gave the citizens tax relief, but the city never fully recovered.

Sardis, like Ephesus, had a large temple devoted to Artemis. Archaeologists have discovered ruins of this temple, and right beside it are ruins of a Christian church. Yet at the writing of Revelation, the church was already in a spiritual slump. It still had a good reputation, but had stopped growing. Like a grand old tree that seems fine in winter, yet has little if any life come spring, the church in Sardis had reached a point where it would either need some serious attention or soon become firewood.

Apoca-Lips Now

"It is common for those that are farthest from God, to boast themselves most of their being near to the Church."

—Matthew Henry

The repeated message of Jesus to this church was to "Wake up!" Although it was mostly a dead church, it still had some life in it in the form of "a few people ... who have not soiled their clothes." Anyone else willing to overcome the spiritual lethargy in Sardis could join them. Jesus promised to publicly endorse those people before his heavenly Father, and to never blot their names from the book of life.

The Church at Philadelphia: Weak Enough to Be Strong

To the angel of the church in Philadelphia write:

These are the words of him who is holy and true, who holds the key of David. What he opens no one can shut, and what he shuts no one can open. I know your deeds. See,

I have placed before you an open door that no one can shut. I know that you have little strength, yet you have kept my word and have not denied my name. I will make those who are of the synagogue of Satan, who claim to be Jews though they are not, but are liars—I will make them come and fall down at your feet and acknowledge that I have loved you. Since you have kept my command to endure patiently, I will also keep you from the hour of trial that is going to come upon the whole world to test those who live on the earth.

I am coming soon. Hold on to what you have, so that no one will take your crown. Him who overcomes I will make a pillar in the temple of my God. Never again will he leave it. I will write on him the name of my God and the name of the city of my God, the new Jerusalem, which is coming down out of heaven from my God; and I will also write on him my new name. He who has an ear, let him hear what the Spirit says to the churches (Revelation 3:7–13).

Once upon a time, about 150 B.C.E., a king named Attalus II Phildelphus was known for two things: (1) He founded a city; and (2) he dearly loved his brother Eumenes. As a result, the city he started became known as Philadelphia, "the city of brotherly love." The city was built on a hill that made it easy to defend, which was the good news. The bad news was that the hill was right above the fault line of the earthquake that destroyed Sardis in 17 C.E., and Philadelphia was ruined, too. In addition, 20 years of aftershocks kept interfering with rebuilding efforts. Vineyards did well, however, so the area became a center of worship for the god Dionysius.

Clanging Symbols

The symbol of "keys" is used throughout the Bible. Possession of a key allows access to places denied others. In this respect, the fear of the Lord is the "key" to "a rich store of salvation and wisdom and knowledge" (Isaiah 33:6). The "key of David" in Revelation 3:7 may be a reference to Isaiah 22:22 where Scripture speaks of "the key to the house of David." The messianic line continued from the house of David, so later on Jesus would speak of the "keys to the kingdom" (Matthew 16:19) that he was passing on to Peter. You might also remember that when Jesus first appeared to John on Patmos, he held "the keys of death and Hades" (Revelation 1:18).

But even though the city was on shaky ground, the church there was amazingly solid. It wasn't that it appeared strong—just the opposite. While the church at Sardis had appeared alive but was dead, the Philadelphians were very much alive in spite of everything they had been through. In standing firm for what they believed, they had had the wind knocked out of them so often that they had little stamina left. Yet they kept at it.

To this church of holiness and truth, Jesus described himself as "him who is holy and true." He also said much about doors and keys. He held the "key of David." He spoke of an open door before them that no one could shut. Some understand this door to represent the opportunities given to this faithful church; others feel this symbolizes their automatic entrance into his kingdom when their struggle is over.

And indeed, the church at Philadelphia was struggling. Like most of the other churches addressed, it was combating lies from other sources. During Jesus' life on earth, he hadn't always been welcome at the Jewish synagogues. Now it seemed that the Philadelphian church was also at odds with a local synagogue. Yet Jesus made the Philadelphians a number of prom- ises. With earthquakes shaking the ground around them, he promised they would be a pillar in God's temple—one that surely would never topple! In a time when many wanted to rename their city Neocaesarea (in a blatant political kiss-up to the emperor Tiberius for lots of earthquake relief funds), Jesus turned the attention of the church from "New Caesarville" to the new Jerusalem.

You may have noticed that Philadelphia didn't get any divine criticism. And we need to notice some- thing else. Among the other promises Jesus made to them was this one: "Since you have kept my command to endure patiently, I will also keep you from the hour of trial that is going to come upon the whole world to test those who live on the earth" (Revelation 3:10). Later, when we begin to address broad concepts like the rapture and the great tribulation, this promise will come up again.

A Bright Spot

Some of these promises to the churches might not sound like much to us—especially since we're breezing past them so quickly. But to the suffering church members, they would have meant a lot. Not only were the promises reminders that God saw what had been going on since Jesus had as- cended, but that he would cer- tainly reward faithfulness. After six or seven decades, this was no small piece of good news.

The Church at Laodicea: They Make Jesus Want to Puke!

To the angel of the church in Laodicea write:

These are the words of the Amen, the faithful and true witness, the ruler of God's cre- ation. I know your deeds, that you are neither cold nor hot. I wish you were either one or the other! So, because you are lukewarm—neither hot nor cold—I am about to spit you out of my mouth. You say, "I am rich; I have acquired wealth and do not need a thing." But you do not realize that you are wretched, pitiful, poor, blind and naked. I counsel you to buy from me gold refined in the fire, so you can become rich; and white clothes to wear, so you can cover your shameful nakedness; and salve to put on your eyes, so you can see.

Those whom I love I rebuke and discipline. So be earnest, and repent. Here I am! I stand at the door and knock. If anyone hears my voice and opens the door, I will come in and eat with him, and he with me.

To him who overcomes, I will give the right to sit with me on my throne, just as I overcame and sat down with my Father on his throne. He who has an ear, let him hear what the Spirit says to the churches (Revelation 3:14–22).

When it comes to the seven churches in Revelation, it's probably safe to say that the last is also the least. The church at Laodicea doesn't come off sounding like the best place for worship or ministry.

The *city* of Laodicea was in good shape, however. The earthquakes that ravaged some of the other cities also hit here with equal severity, but the Laodiceans had the capital to recover with no help from the Romans. The city not only was a big provider of glossy black woolen cloth (a popular source of carpets and cloaks), but it also lay on a major Asian trade route that ensured good sales. It was a noted banking center (where Cicero once cashed some checks). In addition, a medical school was located there, and the area had become famous for producing a medicinal eye salve.

The Laodicean citizens didn't have to depend on anyone else for their livelihood, and it seems the Laodicean church had stopped depending on Jesus for their spiritual needs as well. It wasn't a "cold" church; it simply wasn't "hot." In an interesting statement, Jesus expressed that he would have preferred their being cold to their being lukewarm. Presenting himself as "the Amen, the faithful and true witness," Jesus could not condone a witness who was only half faithful and half true.

Apoca-Lips Now

"The forces of good in the world are immobilized less by their adversaries than by their sleep."

—E.M. Poteat

Consequently, he warned that he was "about to spit you out of my mouth." And lest we think *spitting* is a disgusting habit, the literal translation of the word is *vomit*. This church that was satisfied to remain lukewarm rather than "on fire" was enough to make Jesus want to vomit.

From all outer appearances, the church was rich, successful, and a credit to the community. But from the spiritual perspective of Jesus himself, it was "wretched, pitiful, poor, blind and naked." This church received no commendation from Jesus at all.

But that didn't mean he had given up on his people in Laodicea. On the contrary. If he didn't love the people there, he wouldn't have bothered to rebuke them. His words were meant to encourage them to repent and discover the truly important things in life. If the door between them was closed, it was locked from inside the church. He leaves them with an image of the omnipotent Lord of the universe patiently knocking on the door, eager to share a meal, but waiting for *them* to open the door. He had opened the door to the kingdom of heaven to the church in Philadelphia, but to do the same for the Laodiceans, they had to choose to come out of seclusion.

Flashback

So many of us have had lousy bosses or maybe even bad parents that we've come to associate correction with harsh criticism. This is not a biblical standard. For the record, the Bible says, "'My son, do not make light of the Lord's discipline, and do not lose heart when he rebukes you, because the Lord disciplines those he loves, and he punishes everyone he accepts as a son.' ... No discipline seems pleasant at the time, but painful. Later on, however, it produces a harvest of righteousness and peace for those who have been trained by it" (Hebrews 12:5–6, 11).

Yet as with all the others, he left the Laodiceans with a promise. In their case, he said they would sit with him on his throne if they overcame their spiritual obstacles. He holds out hope for all the people in all the churches—if they "overcome" and find their sense of purpose in him.

Why These Seven Churches?

The authors are well aware you probably didn't pick up a book about Revelation to get a long chapter on church history and problems. Yet had we skipped this section of the book, we would only have to come back to it again and again. For one thing, the rest of the Book of Revelation was to accompany these letters to the churches. We need to keep in mind that the apocalyptic drama is primarily addressed to believers.

Second, the promises and warnings made to the individual churches have become favorite portions of Scripture for some believers. The image of Jesus standing at the door and knocking (Revelation 3:20) is a popular verse to memorize, and has been portrayed artistically as well. And certainly the repeated emphasis on overcoming is something many Christians find helpful.

But perhaps even more important to our examination of Revelation is the speculation of why these seven churches were singled out. Other churches were bigger or better. Paul had already paved the way with letters to churches at Rome, Corinth, Philippi, Thessalonica, and other places. Why did Jesus single out Ephesus, Smyrna, Pergamum, Thyatira, Sardis, Philadelphia, and Laodicea?

Apoca-Lips Now

"The Church is a symbol of eternity in the midst of the self-sufficient world."

—Rudolf Bultmann

Some people feel these seven churches are prototypical of most churches. Wherever we attend, we can probably find a similar profile to one of these churches, and can adapt the promises and/or words of warning to ourselves. Who among us can't point to a church we've attended that seems to have lost its first love, or has even reached a point of spiritual deadness? Maybe we've seen other groups that are small and suffering, yet have what surely must be a supernatural source of joy and stamina. Perhaps that's primarily why these seven churches were chosen.

Other people, however, suggest an even greater possibility of intentionality. In reviewing the history of the church from the first century until the present day, they see a more-than-coincidental pattern between the series of churches in Revelation and stages the church has gone through. Consequently, they see the choice of the seven churches as prophetic.

During the first century, the church remained fairly strong, but perhaps began to lose its first love a bit as the original apostles died off. Next followed a couple of centuries of intense persecution. During the next few centuries, false teachers began to influence the church. In following centuries, the church has at times seemed close to spiritual death, yet has recovered and become active in missions and outreach. Finally, perhaps the current church is working toward a state of lukewarm self-satisfaction.

So, while the seven churches were certainly historical ones, you can speculate if you wish that they might also have been chosen for other reasons. Like much of the rest of Revelation, people will differ to great degrees on their interpretations and speculations.

Back to the Future

But the history lesson is over. Whether or not you wanted to learn it, it's important to ground ourselves in the present to get a little bit of context. From this point onward, however, Revelation kicks into the future. And if you thought the symbolism has created a problem in understanding the messages to the churches, just wait.

Any reference to churches disappears at this point. We'll find some believers along the way, but in most cases they aren't going to be in much of a Sunday-go-to-meeting mood. As time winds down for the world as we know it, freedom of religion will be one of the first things to go. Yet for the few who overcome, all the things Jesus promised still apply. But let's move on and you can see for yourself.

The Least You Need to Know

➤ Before the Book of Revelation looks at future conditions, it deals with the present in which it was written.

➤ John was asked by Jesus to take dictation for letters to seven specific churches.

➤ The seven churches were most likely selected for a particular reason, but scholars disagree as to exactly what that reason was.

➤ No matter how good or bad the description of the church, Jesus made bold promises "to him who overcomes."

Part 2

The Storm Clouds Gather

So far what you've been learning about Revelation—the background and introduction—has been rather tame and perhaps not what you were expecting. But in this section things intensify quickly.

As you read about the four horsemen of the apocalypse, plagues, wars, famines, and more, it may feel very dark, frightening, and negative. It is. It's like watching the dark clouds roll in and realizing there's nothing you can do to avoid the coming storm.

During such times, the best you can do is hunker down, expect the worst, and keep an eye on the horizon until things lighten up. The storm in Revelation is about to hit. But as you look at the gathering clouds, keep in mind that there's a bright day coming.

Chapter 5

Scrolled, Sealed, Delivered

In This Chapter

➤ A look at Revelation 4–5

➤ John's invitation to visit heaven for a while

➤ A description of a number of heavenly beings

➤ A scroll with seven seals

A major factor in how much you believe (or pooh-pooh) what you read in the Book of Revelation will be how much trust you place in the credentials of the people involved. If you go along with the tradition that the author is indeed John, who had been a primary apostle of Jesus and who writes because he is inspired by God's Spirit, you'll have a different perspective than someone who thinks the whole Bible springs from the sheer imagination of men. If you believe that Jesus actually appeared to John and showed him some amazing and confusing things, you'll have a higher respect for what is being said than if you assume John was simply smoking whatever he could find growing on Patmos.

We saw in Chapter 4, "Seven Churches Get a Performance Review," that Jesus opened his letters to the churches with a different set of credentials in each case: "him who is the First and Last," "him who is holy and true," and so forth. And as Revelation shifts dramatically from John's present to his future, we will again see an emphasis on credentials. Since we're going to be talking about the end of the world, final judgment, eternal promises, and other matters of extreme importance, it's helpful to know who's in charge here. And that's exactly where the future segment of Revelation begins.

Knock, Knock, Knockin' on Heaven's Door

After this I looked, and there before me was a door standing open in heaven. And the voice I had first heard speaking to me like a trumpet said, "Come up here, and I will show you what must take place after this." At once I was in the Spirit, and there before me was a throne in heaven with someone sitting on it. And the one who sat there had the appearance of jasper and carnelian. A rainbow, resembling an emerald, encircled the throne (Revelation 4:1–3).

Clanging Symbols

A door is one of the symbols used by Jesus to describe himself: "I tell you the truth, I am the gate [door] for the sheep .... I am the gate [door]; whoever enters through me will be saved" (John 10:7, 9). The promise is also held out to "Knock and the door will be opened to you" (Matthew 7:7). Some people might suggest that the open door in Revelation symbolically reflects these previous references to Jesus.

Apoca-Lips Now

"Many are in high place, and of renown: but mysteries are revealed unto the meek."

—The Apocrypha, Ecclesiasticus 3:19

John had faithfully recorded letters to all seven churches as instructed. It was "after this," perhaps as he was shaking his wrist to relieve his writer's cramp, that he saw an open door in heaven. He not only saw the door, but heard a clear invitation to "come up here." The voice was the same as the one that had been speaking to him—based on all the descriptions, clearly the speaker must have been Jesus.

John stated simply that "At once, I was in the Spirit." What this means, exactly, is less simple. Most likely, he wasn't claiming to be whisked away bodily, like an alien abductee. Rather, the things he witnessed were probably on a spiritual plane while his body remained earthbound, on the island.

And if you want to nitpick with the language, it seems the sense of urgency has shifted just a bit. When being asked to write the letters to the churches (in the present), John had been told that the events to be described in Revelation were things that *will* take place later (Revelation 1:19). Here (stepping into the future) the word is a bit more emphatic. Those events have become the things that *must* take place (Revelation 4:1).

The first thing observed by John was a throne with a figure on it. Based on the description, the figure must surely be God, and this assumption is borne out partially because of the indirect description used. Throughout Scripture, we are told that mere humans are incapable of viewing the full glory of God. In most angel encounters, humans find themselves prostrate and quivering like 170-pound blobs of Jell-O. A face-to-face encounter with God is simply impossible.

The Old Testament Israelites were told, "You cannot see my face, for no one may see me and live" (Exodus 33:20). Moses was the closest thing to an exception to this rule. While it is said that he spoke to God "face to face, as a man speaks with his friend" (Exodus 33:11), he was never shown the full glory of God. When he asked to do so, God directed him to a cleft in a rock. God agreed to walk by, shielding Moses with his hand until he went past, and then removed his hand to allow Moses to see his back (Exodus 33:18–23). It seems John is witnessing a similar radiance, though without seeing clearly the face of God.

So John describes God in terms of his surroundings. Regular words just don't seem to get the job done, so John leans heavily on images of precious metals and precious stones. The figure on the throne had "the appearance of jasper and carnelian." We are familiar with jasper as the component of much of the petrified wood found in the American southwest. But while that form is primarily earth-toned (yellow, brown, red, and green), John describes jasper as "clear as crystal" (Revelation 21:11). Carnelian (also translated as *ruby* or *sardius*) is usually red or brownish red, deriving its color from iron oxide. The throne John saw was encircled by a rainbow, resembling an emerald, which would have been primarily a deep green color.

It's interesting to see that a rainbow surrounds the throne of God. You're probably familiar enough with the story of Noah to remember that the rainbow was given as a sign from God that he would never again destroy the world with water (Genesis 9:12–16). But as we will see, there are numerous other ways to express divine judgment.

Who Are Those Guys?

Surrounding the throne were twenty-four other thrones, and seated on them were twenty-four elders. They were dressed in white and had crowns of gold on their heads. From the throne

Flashback

Other biblical characters had close encounters with God. For example, both Isaiah (Isaiah 6:1–8) and Ezekiel (Ezekiel 1) saw things similar to what John describes. Ezekiel even writes of a similar radiance surrounding God "like the appearance of a rainbow in the clouds on a rainy day." And the Apostle Paul was "caught up to the third heaven" where he "heard inexpressible things, things that man is not permitted to tell" (2 Corinthians 12:2–4).

Flashback

In the Old Testament, the official dress of the high priest (designed by God and described in detail to Moses) included a breastplate of precious stones (Exodus 28:15–30). The first stone was a carnelian (ruby) and the last was a jasper. An emerald was also among the 12 stones listed.

came flashes of lightning, rumblings and peals of thunder. Before the throne, seven lamps were blazing. These are the seven spirits of God. Also before the throne there was what looked like a sea of glass, clear as crystal. In the center, around the throne, were four living creatures, and they were covered with eyes, in front and in back. The first living creature was like a lion, the second was like an ox, the third had a face like a man, the fourth was like a flying eagle. Each of the four living creatures had six wings and was covered with eyes all around, even under his wings. Day and night they never stop saying: "Holy, holy, holy is the Lord God Almighty, who was, and is, and is to come."

Whenever the living creatures give glory, honor and thanks to him who sits on the throne and who lives for ever and ever, the twenty-four elders fall down before him who sits on the throne, and worship him who lives for ever and ever. They lay their crowns before the throne and say: "You are worthy, our Lord and God, to receive glory and honor and power, for you created all things, and by your will they were created and have their being" (Revelation 4:4–11).

Around the main throne was a circle of 24 other thrones on which sat "elders." They were dressed in white clothing and wore crowns of gold. To accentuate this splendor came lightning and thunder from the throne, an expansive "sea of glass, clear as crystal," and the presence of seven blazing lamps that are identified as "the seven spirits of God" (or in other translations, "the sevenfold Spirit of God"). Some people suggest the burning lamps represent the Holy Spirit who came as "tongues of fire" on the Day of Pentecost (Acts 2:1–4). If so, the seven lamps would again symbolize completeness/perfection.

And who are these "elders"? Two popular theories are that they are either …

1. A special class of angels who have been designated for special service to God.

2. Resurrected human beings who have been judged and rewarded, and now represent all who believe in Jesus as savior.

The number 24 in this instance is often thought to be symbolic of the 12 tribes of Israel in the Old Testament and the 12 New Testament apostles.

We have a better clue as to the identity of the "four living creatures." In John's description, one appeared as a lion, one as an ox, one as an eagle, and one with the face of a man. Each had six wings and was covered with eyes. Ezekiel had described very similar creatures in his vision of heaven. In his case, however, all

Apoca-Lips Now

"Christians should never fail to sense the operation of an angelic glory. It forever eclipses the world of demonic powers, as the sun does a candle's light."

—Billy Graham

of the creatures had four faces: one face like a man, one like a lion, one like an ox, and one like an eagle. They, too, had numerous wings and eyes (Ezekiel 1:4–18). Later in his book, Ezekiel identifies these beings as cherubim (Ezekiel 10)—a special class of angels. The cherubim were the angels carved into the lid of the Ark of the Covenant, and are mentioned in numerous other places throughout Scripture.

Both groups—the elders and the living creatures—perpetually offered glory to God. The concept of eternity comes through clearly in this passage. The one on the throne "lives for ever and ever." The four living creatures offer praise "day and night" and never stop. The 24 elders respond to such praise by falling before the one on the throne, laying their crowns before him, and worshipping him "who lives for ever and ever." The credentials of this figure are not only unique, but also everlasting.

Scroll Call

> *Then I saw in the right hand of him who sat on the throne a scroll with writing on both sides and sealed with seven seals. And I saw a mighty angel proclaiming in a loud voice, "Who is worthy to break the seals and open the scroll?" But no one in heaven or on earth or under the earth could open the scroll or even look inside it. I wept and wept because no one was found who was worthy to open the scroll or look inside* (Revelation 5:1–4).

So far, we've seen some very impressive characters in the heavenly scene that John describes. They appear to be highly respected beings who are beyond reproach. Yet in this matter of credentials, we've still run into a problem.

The figure on the throne, assumed to be God himself, is holding a sealed scroll. It is obviously of great importance. It is covered with writing, front and back, yet no one is found worthy to pop the seals and see what it says.

Until the second century, essentially any reference to a "book" was actually a scroll. The material used could be leather, parchment, or papyrus that was glued or sewn together to provide sufficient length for the writer. Then the finished product was rolled around a rod so the writing (which was in columns) could be read as the manuscript was unrolled.

Flashback

In an Old Testament prophecy anticipating a future time of judgment, one of the warnings is that the stars will dissolve and fall and "the sky [will be] rolled up like a scroll" (Isaiah 34:4).

This particular scroll was sealed, which would not have been unusual during these times. The use (and popularity) of seals has been traced to the fourth millennium B.C.E. Usually a design (or name or statement) would be engraved into a hard substance (rock, metal, precious stones), which was then pressed into clay or soft wax to harden.

Seals were used to authenticate the source of letters, to formalize agreements, to verify disputed authorship, to indicate ownership, and to deny access to certain people. (Jesus' tomb was sealed, much for the same reason police put yellow tape across the doors at a crime scene.) In the case of this scroll in Revelation, the purpose of the seals would be to protect the document from being tampered with by people who had no business reading what was inside.

So the obvious question was posed by a mighty angel: "Who is worthy to break the seals and open the scroll?" When no answer was immediately forthcoming, John "wept and wept." Here he had been summoned into heaven itself to witness great things, and he had come across the most glorious and impressive figures he had ever seen. Now he was being taunted with a scroll that obviously concealed a message of utmost importance, and no one was stepping forward with the right credentials to open it. The disappointment he felt was enough to cause open weeping. But not for long.

Nothing Sheepish About This Lamb

Then one of the elders said to me, "Do not weep! See, the Lion of the tribe of Judah, the Root of David, has triumphed. He is able to open the scroll and its seven seals."

Clanging Symbols

For anyone who has run with the bulls in Pamplona, startled a moose in the wilderness, or gotten on the bad side of a goat in the barnyard, it should come as no surprise that horns were a symbol of strength and power. The number seven represented completion or perfection. What is a bit unusual is that this symbol of absolute power is attached to a *lamb*.

Then I saw a Lamb, looking as if it had been slain, standing in the center of the throne, encircled by the four living creatures and the elders. He had seven horns and seven eyes, which are the seven spirits of God sent out into all the earth. He came and took the scroll from the right hand of him who sat on the throne. And when he had taken it, the four living creatures and the twenty-four elders fell down before the Lamb. Each one had a harp and they were holding golden bowls full of incense, which are the prayers of the saints. And they sang a new song: "You are worthy to take the scroll and to open its seals, because you were slain, and with your blood you purchased men for God from every tribe and language and people and nation. You have made them to be a kingdom and priests to serve our God, and they will reign on the earth" (Revelation 5:5–10).

Although John was forlorn and weepy, those around him seemed to know something he didn't. One of the elders strolled over to encourage him, and told him that "the Lion of the tribe of Judah" would be able to open the scroll. When the Old Testament figure Jacob

(Israel) blessed his children, he called his son Judah "a lion's cub" (Genesis 49:9). Centuries had passed, but now the heavenly figure is identified as the "Lion of the tribe of Judah"—a symbol of highest honor. But when John turned to look, he didn't see a lion. Instead he saw a most peculiar-looking lamb. To begin with, it looked as if it had been killed. And on closer inspection, it had seven horns and seven eyes.

In addition to all the symbolic imagery, a clue to the identity of this Lion/Lamb is its location. It was "standing in the center of the throne, encircled by the four living creatures and the elders." Who could this figure symbolize other than Jesus? He had come from the line of Judah, he had been killed but came back to life, and he possessed unlimited power (seven horns) and the fullness of the spirit of God (seven eyes).

In addition to the physical description is the endorsement of the heavenly beings who attested: "with your blood you purchased men for God from every tribe and language and people and nation." If this isn't Jesus who stands in the center of the throne of God, Christianity is in for some serious reconsideration. It is Jesus alone who has the credentials to open the scroll taken from the right hand of God.

The Heavenly Huddle

Then I looked and heard the voice of many angels, numbering thousands upon thousands, and ten thousand times ten thousand. They encircled the throne and the living creatures and the elders. In a loud voice they sang: "Worthy is the Lamb, who was slain, to receive power and wealth and wisdom and strength and honor and glory and praise!"

Then I heard every creature in heaven and on earth and under the earth and on the sea, and all that is in them, singing: "To him who sits on the throne and to the Lamb be praise and honor and glory and power, for ever and ever!" The four living creatures said, "Amen," and the elders fell down and worshipped (Revelation 5:11–14).

A Bright Spot

It's interesting to note in this passage that the image of people playing harps in heaven does indeed come from the Bible (Revelation 5:8). In addition is the confirmation that our prayers get beyond the ceiling. Each of the 24 elders held a golden bowl "which are the prayers of the saints."

Apoca-Lips Now

"Millions of spiritual creatures walk the earth unseen, both when we sleep and when we awake."

—John Milton

For those outside of Christianity who don't believe Jesus to be the only way to God, this can be an irritating or troubling passage. Previously we have seen the heavenly hoard offering loud verbal praise to God the Father, who sits on the throne in heaven (Revelation 4:8, 11). Here, however, they turn equal attention to the Lamb (Revelation 5:9–14).

An enormous huddle begins to form. The throne with the radiant figure and the Lamb remain in the center. Around them stand the four living creatures and 24 elders. And at this point, an uncountable number of angels gravitate to the same location, crowding around the throne. The best estimate John could give was, "thousands upon thousands, and ten thousand times ten thousand."

And that still wasn't all. John also noted the voices of "every creature in heaven and on earth and under the earth and on the sea, and all that is in them." This entire crowd began to sing loud praises to the Lamb. All the praise and attention that had previously been bestowed on God the Father was now directed to the Jesus the Lamb. And since each of the 24 elders had a harp, apparently all the singing being done had some musical accompaniment as well.

Their song was a "new" one. (Just as Revelation contains a lot of "sevens," it also speaks of many "new" things—even more heavily as we get closer to the end.) The anticipation seemed to grow as this heavenly crowd realized that once the mysterious scroll was opened, things would never be the same.

Again, we need to notice the degree of detail John includes in his observations. For those who believe John's credentials as a writer and his account of what happened, it is amazing to consider what it might have been like to be beamed up to heaven and immediately start taking notes. What kind of reporters would most people make under similar circumstances?

For those who don't place any stock in John's credentials—or the divine inspiration of the Bible in general—it's easy to pick and choose what to believe and what to ignore. But now that we've dealt with the issue of credentials, let's not lollygag.

In the next chapter, the seals start popping.

A Bright Spot

The entire section of Revelation covered in this chapter is not only a bright spot, but perhaps a brilliant and blinding spot in places. This will not be true of much of the rest of the Book of Revelation. So if you think this section seemed a bit too sugary and churchy, the tone is quickly going to change.

Apoca-Lips Now

"I had a million questions to ask God: but when I met Him, they all fled my mind; and it didn't seem to matter."

—Christopher Morley

The Least You Need to Know

➤ John was invited into heaven, and responded "in the Spirit" to record what he saw and heard.

➤ Heaven appears to be populated by many kinds of strange and wonderful creatures.

➤ John's initial focus of attention was the activity that took place around a brilliant throne in heaven.

➤ Not only was God receiving intense praise from the heavenly population, but so was a Lamb who appeared to have been previously killed.

Chapter 6

Sealings, Nothing More Than Sealings

In This Chapter

➤ A look at Revelation 5–6

➤ What's under the first six seals on the heavenly scroll

➤ The four horsemen of the apocalypse

➤ A large group of people are sealed for their own protection

---

As we continue with Revelation in this chapter, we will see seals used in regard to both good news and bad news. Some will be protecting our eyes from bad things, and as the seals get broken we will witness terrible events. But we will also see another kind of seal used in a most positive way.

Our Lids Are Sealed

Before we jump right into the seals on the scroll that we saw in Chapter 5, "Scrolled, Sealed, Delivered," let's spend a moment considering what importance we place on seals even today. We may at first tend to think that wax seals on a scroll are ancient, dated, and irrelevant. Yet we continue to depend on seals as much as ever.

A few decades ago, when "canned foods" referred more frequently to glass jars with metal or paraffin seals across the top than to factory-sealed aluminum cans, the seal was of utmost importance. A can with a broken seal would alert the owner to potential accidental food poisoning. And after the Tylenol scare of a few years ago, most of us are by now wary of *intentional* tampering of edible products. If we pop the lid to discover the foil seal peeled halfway back, we're likely to reject that carton of milk, bottle of aspirin, or whatever. We prefer, if not demand, our food products sealed and tamper-proof.

In other cases, seals protect us by keeping us unaware of what they hide. Just as we seal our basements because we don't want our carpets and prized possessions to see water damage, we seal other things to keep them from being seen and/or available for use. Trigger locks prevent guns from accidentally being fired by the wrong hands. Parents can scramble certain cable stations to "seal" them from being viewed by too-young eyes. Child-resistant caps prevent the accidental over-consumption of even good things like vitamins or medicine.

Apoca-Lips Now

"Has this world been so kind to you that you should leave with regret? There are better things ahead than any we leave behind."

—C.S. Lewis

Those are a few of the potential bad-news connotations of seals. Yet in other ways, we use seals for only the most positive things. We slap them on diplomas and passports to make such documents official and harder to forge. Only our most special letters (for those few who still use pen and paper) are "sealed with a kiss." And many businesses have an official seal for their most special documents.

God's Housecleaning Seals of Disapproval

I watched as the Lamb opened the first of the seven seals. Then I heard one of the four living creatures say in a voice like thunder, "Come!" I looked, and there before me was a white horse! Its rider held a bow, and he was given a crown, and he rode out as a conqueror bent on conquest.

When the Lamb opened the second seal, I heard the second living creature say, "Come!" Then another horse came out, a fiery red one. Its rider was given power to take peace from the earth and to make men slay each other. To him was given a large sword.

When the Lamb opened the third seal, I heard the third living creature say, "Come!" I looked, and there before me was a black horse! Its rider was holding a pair of scales in his hand. Then I heard what sounded like a voice among the four living creatures, saying, "A quart of wheat for a day's wages, and three quarts of barley for a day's wages, and do not damage the oil and the wine!"

When the Lamb opened the fourth seal, I heard the voice of the fourth living creature say, "Come!" I looked, and there before me was a pale horse! Its rider was named

Death, and Hades was following close behind him. They were given power over a fourth of the earth to kill by sword, famine and plague, and by the wild beasts of the earth (Revelation 6:1–8).

A Bright Spot

If our focus remains only on the scary figures riding the horses, we may develop an incomplete perspective on Revelation. But it is the intentional activity in heaven that orchestrates the entire apocalyptic holocaust that follows. The Lamb is the one breaking the seals, and each of the four living creatures summons one of the horsemen upon the breach of the seal. As John records the behind-the-scenes activities, he makes it clear that not only is God aware of what's going on, he is also in charge of even the worst that is about to happen.

We know the scroll had a total of seven seals (Revelation 5:1). As each of the first four seals was opened, a rider on a horse appeared. By their appearance, it was clear these guys weren't looking for a game of polo—their missions (as well as their modes of transportation) were a horse of a different color. The riders have come to be called the Four Horsemen of the Apocalypse. It is at their appearance in the Book of Revelation that things really begin to get nasty.

The first rider is on a white horse. Normally a symbol of victory, this figure is sometimes assumed to be Jesus. However, as we will see when we try to assemble a workable chronology of Revelation, many people feel this interpretation does not make sense. They suggest just the opposite—that the bold figure is the antichrist. If we limit ourselves to this description only, an argument can be made either way.

However you want to look at it, the rider is described as "a conqueror bent on conquest." He also wears a crown and carries a bow. Since no arrow is mentioned, it is assumed by some that his conquest will be a peaceful one (at first).

Flashback

The Old Testament prophet Zechariah had a series of visions in a single night. The first and last were both similar to this portion of John's vision in that they included imagery of divinely designated, different-colored horses supporting riders or pulling chariots (Zechariah 1:7–11; 6:1–8).

The breaking of the second seal summoned a second rider, this one on a fiery red horse and wielding a large sword. Rider #2 had the special talent of making people kill each other, removing peace from the earth. If indeed the first rider had based his success on peace, it would be only temporary as he is followed by this second symbol—obviously one of war.

The third seal was opened, the third horseman was summoned, and a black horse came riding out. Rather than a weapon, this rider was holding a pair of scales. A clue to the significance of this rider is provided by the four living creatures, who associated his presence with vastly inflated prices for basic foods.

A day's wages should have bought 10 good meals during this time, but at these prices would provide only one. Wheat was preferable to barley, but barley was considerably cheaper and could be stretched further on low incomes. The reference to not damaging the oil and wine might indicate that divine limits will be imposed on the extent of the famine. Or it may simply mean that when famine hits in the Middle East, the grain crops tend to fail before the olives and grapes.

If we consider that this portion of Revelation might be chronological—which isn't too much of a stretch given the sequence of riders, one after another—it makes sense that famine would follow war. We've seen as much on the evening news in Africa, Eastern Europe, and other places. It also makes sense when we turn our attention to the next rider.

Apoca-Lips Now

"There will not cease to be ferment in the world unless people are sure of their food."

—Pearl S. Buck

The breach of the fourth seal revealed a pale (or, literally translated, a "pale green") horse, and the text leaves little doubt as to who the horseman is. The rider is clearly identified as "Death, and Hades was following close behind him." The personifications of death and hell make a nasty little tag team, and when their work is done, a fourth of the world's population lies dead. The wars and famines have taken their toll, and in addition we see carnage brought about by plagues and even rampaging wild animals. As these horsemen ride, there are all kinds of ways to die.

Are You Sure You Want to Go Through with This?

Let's pause here for just a moment to point out the challenge of interpreting Revelation. You can see that trying to assign specific identities to the horsemen is no small matter. Is the first rider indeed the antichrist? If so, how do we know? Can we determine not only his title, but his identity as well? *Should* we attempt to discern such things?

To begin with, we have very little to go on. People can't even agree if the events just described are in our past or future. If in the past, we cannot point to a specific time when a fourth of the population died, even during the worst wars and plagues. Yet if these are future events, and if we want to take them at face value, the math involved is terrifying. Look at a recent census and determine the number of deaths if a quarter of the population died within a relatively short time period.

So at this point, one of the simplest ways to interpret the significance of these horsemen is to avoid getting too specific. Let's resist any urge to speculate that Rider #3 might be Joe, your loner neighbor with ties to a secret militia. For now, let's simply identify the riders as the spirits of conquest, war, famine, and death. Later, as we gather more information, we will be better equipped to attempt some interpretations.

Flashback

When Jesus was asked about the signs of the end of the age, he gave a verbal picture surprisingly close to the sequence of events we have just witnessed:

"Watch out that no one deceives you. For many will come in my name, claiming, 'I am the Christ,' and will deceive many. You will hear of wars and rumors of wars, but see to it that you are not alarmed. Such things must happen, but the end is still to come. Nation will rise against nation, and kingdom against kingdom. There will be famines and earthquakes in various places. All these are the beginning of birth pangs. Then you will be handed over to be persecuted and put to death, and you will be hated by all nations because of me. At that time many will turn away from the faith and will betray and hate each other, and many false prophets will appear and deceive many people" (Matthew 24:4–11).

White Clothes and Dark Skies

When he opened the fifth seal, I saw under the altar the souls of those who had been slain because of the word of God and the testimony they had maintained. They called out in a loud voice, "How long, Sovereign Lord, holy and true, until you judge the inhabitants of the earth and avenge our blood?" Then each of them was given a white robe, and they were told to wait a little longer, until the number of their fellow servants and brothers who were to be killed as they had been was completed.

I watched as he opened the sixth seal. There was a great earthquake. The sun turned black like sackcloth made of goat hair, the whole moon turned blood red, and the stars in the sky fell to earth, as late figs drop from a fig tree when shaken by a strong wind. The sky receded like a scroll, rolling up, and every mountain and island was removed from its place.

Then the kings of the earth, the princes, the generals, the rich, the mighty, and every slave and every free man hid in caves and among the rocks of the mountains. They called to the mountains and the rocks, "Fall on us and hide us from the face of him who sits on the throne and from the wrath of the Lamb! For the great day of their wrath has come, and who can stand?" (Revelation 6:9–17).

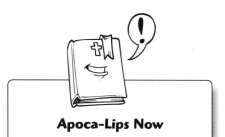

Apoca-Lips Now

"I am God's wheat, and I am ground by the teeth of wild beasts that I may be found pure bread of Christ."

—St. Ignatius of Antioch

The four grim horsemen of the apocalypse are the results of the first four seals that were opened, but there are still three seals to go. The scene changes dramatically as the fifth seal is opened by the Lamb in heaven. Rather than further gloom and doom on horseback, we see the results of some of the gory doings that have already taken place. A number of people whose "testimony" had remained faithful to God had been killed, and they weren't very happy about it.

Now in heaven, they cried out to God, wondering how long it would be before he avenged their unjust deaths. In response, white robes were passed out for them to wear and they were asked to wait "a little longer." The killing wasn't quite over, but the end was drawing near. (We will learn more about this group when we get to Revelation 7:9–17.)

But turning our attention to the opening of the sixth seal, we see the forces of nature affected. A great earthquake struck. The sun turned black. The moon turned blood red. Stars started shooting across the skies "as late figs drop from a fig tree." Mountains and islands were shaken. The sky itself seemed to be collapsing.

At this point we get the first indication of how the people on earth are responding to all the activity that has been taking place. Apparently their survival instincts have kicked in, for we see them hiding in caves and among rocks. Yet at the same time they are praying for death, asking the mountains to fall on them. They seem to suspect that their geologic problems have a divine source.

But as we will soon see, this is only the first in a series of judgments. Things are going to get even worse, and as they do, people's attitudes will become more callous. Now, however, the big question is, "Who can stand?" We're about to find out.

After Six Terrible Seals, 144,000 Good Ones

After this I saw four angels standing at the four corners of the earth, holding back the four winds of the earth to prevent any wind from blowing on the land or on the sea or on any tree. Then I saw another angel coming up from the east, having the seal of the living God. He called out in a loud voice to the four angels who had been given power to harm the land and the sea: "Do not harm the land or the sea or the trees until we put a seal on the foreheads of the servants of our God." Then I heard the number of those who were sealed: 144,000 from all the tribes of Israel.

From the tribe of Judah 12,000 were sealed, from the tribe of Reuben 12,000, from the tribe of Gad 12,000, from the tribe of Asher 12,000, from the tribe of Naphtali 12,000, from the tribe of Manasseh 12,000, from the tribe of Simeon 12,000, from the tribe of Levi 12,000, from the tribe of Issachar 12,000, from the tribe of Zebulun 12,000, from the tribe of Joseph 12,000, from the tribe of Benjamin 12,000 (Revelation 7:1–8).

As tremendous numbers of people are dropping dead from war, famine, plagues, and such, the survivors wonder who can stand. Here we have an answer. God has determined to protect at least 144,000 people. But who are they?

Like any other question in Revelation, this query has more than one possible answer. Some say this group of 144,000 symbolizes the people who will remain faithful to God in spite of all the terrible things happening to them and around them during the end times. (Note: Technically, references to the "end times" or "last days" can include the time between Jesus' first coming and second coming. Yet more often than not, the terms are used in reference to a future near-the-end-of-the-world time.)

Flashback

After he killed Abel, Cain soon began to fear that his own life was in danger, but God promised to protect him. We are told, "Then the Lord put a mark on Cain so that no one who found him would kill him" (Genesis 4:15). Here in Revelation, we find a similar protective mark 144,000 times over. After the devastation connected with the seals on the scroll, it is refreshing to see that God "seals" people in positive ways as well.

Others disagree. They point to the details provided in this account and propose that such specificity allows for a much more literal interpretation. They would argue that this group is indeed a Jewish contingent, and that even in the turbulent times of the Great Tribulation, God will uphold Old Testament promises to protect and reward his people.

One reason for the different interpretations is that we have lost track of many of the Jewish genealogies. When the Israelites were carried into captivity after the series of kings of Israel and Judah, many of them became "lost" tribes. While they had previously lived in separate, clearly designated tribal territories, they never returned to that system. Most contemporary Jewish people cannot trace their lineage to specific tribes. So is the number of "sealed" people in each tribe a moot point?

Some say yes. Others say that even though *they* no longer know which tribe they are descended from, God knows. It is no problem for him to select a specific number from each ancient tribe if he so wishes.

To further the speculation on this passage, we might note that the tribes mentioned don't correspond exactly with the sons of Israel. Most of the 12 tribes were named for one of the sons of Jacob (Israel), but there was no geographic area named after Joseph or Levi. The Levites were scattered among the other tribes to attend to the spiritual needs of the people. And Joseph actually received a double dose of God's blessing, with land going to each of his sons, Manasseh and Ephraim. So starting with the 12 sons of Jacob (Israel) minus Joseph and Levi, plus Manasseh and Ephraim, there were still 12 tribes.

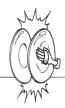

Clanging Symbols

The "seal" was used as a symbol throughout the Bible. In the classic love story recorded in Song of Songs, the bride tells her lover, "Place me like a seal over your heart, like a seal on your arm" (Song of Songs 8:6). Jesus speaks of God's seal of approval placed on certain people (John 6:27). Paul referred to believers as the "seal of [his] apostleship" (1 Corinthians 9:2) and to the Holy Spirit as "a seal ... who is a deposit guaranteeing our inheritance" (Ephesians 1:13). In the context of these passages, it seems clear that God's seals are tamper-proof, which is good news for the 144,000 sealed people in Revelation.

This passage in Revelation also lists 12 tribes. However, this one includes Joseph and Levi, and also includes one of Joseph's sons, Manasseh. The tribe of Dan, for some reason, is missing. The people in Dan's tribe had been among the first to entangle themselves in idolatry long ago (Judges 18:30–31), yet Old Testament prophecies list Dan among the tribes to be rewarded at a future time (Ezekiel 48:1–2, 32). As people ponder why poor Dan is left out of the listing in Revelation 7:5–8, some of them conjecture that the antichrist may come from that particular tribe. We have no proof one way or the other.

But in the jumble of specifics that we're unclear about, let's not miss the big picture, which remains clear: According to Revelation, God is going to see a significant number of people through to the end. In spite of widespread natural disasters and intense personal persecution, they will be survivors. (The seal of God ensures one's survival more certainly than even an immunity necklace!)

So to answer the question, "Who can stand?" we have one group for sure (whether a literal 144,000, or a symbolic different number). There's a second group as well, but they don't have it quite as good as this first one.

Tonight We're Going to Party Like It's When We Were Alive

After this I looked and there before me was a great multitude that no one could count, from every nation, tribe, people and language, standing before the throne and in front of the Lamb. They were wearing white robes and were holding palm branches in their hands. And they cried out in a loud voice: "Salvation belongs to our God, who sits on the throne, and to the Lamb." All the angels were standing around the throne and around the elders and the four living creatures. They fell down on their faces before the throne and worshiped God, saying: "Amen! Praise and glory and wisdom and thanks and honor and power and strength be to our God for ever and ever. Amen!"

Then one of the elders asked me, "These in white robes—who are they, and where did they come from?"

I answered, "Sir, you know." And he said, "These are they who have come out of the great tribulation; they have washed their robes and made them white in the blood of the Lamb. Therefore, they are before the throne of God and serve him day and night in his temple; and he who sits on the throne will spread his tent over them. Never again will they hunger; never again will they thirst. The sun will not beat upon them, nor any scorching heat. For the Lamb at the center of the throne will be their shepherd; he will lead them to springs of living water. And God will wipe away every tear from their eyes" (Revelation 7:9–17).

While a small sampling of the population is sealed to prevent harm from coming to them during the great tribulation, a much larger group appears destined to suffer and/or die as a result of their faith. The first group was identified as Jewish tribes (though some consider the reference to be symbolic). In this case, however, the group is comprised of "every nation, tribe, people, and language."

More than likely, this is a more detailed description of the group we saw at the opening of the fifth seal—"those who had been slain because of the word of God and the testimony they had maintained" (Revelation 6:9). The white robes had been handed out at that time, and now the group is all properly dressed. They seem to fit in well with the others in heaven because they stand before the throne and loudly proclaim glory to God and to the Lamb.

One of the 24 elders gave John a pop quiz: "Who are they, and where did they come from?"

John dodged the question with the first-century equivalent of, "Why don't *you* tell *me?*" So we get another direct piece of information to help us understand Revelation: "These are they who have come out of the great tribulation." And since they are seen in heaven, they apparently are martyrs. Because they held to their faith, even unto death, they are now privileged to have a position before the throne of God to be in his presence "day and night."

Apoca-Lips Now

"I would willingly endure all the sufferings of this world to be raised a degree higher in heaven, and to possess the smallest increase of the knowledge of God's greatness."

—St. Teresa of Avila

The additional information seems to suggest the manner in which some of them died—hunger, thirst, and scorching heat, among other things. But never again for eternity will they experience pain or discomfort. Not only will any physical needs be attended to ("he will lead them to springs of living water"), but their emotional/spiritual needs will be met as well. God himself will wipe away every tear from their eyes.

We will see this group again before we get out of Revelation. For now, let's let them enjoy themselves in the presence of God. We need to get back to less pleasant undertakings. You may have noticed that while the scroll contained seven seals, we've seen what's beneath only six of them. The next chapter will deal with what's under that last seal. And let's just say it's likely to dispel any notions you might have about seven being a lucky number.

The Least You Need to Know

➤ Of the seven seals on the heavenly scroll, the first four reveal the four horsemen of the apocalypse—conquest, bloodshed (war), famine, and death.

➤ The fifth seal reveals a heavenly crew eager for justice to be done on those who had killed them.

➤ The sixth seal unleashes grave natural disasters on the people on earth.

➤ A significant group of people is sealed by God and promised protection during the terrible events scheduled to take place.

Chapter 7

Horns of Plenty
(of Trouble)

In This Chapter

➤ A look at Revelation 8–9

➤ A short period of dead silence in heaven

➤ The seventh seal (the seven trumpet judgments)

➤ Weird locusts, bizarre horses, and a host of other strange things

---

Perhaps we need to consult an expert before going any further with Revelation—Mel Brooks. His classic movie *Young Frankenstein* contains a scene where Dr. Frankenstein and Igor ("eye-gore") are doing the most detestable job imaginable. In order for the doctor's work to advance, they are in a cemetery in the dead of night, digging up a recently interred corpse. Igor comments that things could be worse. The doctor, exasperated, asks how things could possibly be worse. Igor shrugs and says, "Could be raining." Immediately the thunder booms and the skies open with torrential rain.

Reading through the Book of Revelation can evoke a similar emotional response. We read of unimaginable sufferings, shocking death statistics, and other terrible judgments. Like sitting through a horror movie, we are quite relieved with the end of each graphic scene, hoping for a break where we can unclench our fists and let our heart rates get back to normal. But as soon as we begin to let down our guard, some unexpected figure jumps out and once more shakes us to the core.

Having bravely made it through six seals, we're prepared for the final one. We can take one more seal, no matter how bad. Right?

You might think so, yet the seventh seal begins a *new* series of judgments known as the seven trumpets. So here we go again. (And if you're familiar with how horror movies work, you might begin right now to be concerned with what's going to happen once that seventh trumpet sounds.)

The Calm Before the Storm

When he opened the seventh seal, there was silence in heaven for about half an hour.

And I saw the seven angels who stand before God, and to them were given seven trumpets.

Another angel, who had a golden censer, came and stood at the altar. He was given much incense to offer, with the prayers of all the saints, on the golden altar before the throne. The smoke of the incense, together with the prayers of the saints, went up before God from the angel's hand. Then the angel took the censer, filled it with fire from the altar, and hurled it on the earth; and there came peals of thunder, rumblings, flashes of lightning and an earthquake.

Then the seven angels who had the seven trumpets prepared to sound them (Revelation 8:1–6).

Apoca-Lips Now

"We are afraid
Of pain but more afraid of
   silence; for no nightmare
Of hostile objects could be
   as terrible as this void.
This is the abomination. This is
   the wrath of God."

—W.H. Auden

An old proverb tells us that "Silence is golden." But most of us will never know first-hand. How often do you get a half-hour, when you are both awake and conscious, of complete silence? We doze off with sleep timers on the television and awaken to radio alarms. Cars, elevators, and offices are filled with music or news. If we dare break away from the noise for some solitude, we tend to pack beepers and cell phones to keep our personal conversations going. Silence may be golden, but it's well-hidden gold.

Deafening Silence

So far in our trip through the Book of Revelation, essentially every reference to heaven has included loud and verbal praise to God from everyone present. But suddenly, at the opening of the seventh and final seal on the scroll, we witness "silence in heaven for about half an hour."

Perhaps the estimate was John's best guess, but in the context of eternity, what we know as time is a tricky concept. We are told elsewhere in the Bible that, "With the Lord a day is like a thousand years, and a thousand years are like a day" (2 Peter 3:8). On this timetable, what seems like a half-hour might be closer to 21 years. On the other hand, a couple of minutes of sudden silence after all the jubilant noise might have seemed much longer.

But suffice it to say that for a considerable period of time the heavenly beings stopped their praises, somber if not stunned at what was about to happen. The marked silence reveals the gravity of the situation. Most of what happens in the rest of the Book of Revelation is the result of the opening of this final seal.

Censered

Eight angels have assignments in this passage. Seven are handed trumpets. They will each eventually have a short solo. But the other angel holds a golden censer, and he goes first.

Flashback

An interesting censer story that surprisingly wasn't censored from the Bible is found in Numbers 16. While Moses was leading the Israelites from Egypt to the Promised Land, his authority was challenged by a group of 250 priest wannabes and their ringleader, Korah. The showdown to determine who God wanted in the primary position of spiritual authority involved having everyone offer incense in a censer. Moses explained that if nothing happened to the rebels, then Moses' authority wasn't God-ordained, but that if "something totally new" took place, the people would know that Korah was an imposter.

As everyone presented their fiery censers to God, an earthquake hit with Korah at the epicenter, swallowing his household and his possessions so quickly that "they went down alive into the grave." Meanwhile, "Fire came out from the Lord" (perhaps lightning?) and fried Korah's 250 supporters. And even though Korah's group had misused their censers, the censers themselves were considered holy and salvaged from the smoldering rubble. Aaron also used his censer to miraculously stop a plague spreading through the camp of the grumbling Israelites (vv. 46–50). A total of almost 15,000 people died in this biblical account.

A censer is a saucepan-shaped metal doodad that holds incense while it is burning. During worship, coals would be carried in a censer from the outdoor altar where animals were sacrificed to an altar of incense inside the temple or tabernacle. There incense would be poured on the coals, producing smoke. The smoke symbolized the prayers of the people, rising up to God.

In John's description, the angel serves at a golden altar before the throne of God. He is given "much incense to offer, with the prayers of all the saints." There, in God's presence, the smoke/prayers rose. After this act, however, the angel refilled the censer with fresh hot coals and hurled it to the earth, producing loud thunder, lightning, and an earthquake. And just as distant thunder warns of an approaching storm, this action preceded the sounding of the seven trumpets.

A Bright Spot

In spite of all the devastation about to take place in this portion of Revelation, the trumpet judgments are preceded by a powerful image suggesting that the prayers of God's people are still being heard. It may not be too much of a stretch to consider that the trumpet judgments are God's response to a lengthy accumulation of prayers for justice. (See Revelation 6:9–10.)

Torched by an Angel

The first angel sounded his trumpet, and there came hail and fire mixed with blood, and it was hurled down upon the earth. A third of the earth was burned up, a third of the trees were burned up, and all the green grass was burned up.

The second angel sounded his trumpet, and something like a huge mountain, all ablaze, was thrown into the sea. A third of the sea turned into blood, a third of the living creatures in the sea died, and a third of the ships were destroyed.

The third angel sounded his trumpet, and a great star, blazing like a torch, fell from the sky on a third of the rivers and on the springs of water—the name of the star is Wormwood. A third of the waters turned bitter, and many people died from the waters that had become bitter.

The fourth angel sounded his trumpet, and a third of the sun was struck, a third of the moon, and a third of the stars, so that a third of them turned dark. A third of the day was without light, and also a third of the night (Revelation 8:7–12).

In spite of what you might think about the music of Herb Alpert, Miles Davis, Dizzy Gillespie, or Barry Glickman and his Golden Cornet, trumpet players of the Bible normally command a lot of respect. The seven angelic hornsmen of Revelation are no exception. And based on the severity of the trumpet judgments, let's just be glad they aren't playing tubas.

Clanging Symbols

Throughout the Bible, trumpets are used to initiate or announce big events. Gideon once defeated a huge army with a band of 300 men "armed" not with swords, but with trumpets, torches, and clay pitchers (Judges 7:15–25). King Saul used a trumpet to assemble his troops (1 Samuel 13:3). Ezekiel the prophet was compared to a watchman whose job it was to sound a trumpet when he saw trouble approaching (Ezekiel 33:1–9). Zechariah writes of a trumpet announcing the appearance of God (Zechariah 9:14). Paul writes of the resurrection of the dead, summoned by "the voice of the archangel and with the trumpet call of God" (1 Thessalonians 4:16–17). And Jesus speaks of his return preceded by angels providing a "loud trumpet call" (Matthew 24:30–31).

At the sound of the trumpet of the first angel, hail and fire descended upon the earth, affecting the vegetation. A third of the trees, grass, and land was burned up.

The second angel's trumpet had a similar effect on the seas. A mountain-sized meteorite (or some equivalent) plunged into the ocean, turning it to blood and killing a third of the animal life, as well as taking out a third of the boats. Many feel the water-to-blood imagery is not necessarily literal. More likely, they say, the water had the *appearance* of blood. For example, the King James Version of Revelation 6:12 says, "the moon became like blood." More recent translations read, "the whole moon turned blood red."

The third trumpet blast likewise polluted a third of the fresh water on earth. Something fell from the sky that John described as "a great star, blazing like a torch." He called the star Wormwood, and it made a third of the fresh water bitter, killing many who drank it. While polluting fresh water is not hard to do, this event is sometimes thought to reflect a miracle performed while the Israelites were in the wilderness on the way to the Promised Land. At one of the first places they stopped after crossing the Red Sea, the only water they found

Flashback

The water-to-blood judgment is nothing new here in Revelation. It was one of the first signs Moses performed attempting to convince Pharaoh to let the Israelites leave Egypt (Exodus 7:14–24). Whatever happened made the Nile water stinky and undrinkable, and killed the fish in it.

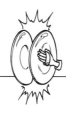

Clanging Symbols

Wormwood means little to most people today, but it would have been a significant symbol to people receiving John's original writing. Wormwood is a plant that produces a bitter-flavored oil. (The liqueur absinthe is derived from one form of this plant, and is forbidden in many countries because excessive use can cause mental problems and/or death.) In a biblical context, wormwood came to symbolize bitterness.

was rank and bitter. At God's instructions, Moses threw a specific piece of wood into the water and it became pure (Exodus 15:22–27). So the pollution of the water in Revelation is perceived by some people to be just as divine and miraculous as the sudden purification of the water in the wilderness.

In another action that paralleled one of the plagues in Egypt, the fourth angel brought darkness as he blew his trumpet and a third of the light was diminished from the sun, moon, and stars. Psychological studies teach us about the importance of light in our daily and weekly cycles. Assuming that these trumpet judgments are taking place in the order stated, it must be quite devastating to experience so much natural disaster only to then have the skies themselves turn dark and gloomy. It certainly wouldn't do much to build morale.

And the worst is still ahead. The trumpets yet to come (#5, #6, and #7) are equated with Woes #1, #2, and #3. They are so designated because of the increased severity of the judgments associated with them.

Woe, Woe, Woe, Your Boat Sank at Trumpet #2

As I watched, I heard an eagle that was flying in midair call out in a loud voice: "Woe! Woe! Woe to the inhabitants of the earth, because of the trumpet blasts about to be sounded by the other three angels!"

The fifth angel sounded his trumpet, and I saw a star that had fallen from the sky to the earth. The star was given the key to the shaft of the Abyss. When he opened the Abyss, smoke rose from it like the smoke from a gigantic furnace. The sun and sky were darkened by the smoke from the Abyss. And out of the smoke locusts came down upon the earth and were given power like that of scorpions of the earth. They were told not to harm the grass of the earth or any plant or tree, but only those people who did not have the seal of God on their foreheads. They were not given power to kill them, but only to torture them for five months. And the agony they suffered was like that of the sting of a scorpion when it strikes a man. During those days men will seek death, but will not find it; they will long to die, but death will elude them.

The locusts looked like horses prepared for battle. On their heads they wore something like crowns of gold, and their faces resembled human faces. Their hair was like women's hair, and their teeth were like lions' teeth. They had breastplates like breastplates of iron, and the sound of their wings was like the thundering of many horses and chariots rushing into battle. They had tails and stings like scorpions, and in their tails they had power to torment people for five months. They had as king over them the angel of the Abyss, whose name in Hebrew is Abaddon, and in Greek, Apollyon.

The first woe is past; two other woes are yet to come (Revelation 8:13–9:12).

The early trumpet judgments had sent lots of stuff plummeting from the sky to the earth. We've seen a fiery censer (Revelation 8:5), hail and fire mixed with blood (v. 7), something like a huge mountain, all ablaze (v. 8), and a great star blazing like a torch (v. 10). Now, at the sounding of the fifth trumpet, we see another star. But this one appears to be quite different from anything that has come previously.

A "Star" Is Born

The "star" that falls in this case is given personal attributes. It is referred to as "he" (Revelation 9:2) and performs intentional actions. Apparently, this so-called star is no inanimate object. "He" had a key and headed straight for the Abyss.

Flashback

This is not the Bible's first mention of the Abyss. When Jesus was teaching and healing people, he came upon a young man who was possessed by a number of evil spirits known as "Legion." Jesus was going to cast these demons out of the man, and they begged him not to order them to go to the Abyss (Luke 8:31). Instead, they went into a large herd of pigs feeding nearby, and the entire herd ran into a lake and drowned.

A word of warning: This isn't the last mention of the Abyss, either. We will hear more about it later in Revelation.

The name of the Abyss is taken from the Greek word *abyssos,* which means bottomless. It's where we get the concept of a bottomless pit, and it's a place even demons despise to go. In this passage, however, a number of horrible spirits are being released. The "star" that fell from the heavens had a key and opened the Abyss. As he did, smoke rose that was sufficient to blot the sunlight for a while.

We know that the Abyss was a type of holding cell for evil spirits, yet what John described appearing at this juncture were "locusts." His peculiar description of the locusts cause many people to assume they were the form taken by the demons who had been released from the Abyss.

A Bright Spot

This portion of Revelation has precious little to highlight as positive. Yet if we read closely we see that the key to the Abyss "was given" to the ominous "star" (Revelation 9:1). He didn't have it of his own accord, nor did he take it from its owner. It appears that the tremendous powers described, as horrendous as they are, continue to be orchestrated by an even more powerful source.

Apoca-Lips Now

"When all the world dissolves,
And every creature shall be
   purified,
All place shall be hell that is not
   heaven."

—Christopher Marlowe

Day of the Locust

Regular locusts are grasshopper-like insects. What John described, however, doesn't sound at all like grasshoppers—or even insects, for that matter. He compared them to "horses prepared for battle." They wore something like crowns of gold. Their faces seemed human. They had teeth like lions, and hair like women. They had an armor-like protection, made a lot of noise when they moved, and had tails that could sting like scorpions.

Regular locusts were feared by most biblical civilizations because one large swarm could strip away most crops in a matter of minutes, creating an almost certain famine to follow. In addition, the females laid large quantities of eggs deep in the soil that would hatch in the spring, resulting in larval nymphs that would eat whatever had grown back.

These "locusts" of Revelation, however, did not attack plant life. Instead, they turned their attention to human beings. The "sting" of these things, whatever they were, was not fatal. However, during a five-month period they created great pain—so much pain, in fact, that their victims *wished* for death. Those who had the seal of God were not afflicted by these beings.

Another hint that these "locusts" might not be mere insects is the fact that they had a "king" identified as "the angel of the Abyss" (Revelation 9:11). Perhaps this is the figure who released them in the first place. He even had a name, "Abaddon" or "Apollyon." Those are his Hebrew and Greek names. In English, he would be named Destroyer.

Regardless of how we interpret this portion of Revelation—insects, demons, or whatever—we can surely infer that something significant is taking place. John described the events connected with each of the first four trumpets with just a short paragraph or so.

Here, however, he begins to add more detail and become more specific. We might not have a clue what's going on, but the attention given it by the writer creates a natural emphasis on its importance.

If You Thought the Locusts Were Bad, Take a Look at These Horses!

The sixth angel sounded his trumpet, and I heard a voice coming from the horns of the golden altar that is before God. It said to the sixth angel who had the trumpet, "Release the four angels who are bound at the great river Euphrates." And the four angels who had been kept ready for this very hour and day and month and year were released to kill a third of mankind. The number of the mounted troops was two hundred million. I heard their number.

The horses and riders I saw in my vision looked like this: Their breastplates were fiery red, dark blue, and yellow as sulfur. The heads of the horses resembled the heads of lions, and out of their mouths came fire, smoke and sulfur. A third of mankind was killed by the three plagues of fire, smoke and sulfur that came out of their mouths. The power of the horses was in their mouths and in their tails; for their tails were like snakes, having heads with which they inflict injury.

The rest of mankind that were not killed by these plagues still did not repent of the work of their hands; they did not stop worshiping demons, and idols of gold, silver, bronze, stone and wood—idols that cannot see or hear or walk. Nor did they repent of their murders, their magic arts, their sexual immorality or their thefts (Revelation 9:13–21).

The death count had leveled off during the events associated with the fifth trumpet, although the stinging locusts (whatever they may be) had created a tortuous kind of pain for many people. But after the sounding of the sixth angel's trumpet, another significant percentage of the population would soon die.

The trumpet blew, a voice spoke, and the sixth trumpet-playing angel was told to release four other angels who had been bound. Since good angels wouldn't have needed a timeout for misbehavior, the four bound angels were probably up to no good. Their location was near the Euphrates River, and the purpose of their release was "to kill a third of mankind."

A Bright Spot

In another tiny clause within the harsh trumpet judgments is a notation that these four awful angels "had been kept ready for this very hour and day and month and year." With all that's going on, nothing is random or out of control.

At this point the narrative suddenly begins to describe warfare. There seems to be a correlation with the release of the four angels and the hostile activity on earth, but the connection is unclear. Assembled for war was an enormous contingent of mounted troops numbering 200 million. John, in his account, makes it clear that, "I heard their number." It would have been most difficult to make estimates by merely observing such a horde. And while the number sounds a bit on the high side at first, China, for example, boasted an army of 200 million soldiers as early as 1965.

The locusts in the previous section were compared to horses (9:7), so it should come as no surprise that horses are likewise described in extreme terms. Not since the Trojan horse have equines been responsible for so much damage. Their heads looked more like those of lions, and from their mouths came fire, smoke, and sulfur. It was this substance or mixture of substances that killed a third of the population. In addition to the deadly "mouths" of the horses, their tails were also bizarre—like snakes with heads of their own that could also injure others. The colors associated with the horses and their riders were fiery red, dark blue, and bright yellow.

The description of fire, smoke, and sulfur have led some people to believe that John was giving his best description of machinery (tanks, missiles, or some other war tools) which he would have had no other way of explaining. If literal animals, both the locusts and the horses would have to be some kind of mutants to fit the descriptions provided for them. But in the apocalyptic world of Revelation, it's hard to rule out anything for sure.

The effect of the harm done by these "horses" is described as a plague. And at this point we are shown the spiritual state of people during this time. We've seen that many of those who had expressed faith in God had been martyred. Now we see that the majority of those still on earth were active in idolatry, demon worship, murder, occult practices, stealing, and sexual immorality. Although the extreme difficulties they were facing might be viewed as divine judgments, they didn't care. They refused to repent or to stop what they were doing. Of course, with the world in the shape that has been described so far, it shouldn't be surprising if most of its inhabitants have adopted the motto of "Every man for himself."

Apoca-Lips Now

"It is a painful thing
To look at your own trouble and
know
That you yourself and no one
else has made it."

—Sophocles

Apoca-Lips Now

"The bow of God's wrath is bent, and the arrow made ready on the string, and justice bends the arrow at your heart, and strains the bow, and there is nothing but the mere pleasure of God, and that of an angry God, without any promise or obligation at all, that keeps the arrow one moment from being made drunk with your blood."

—Jonathan Edwards

Time for an Intermission in the Trumpet Recital

In the description of the seven seals, you may remember there was a parenthetical account between the sixth and seventh ones. Similarly, we have now been through the first six trumpets, and we're going to put the progress on pause for a chapter in order to accumulate a bit more information as to what is going on.

If you've been keeping score in the meantime, you will have noticed that the world's population is rapidly decreasing. We first saw a fourth of everyone killed (Revelation 6:8) and then another third of those left (Revelation 9:18). If you do the math, that leaves us with only half of those we started with. (And if you talk to certain people, they'll tell you all the Christians disappeared before any of this started. We'll deal with that particular interpretation later, but we can acknowledge that such a viewpoint would account for another considerable loss of population by this point in time.)

And still we have another trumpet left to hear from. By now, surely no one can remotely think it might signal good news.

The Least You Need to Know

➤ The seventh seal initiates a second series of judgments—the seven trumpets.

➤ The severity of the trumpet judgments is marked by an extended silence in heaven.

➤ Increased demonic activity is anticipated during this time.

➤ Another third of the population is expected to die during these judgments.

Chapter 8

Witness for the Persecution

In This Chapter

➤ A look at Revelation 10–11:14

➤ Yet another angel, yet another scroll

➤ John is assigned some chores

➤ The fall and rise of two powerful witnesses

If you're an aspiring screenwriter, it's hard to go wrong if your pitch includes a bedraggled yet determined underdog standing up against a much more powerful force. Outclassed, outnumbered, and out of options, your hero must make his (or her!) stand and somehow come out victorious. Or add a twist that's even more certain to succeed: Have your hero sacrifice himself for the group he is fighting for.

Think about the movies using this formula that have become classics: *Rocky. Norma Rae. Erin Brockavich. Mr. Smith Goes to Washington. Titanic. Star Wars. Braveheart.* The list goes on and on. The names, faces, and settings change, but the basic plot remains the same. The next section of Revelation contains a similar scene that predates all these others.

Before we meet our heroes, however, let's see what John's up to as he awaits the sounding of the seventh trumpet.

A Mightier Angel, a Tinier Scroll

Then I saw another mighty angel coming down from heaven. He was robed in a cloud, with a rainbow above his head; his face was like the sun, and his legs were like fiery pillars. He was holding a little scroll, which lay open in his hand. He planted his right foot on the sea and his left foot on the land, and he gave a loud shout like the roar of a lion. When he shouted, the voices of the seven thunders spoke. And when the seven thunders spoke, I was about to write; but I heard a voice from heaven say, "Seal up what the seven thunders have said and do not write it down."

Then the angel I had seen standing on the sea and on the land raised his right hand to heaven. And he swore by him who lives for ever and ever, who created the heavens and all that is in them, the earth and all that is in it, and the sea and all that is in it, and said, "There will be no more delay! But in the days when the seventh angel is about to sound his trumpet, the mystery of God will be accomplished, just as he announced to his servants the prophets."

Then the voice that I had heard from heaven spoke to me once more: "Go, take the scroll that lies open in the hand of the angel who is standing on the sea and on the land."

So I went to the angel and asked him to give me the little scroll. He said to me, "Take it and eat it. It will turn your stomach sour, but in your mouth it will be as sweet as honey." I took the little scroll from the angel's hand and ate it. It tasted as sweet as honey in my mouth, but when I had eaten it, my stomach turned sour. Then I was told, "You must prophesy again about many peoples, nations, languages and kings" (Revelation 10:1–11).

What do you suppose it would take for an angel to stand out among all the others we've witnessed so far? John has previously described the four living creatures (whom we have assumed to be angels) standing around God's throne, and how 10,000 times 10,000 other angels huddled around to sing praises. He has told us about an angel slinging a fiery censer to earth, and seven others playing trumpets. Powerful, defiant angels have been unbound to wreak unimaginable havoc among the inhabitants of earth. It seems everywhere John looks, angels are performing magnificent and sometimes quite frightening feats.

Yet now he comes upon a figure he describes as a *mighty* angel. What must a heavenly being have to do to stand out among the run-of-the-mill angels John has already been describing?

Apoca-Lips Now

"Perhaps there is no happiness in life so perfect as the martyr's."

—O. Henry

Indeed, John had to borrow from the images of a glorious day among nature to describe this figure. The mighty angel had a face like the sun, a rainbow forming a "crown" of sorts, and was clothed "in a cloud." His legs were "like fiery pillars" with one foot planted on the land and the other foot upon the sea. When he spoke, it sounded like "the roar of a lion" and "the voices of the seven thunders." No doubt that this particular angel was likely to stand out in a crowd.

John was just about to record what this angel said, but for the first time he was forbidden to do so. In spite of all the "revealing" contained in the Book of Revelation, it appears there are certain things that will continue to be secret until a yet-to-be-designated time.

What John *did* describe was what the angel was holding—"a little scroll." This isn't the sealed scroll. Its size makes it distinctive—so much so that different words are used for the two scrolls in the original language. Besides, we last saw the Lamb holding the sealed scroll, and the series of judgments contained in it have not yet run their course.

And just as the silence in heaven had marked the opening of the seventh seal, it appears that this mighty angel has been sent to denote the significance of the seventh trumpet about to sound. The message of the angel: "There will be no more delay!"

Got Any Good Recipes for Scroll?

John had been a good sport up till now, doing everything he was told. He had faithfully recorded the letters to the churches. He had entered that open door in heaven and had overcome his fear as he kept observing all the sights and sounds of this strange and wonderful world. When asked his opinion of everything that was going on, he humbly deferred to the obviously more knowledgeable heavenly beings to provide an answer. But now he's about to get a bit more involved.

To begin with, he is challenged to approach the mighty angel and take the little scroll he is

Apoca-Lips Now

"Then if angels fight, weak men must fall: for heaven still guards the right."

—William Shakespeare

A Bright Spot

Centuries had passed since God had promised his prophets and his people that he would balance the scales of justice for them. In all that time, no one had fully understood what he had in mind, or when they could expect to see something happen. This mighty angel, however, promises that with the sounding of the final trumpet, "the mystery of God will be accomplished, just as he announced to his servants the prophets."

holding. Remember his description of this angel, and don't forget that the heavenly being is still standing with one foot on the land mass of earth and the other foot on the sea. Most people would sooner attempt to take a bone away from a ravenous pit bull.

But John responded as the voice instructed him to do. He did, however, *ask* the mighty angel for the scroll rather than attempting to wrestle him for it. The angel readily handed him the scroll, but gave him some unusual instructions: "Take it and eat it." Who was John to argue with him?

Flashback

"Eating" the words of God might not have been a novel concept to John, who was familiar with the Old Testament. In one of the psalms, David had written: "The ordinances of the Lord are sure and altogether righteous. They ... are sweeter than honey, than honey from the comb" (Psalm 19:9–10). Jeremiah wrote of eating the words of God, resulting in "my joy and my heart's delight" (Jeremiah 15:16). Ezekiel, like John, had been instructed to eat a scroll, and in his case, "It tasted as sweet as honey in my mouth" (Ezekiel 2:8–3:3).

Clanging Symbols

Eating is an action that implies total consumption for the purposes of both taste and nutrition. So the symbolism of "eating" God's words is to fully "digest" what God is saying, which should certainly have better results than taking a binge-and-purge approach to Scripture.

John ate the scroll, which was deliciously sweet (and probably quite low in calories). His initial response was similar to what Old Testament people had noted in similar circumstances: "It tasted as sweet as honey in my mouth." But the sweet experience didn't last long, because as an aftereffect, John got an upset stomach.

This gastronomic response is frequently explained by the fact that "digesting" God's will is a sweet experience. To get a sudden burst of spiritual understanding or insight into something that has always puzzled you is like sinking your teeth into the world's best hot fudge sundae or slice of key lime pie. And since John was beginning to see not only God's plan, but perhaps a sense of his timing as well, this would have indeed been a sweet treat. Yet as the full effect of what he was being told began to sink in, the facts were more than a little unsettling. The good news was that God had a definite plan and was about to take action. The bad news was that God had a definite plan and was about to take action. Whether the news was ultimately good or bad for a particular individual would depend on that person's relationship with God.

John was being called to "prophesy again," and like many of the prophets before him, his would be a sweet and sour message. That's why, even today, some people read the Book of Revelation with dread, fear, and trembling—and it leaves a bad taste in their mouths. Others "eat it up" as a promise of a final countdown to a time when every injustice will be made right.

The Man of a Measure

> *I was given a reed like a measuring rod and was told, "Go and measure the temple of God and the altar, and count the worshipers there. But exclude the outer court; do not measure it, because it has been given to the Gentiles. They will trample on the holy city for 42 months. And I will give power to my two witnesses, and they will prophesy for 1,260 days, clothed in sackcloth" (Revelation 11:1–3).*

After dining on a fine fillet of scroll, John was given a job to do. Some people like to say that God never assigns anyone a task without also giving him or her the tools to accomplish it, so along with the job assignment John was handed a measuring rod and told to measure the temple.

Flashback

The task of measuring had also been given to Ezekiel at one time. In circumstances similar to John's, he was told to measure a temple (which, many believe, was also a not-yet-seen temple of the future). In Ezekiel's case (Ezekiel 40–43), he was accompanied by an angel with a measuring rod about 10$^1/_2$ feet long. And although Ezekiel witnessed God's glory departing from Solomon's temple (Ezekiel 10:18), it returned to this new temple he had measured (Ezekiel 43:5).

The presence of a temple seems to be another clear reminder, as was the sealing of the 144,000 (Revelation 7:1–8), that God has not forgotten his many promises to the Jewish people. As a matter of fact, the mention of Gentiles in this context is purely negative—they "will trample on the holy city."

Distances during the first century were frequently measured with rods cut to specific lengths. The rods were light, made of reeds not unlike bamboo that grew long and straight. But as important as this task seemed to be, we don't learn much about what John discovered in his job of measuring and census-taking. There is little break between the instructions for John to measure, and an explanation of two witnesses who will appear. We're about to take a closer look at those two, but first note the time periods mentioned by the mighty angel.

As the Gentiles "trample on the holy city for 42 months," God's two witnesses "will prophesy for 1,260 days." Forty-two months translates to three and a half years. And using a 30-day month (based on the Jewish calendar), the 1,260 days equates to the same length of time. (Even though both totals amount to the same *length* of time, they are not necessarily the same *period* of time. For example, in a seven-year period, the witnesses could conceivably prophesy for the first half, and the city could be trampled during the second half.) We need not worry about it too much at this point, but keep the three-and-a-half-year period in mind, because it will be very important later, when considering a number of various possible interpretations of Revelation.

The Power of Two

These are the two olive trees and the two lampstands that stand before the Lord of the earth. If anyone tries to harm them, fire comes from their mouths and devours their enemies. This is how anyone who wants to harm them must die. These men have power to shut up the sky so that it will not rain during the time they are prophesying; and they have power to turn the waters into blood and to strike the earth with every kind of plague as often as they want (Revelation 11:4–16).

Clanging Symbols

Whoever these witnesses are, God refers to them as "the two olive trees and the two lampstands that stand before the Lord of the earth." Olive oil was a common fuel of the time, so the association with the lampstand was a logical one. Yet before olives yielded their oil, they were beaten off the trees with long sticks and then crushed beneath a heavy stone wheel. Perhaps the imagery of what happens to the olives to produce oil was symbolic of what would happen to these two "olive trees."

If these two "witnesses" have a theme song, it must surely be "You and Me Against the World." For a period of three and a half years, they are given power to "prophesy." And while their message will not be at all popular among the masses at the time, they at first appear to enjoy a supernatural immunity to being harmed.

They dress in sackcloth (Revelation 11:3), in a throwback to prophets of old. Sack-cloth was a dark and coarse cloth made of goat or camel hair. Not exactly preferred leisure wear, it soon came to symbolize mourning and repentance. Only those serious about their sorrow would choose to wear this particular material.

In addition, the ability of these two witnesses to perform miraculous feats is surprisingly similar to two specific Old Testament prophets. The power to turn water to blood and inflict plagues on the earth was how Moses eventually persuaded Pharaoh to allow the Israelites to leave Egypt (Exodus 7–12). And withholding rain was a tactic used by Elijah to get the attention of wicked King Ahab (1 Kings 17:1). The parallels in Revelation are so similar that some people have come to speculate that the two witnesses are a literal return of Moses and Elijah. But (surprise!) not everyone agrees.

If there is no rain during the time these two witnesses are prophesying, and if they are prophesying for three and a half years, these two figures are certain to be associated with the drought, and therefore unpopular to begin with. In addition, their "prophetic" message isn't likely to win them many friends. The job of a prophet is to call sinful masses to repentance. Yet if someone attempts to harm either of these two, "fire comes out of their mouths and devours their enemies."

This cryptic reference to fire is puzzling. In a symbolic sense, we are told that God's word is like fire (Jeremiah 23:29), and he had previously told Jeremiah, "I will make my words in your mouth a fire and these people the wood it consumes" (Jeremiah 5:14). In the case of the two witnesses, however, the use of fire seems more literal.

Flashback

Olive oil was the fuel that fired the lampstand in God's temple (see Exodus 27:20–21).

Flashback

In yet another comparison of the two witnesses with Moses and Elijah, you might recall that perhaps Elijah's best-known miracle was the calling down of fire on a waterlogged altar in the presence of hundreds of priests of Baal. In that case, the fire from heaven consumed not only the wet wood, but also the stones and soil around the altar (1 Kings 18:16–39).

The Witness Rejection Program

Now when they have finished their testimony, the beast that comes up from the Abyss will attack them, and overpower and kill them. Their bodies will lie in the street of the great city, which is figuratively called Sodom and Egypt, where also their Lord was crucified. For three and a half days men from every people, tribe, language and nation will gaze on their bodies and refuse them burial. The inhabitants of the earth will gloat over them and will celebrate by sending each other gifts, because these two prophets had tormented those who live on the earth.

But after the three and a half days a breath of life from God entered them, and they stood on their feet, and terror struck those who saw them. Then they heard a loud voice from heaven saying to them, "Come up here." And they went up to heaven in a cloud, while their enemies looked on.

At that very hour there was a severe earthquake and a tenth of the city collapsed. Seven thousand people were killed in the earthquake, and the survivors were terrified and gave glory to the God of heaven.

The second woe has passed; the third woe is coming soon (Revelation 11:7–14).

Clanging Symbols

In this passage we see at last the location of the two witnesses—"where ... their Lord was crucified." This is obviously a reference to Jerusalem, yet the once-proud city is by now being linked to Sodom and Egypt, which had long been symbols of sin, slavery, and judgment.

Apoca-Lips Now

"We need more understanding of human nature, because the only real danger that exists is man himself .... We know nothing of man, far too little. His psyche should be studied because we are the origin of all coming evil."

—Carl Jung

But after three and a half years of preaching and prophesying, the jig is up for the two witnesses. Their work is done, but the people aren't done with them. At that time, they are overcome by "the beast that comes up from the Abyss." We will see more about who this "beast" is in Chapter 9, "A Beauty and Some Beasts," but for now let's simply note that he's not a very nice figure at all.

Not only are the witnesses killed, but they are also denied a decent burial as their bodies lie in the street. The streets must surely be hot, since it hasn't rained for three and a half years. All the better in the attempt of their opponents to humiliate them at last.

For centuries, this next portion of Revelation must have stumped its readers. How could it ever be possible for "every people, tribe, language and nation" to gaze on two bodies lying in the streets of Jerusalem? Surely it was a perplexing consideration for curious Christians throughout the ages. Today, however, it is much less mysterious. If something like this were to happen today, not only would the cable news networks pick up the story and beam it around the world by satellite, but everyone would probably be able to access a live camera on the two bodies by calling up www.twodeadwitnesses.com. Viewing the remains of the two witnesses would not be a problem.

The response of the population to the deaths of these two witnesses is a stark window into the spiritual/emotional state of most people during this time. Not only do the powers that be deny them burial; in addition, a global holiday celebration is spawned, complete with gloating and gift-giving. If indeed this is a look into the future of the world, one must wonder what happened to the self-help craze promoting sensitivity, empathy, and other values that seem to be absent in this Revelationary preview of times to come.

But in a surprise twist to this celebration, after three and a half days the parties are certain to come to a sudden stop as, on their big-screen TVs, the watching world sees the two witnesses stand up. Not only do the witnesses rise from the dead, but they rise into heaven as well, in response to a verbal invitation to ascend.

The people watching are terror-struck at this point, and their situation doesn't get any better as "at that very hour" an earthquake rocks Jerusalem, killing 7,000 of them. Stuff like that tends to put a damper on a good party.

In previous accounts, we saw that people refused to repent in response to the terrible things taking place (Revelation 9:20–21). In this case, however, the stress appears to be too much for even the most callous of them. We are told that the survivors of the earthquake "were terrified and gave glory to the God of heaven." We will soon discover, however, that this was by no means a permanent change of heart for them.

A Bright Spot

In what must be the world's biggest comeback since the resurrection of Jesus himself, these two witnesses pick themselves up off the street after three and a half days of being dead. It is not only a bright spot for the two of them, but the event creates an immediate sobering up of those watching as well.

Apoca-Lips Now

"Can I see another's woe,
And not be in sorrow too?
Can I see another's grief,
And not seek for kind relief?"
—William Blake

Still Waiting for the Grand Finale

The events in this chapter are all connected with the sounding of the sixth trumpet (and second woe) that began in Chapter 7, "Horns of Plenty (of Trouble)." We are told here that "the second woe has passed; the third woe is coming soon."

We still haven't heard the sound of the seventh trumpet, which is the third (and final) woe. But from this point onward, as John begins to cover the events more toward the *very* end of the world as we know it, the account becomes more specific. We've whipped through the first six seals and first six trumpets rather quickly. The pace will slow a bit from this point forward because so much is starting to happen in such a concentrated time.

The Least You Need to Know

➤ A mighty angel appears to John between the sixth and seventh trumpet judgments.

➤ John is asked to measure a temple and eat a scroll.

➤ Two witnesses speak up for God and cannot be stopped for a period of three and a half years.

➤ A beast is introduced who eventually kills God's witnesses.

Chapter 9

A Beauty and Some Beasts

In This Chapter

➤ A look at Revelation 11:15–13

➤ The seventh trumpet is sounded

➤ Pregnant woman vs. red dragon

➤ Two beasts and the number 666

Well, you're at about the halfway point of your trek through the Book of Revelation, and the world hasn't ended yet. However, you may be perplexed or even disappointed at this point. Perhaps you picked up this book eager to get into the juicy parts of the Bible—devils, antichrists, numbers with secret meanings, little girls with spinning heads, and all the other stuff you've heard about and/or seen in the movies.

You've faithfully plodded halfway through, and so far it's been letters to churches, scrolls with seals, goody-goody guys and girls in heaven, and angelic musicians. Okay, there has also been a bit of blood and special effects stuff, but maybe not quite what you were expecting. Don't give up yet—the worst is yet to come. Aside from the little girl with the spinning head, we will see most of the other symbols introduced in this chapter.

In fact, this chapter will be crucial in explaining what a lot of the "big deal" is about Revelation. In addition, from the standpoint of a chronological timetable, this is where we may begin to drift a bit. We've worked our way straight through the seven seals, and the first six trumpets. Now, as we move into the final trumpet blast, we will see things happening that may hark back to some of the things we've already covered, or anticipate some things still ahead. As usual, we're going to stick as closely as possible to what the text says and what appear to be clear interpretations of key symbols.

Who Plays Seventh Trumpet in Handel's Messiah?

The seventh angel sounded his trumpet, and there were loud voices in heaven, which said: "The kingdom of the world has become the kingdom of our Lord and of his Christ, and he will reign for ever and ever." And the twenty-four elders, who were seated on their thrones before God, fell on their faces and worshiped God, saying: "We give thanks to you, Lord God Almighty, the One who is and who was, because you have taken your great power and have begun to reign. The nations were angry; and your wrath has come. The time has come for judging the dead, and for rewarding your servants the prophets and your saints and those who reverence your name, both small and great—and for destroying those who destroy the earth."

Then God's temple in heaven was opened, and within his temple was seen the ark of his covenant. And there came flashes of lightning, rumblings, peals of thunder, an earthquake and a great hailstorm (Revelation 11:15–19).

Apoca-Lips Now

"Wild, dark times are rumbling toward us, and the prophet who wishes to write a new apocalypse will have to invent entirely new beasts, and beasts so terrible that the ancient animal symbols of St. John will seem like cooing doves and cupids in comparison."

—Heinrich Heine

This Christmas as you listen to Handel's Messiah and get to the part that says, "The kingdom of this world has become the kingdom of our Lord and of his Christ," consider that this quote comes from the part of the Bible where the seventh angel blows his trumpet to announce that "the time has come for judging the dead." It's an ultimately triumphant (and melodic) message, but the impact of what these words signify can really put a damper on having a merry Christmas.

At first glance, this passage seems to be merely another chorus of praise to God. But on closer inspection, a few unsettling distinctions can be noted. To begin with, previous praises to God had referred to him as "him who is, and who was, and who is to come" (Revelation 1:4; 4:8). Here, however, God is perceived as "the One who is and who was." No longer do we find the "is to come" part of his title included because, as the 24 elders say, "you have taken your great power and have begun to reign" (Revelation 11:17).

God's great patience and tolerance of sinful humankind has just about reached an end. The nations are angry, but so is God. The actions predicted in this section are his rewarding the faithful, accompanied by his judgment and destruction of others.

Accompanying this bold statement are a host of attention-getting natural activities to accentuate its importance: lightning, thunder, hail, and an earthquake. We're going to be seeing a lot of these signs in the remaining chapters of Revelation. In addition, John was able to see the ark of the covenant in God's temple in heaven—something few people before him had been privileged to do.

A Bright Spot

The earthly scene is looking quite bleak at this point, yet the announcements being made over the heavenly loudspeaker are jubilant.

Flashback

The ark of the covenant was normally the least-seen item in the Jewish Tabernacle or Temple. It symbolized the immediate presence of God, and had a position of honor in a section of the Temple known as the Most Holy Place. Not even priests had access to this sectioned-off area. Once a year the high priest was allowed to enter and make a blood sacrifice on behalf of the people. Otherwise, anyone entering the Most Holy Place would be sentenced to death (Exodus 26:30–34; Leviticus 16:2).

At this point in the text we take another little timeout to get some additional background on what is going on. We'll get back to the action that immediately follows the seventh trumpet in Revelation 16. But now for something completely different ....

And You Think *You* Had a Hard Labor!

A great and wondrous sign appeared in heaven: a woman clothed with the sun, with the moon under her feet and a crown of twelve stars on her head. She was pregnant and cried out in pain as she was about to give birth. Then another sign appeared in heaven: an enormous red dragon with seven heads and ten horns and seven crowns on his heads. His tail swept a third of the stars out of the sky and flung them to the earth.

97

The dragon stood in front of the woman who was about to give birth, so that he might devour her child the moment it was born. She gave birth to a son, a male child, who will rule all the nations with an iron scepter. And her child was snatched up to God and to his throne. The woman fled into the desert to a place prepared for her by God, where she might be taken care of for 1,260 days (Revelation 12:1–6).

When you're ready to give birth, the last thing you want is a red dragon standing around waiting to eat your child. As you can see, we're getting to a portion of Revelation that is clearly symbolic, or at least, we certainly hope so. Let's see what we can do to unscramble these symbols and make sense of them.

Flashback

The temptation of Jesus by the devil is found in Matthew 4:1–11. Three times Satan made Jesus an attractive offer. All three times Jesus quoted an Old Testament scripture and resisted the devil's temptations.

Apoca-Lips Now

"The Egyptians worship God symbolically in the crocodile, that being the only animal without a tongue, like the Divine Logos, which standeth not in need of speech."

—Plutarch

The red dragon is easy. We simply need to read ahead a bit to Revelation 12:9 where it is identified as "that ancient serpent called the devil, or Satan." The child isn't too hard to figure out either. Identified as a male who will rule all the nations with an iron scepter, and who was snatched up to God, this certainly must be a reference to Jesus. But surely this is a reference to the human Jesus while he was on earth in his flesh-and-blood incarnation. From a biblical perspective, at no other time would Jesus have been in any danger from the devil. In his humanity, however, he was vulnerable to the temptations of Satan just like anyone else. And if this *is* the case, the setting of this dragon/woman/child scene is almost certainly on earth.

So, based on these supposed identities of the dragon and the child, many people have come to the conclusion that the woman represents Israel. Jesus was born into Judaism, and Israel has certainly seen its share of sufferings throughout the ages. However, other people believe the identity of the woman might instead be the church, the Virgin Mary, or some other option. Whoever she represents, let's not miss the fact that she hides out for that three-and-a-half-year period of time we saw in the last chapter—1,260 days.

While the woman's identity may be a bit more in doubt, we are provided considerable detail about the red dragon, Satan. He is described as being enormous, with seven heads, seven crowns, and ten horns. We will later see that some interpretations of Revelation will try to make more of these specific numbers, but in a general sense it's safe to say that the multiple heads symbolize wisdom, the horns power, and the crowns position. At other places in the Bible, Satan is called "the prince of this world" (John 12:31) and the "ruler of the kingdom of the air" (Ephesians 2:2), and he apparently works hard for his titles and position.

Clanging Symbols

One of the reasons many people identify the woman as Israel is her association with the sun, moon, and 12 stars. The same symbols are found in Genesis 37:9–11, in a dream Joseph had as a youngster. The interpretation given at that time was that the sun represented Joseph's father, Jacob (Israel). The moon was his mother, Rebekah. The stars were his 11 brothers. Since Jacob and his 12 sons were the beginning of the Israelites, some people assume the symbols in Revelation are a clue that the woman facing down the red dragon must represent Israel.

The color red might symbolize the bloodshed we're about to witness, or it may be an association with other similar mythologized representations of God's enemies. For example, the Egyptians worshiped one particular god who had the form of a red crocodile. The crocodile was a symbol of deity for the ancient Egyptians for a number of reasons. Crocodiles have eyes that allow them to remain underwater, seeing without being seen. Some felt the number of a crocodile's teeth equaled the number of days in a year, and many other legends abounded.

Clanging Symbols

It isn't unusual to find beasts used as symbols of great power, both in the Bible and in ancient civilizations. Sometimes they represent human powers, and sometimes supernatural ones. For example, look at this passage from Psalm 74:13–14 in reference to Egypt: "It was you [God] who split open the sea by your power; you broke the heads of the monster in the waters. It was you who crushed the heads of Leviathan and gave him as food to the creatures of the desert."

In addition to the physical description of the red dragon, we discover that he had "swept a third of the stars out of the sky and flung them to the earth." Some people interpret this passage as meaning that Satan will be granted extensive power over the forces of nature during the end times. Other people suggest this is a reference to Satan's rebellion against God prior to the creation of our world, and his being cast out of heaven, taking with him a significant contingent of angel warrior/followers. Jesus had once commented: "I saw Satan fall like lightning from heaven" (Luke 10:18). Regardless of your preferred interpretation in this matter, the next portion of Revelation definitely gets back to the good-vs.-evil confrontation.

The War Above the Worlds

And there was war in heaven. Michael and his angels fought against the dragon, and the dragon and his angels fought back. But he was not strong enough, and they lost their place in heaven. The great dragon was hurled down—that ancient serpent called the devil, or Satan, who leads the whole world astray. He was hurled to the earth, and his angels with him.

Then I heard a loud voice in heaven say: "Now have come the salvation and the power and the kingdom of our God, and the authority of his Christ. For the accuser of our brothers, who accuses them before our God day and night, has been hurled down. They overcame him by the blood of the Lamb and by the word of their testimony; they did Not love their lives so much as to shrink from death. Therefore rejoice, you heavens and you who dwell in them! But woe to the earth and the sea, because the devil has gone down to you! He is filled with fury, because he knows that his time is short" (Revelation 12:7–12).

Flashback

Michael means "Who is like God?" and continues to be one of the most popular names for boys. The only angel designated in Scripture as an archangel, Michael pops up in various spots, including Daniel (10:13, 21; 12:1), Jude (v. 9), and perhaps 1 Thessalonians (4:16). He is one of only two angels mentioned by name in the Bible, the other being Gabriel.

Little is known for sure about the relationship between God and Satan after Satan's original rebellion. At times there seems to be out-and-out warfare. Other times they appear to operate under détente as in the Book of Job. While we will see that the final outcome of Satan is spelled out quite specifically later in Revelation, in the meantime he appears to have a certain degree of freedom to operate. After all, the very word "Satan" means *accuser* in Hebrew. And in order for him to accuse people, he must have some kind of access to God.

Yet while his access to and relationship with God remain a bit unclear, humankind is warned again and again to beware of him. Ever since that little stunt he pulled in the Garden of Eden, it should be clear he is not to be trusted, and that he by no means has our best interests in mind.

And in spite of past or present liberties Satan has enjoyed, it seems his time is winding down in this passage. A war in heaven takes place after which he and his supporters are bounced from the heavenly realm. Perhaps this is a reference to his original casting out, but most people seem to think that in the context of all the seals and trumpets and such, this is more of a final, end-times housecleaning.

Flashback

Here are just a few biblical words of warning about Satan:

➤ "Satan himself masquerades as an angel of light. It is not surprising, then, if his servants masquerade as servants of righteousness" (2 Corinthians 11:14–15).

➤ "For our struggle is not against flesh and blood, but against the rulers, against the authorities, against the powers of this dark world and against the spiritual forces of evil in the heavenly realms" (Ephesians 6:12).

➤ "Be self-controlled and alert. Your enemy the devil prowls around like a roaring lion looking for someone to devour. Resist him, standing firm in the faith" (1 Peter 5:8–9).

And if so, the fact that Satan and his horde are "hurled to the earth" doesn't bode well for the earth's inhabitants. You might note that one of the key pieces of information in this context is that Satan "leads the whole world astray." The danger to earthlings is confirmed by the loud voice in heaven. While there is rejoicing in heaven that Satan is no longer a tenant and/or neighbor, sympathy is expressed "to the earth and the sea" because Satan is there and is "filled with fury."

We also see in this passage another reference to the victorious martyrs in heaven. They are sharing in the rejoicing taking place. And we are made aware of the presence of Michael, the archangel.

You Go, Girl! (And Go Quickly!)

When the dragon saw that he had been hurled to the earth, he pursued the woman who had given birth to the male child. The woman was given the two wings of a great eagle, so that she might fly to the place prepared for her in the desert, where she would be taken care of for a time, times and half a time, out of the serpent's reach. Then from his mouth the serpent spewed water like a river, to overtake the woman and sweep her away with the torrent. But the earth helped the woman by opening its mouth and swallowing the river that the dragon had spewed out of his mouth. Then the dragon was enraged at the woman and went off to make war against the rest of her offspring—those who obey God's commandments and hold to the testimony of Jesus (Revelation 12:13–17).

With the jury still out about exactly who the woman represents, this is a difficult passage to make sense of. Still, we find a number of clues to add to those we have been accumulating. To begin with, whether the woman represents Israel or the church, it is clear she remains a target for the full fury of the dragon (Satan). He missed out on getting her child (Jesus), so he is now content to go after "the rest of her offspring"—those who are associated with Jesus.

The dragon is on a search-and-destroy mission, but he can't quite catch up with the woman, thanks to what is apparently divine assistance. Not only is she given "the two wings of a great eagle," but she is also saved from almost certain harm when "the earth helped the woman by opening its mouth and swallowing the river that the dragon had spewed out of his mouth."

Apoca-Lips Now

"The Apocalypse of St. John is the majestic image of a high and stately tragedy, shutting up and intermingling her solemn scenes and acts with a sevenfold chorus of hallelujahs and harping symphonies.

—John Milton

We won't at this point attempt to decipher the possible meanings of the wings, the water, or most of the rest of this passage. Some people have speculated so far as to interpret the eagle as a reference to the national symbol of the United States, and predicting U.S. involvement in whatever is taking place at this time. As previously noted, speculation is anyone's prerogative, but there simply aren't enough facts to go on for a well-grounded interpretation at this point.

Clearly, however, the dragon's target goes into hiding for a period of time. And it is that period that raises new interest: "a time, times, and half a time." With a little leeway, many interpreters use a "time" to equal "a year." So, one time plus two times plus a half a time equals that three-and-a-half-year period that is so prevalent in Revelation.

The next couple of characters in Revelation, however, are a bit easier to figure out. We will find we have considerably more to go on.

A New "King of the Beasts"

And the dragon stood on the shore of the sea. And I saw a beast coming out of the sea. He had ten horns and seven heads, with ten crowns on his horns, and on each head a blasphemous name. The beast I saw resembled a leopard, but had feet like those of a bear and a mouth like that of a lion. The dragon gave the beast his power and his throne and great authority. One of the heads of the beast seemed to have had a fatal wound, but the fatal wound had been healed. The whole world was astonished and followed the beast. Men worshiped the dragon because he had given authority to the beast, and they also worshiped the beast and asked, "Who is like the beast? Who can make war against him?"

The beast was given a mouth to utter proud words and blasphemies and to exercise his authority for forty-two months. He opened his mouth to blaspheme God, and to slander his name and his dwelling place and those who live in heaven. He was given power to make war against the saints and to conquer them. And he was given authority over every tribe, people, language and nation. All inhabitants of the earth will worship the beast—all whose names have not been written in the book of life belonging to the Lamb that was slain from the creation of the world.

He who has an ear, let him hear. If anyone is to go into captivity, into captivity he will go. If anyone is to be killed with the sword, with the sword he will be killed. This calls for patient endurance and faithfulness on the part of the saints (Revelation 13:1–10).

The Book of Revelation is something like a roller coaster ride at the end of the Bible. And as such, we've climbed to the top of the highest peak and have just begun the plummet down the steepest slope. As this "beast" comes out of the sea and begins his reign, much of what came before and what follows in Revelation begins to make more sense, and the text will take on a new intensity.

Flashback

John had written about antichrists (plural) in previous writings (1 John and 2 John). For example, he wrote, "Dear children, this is the last hour; and as you have heard that the antichrist is coming, even now many antichrists have come. This is how we know it is the last hour .... Who is the liar? It is the man who denies that Jesus is the Christ. Such a man is the antichrist—he denies the Father and the Son" (1 John 2:18, 22). But the beast in Revelation 13 is generally referred to as *the* Antichrist—the pinnacle of resistance to God.

The word antichrist isn't found in most translations of Revelation. But essentially all interpreters agree that this beast is what our culture has come to call the Antichrist. (We'll give him a capital A for his name to differentiate him from others mentioned in the Bible.)

We have seen martyrs in heaven, but not a lot was said about how they got there. And we've seen a lot of events taking place that initially might seem more natural than spiritual. Yet with the introduction of this beast, many of those events begin to be seen in a different context.

The dragon empowers this beast, and the two are quite similar in description. The dragon was described as having seven heads, ten horns, and seven crowns (Revelation 12:3). The beast has seven heads, ten horns, and ten crowns. But the beast was also described in terms comparing him to a leopard, bear, and lion.

Surely this description is symbolic, because the "beast" is portrayed as a popular and powerful figure. The people on earth not only worshiped the beast himself, but also the dragon who had given him his power. People were astonished at what this figure was able to do, with much of their fascination stemming from the belief that he had apparently recovered from a "fatal" wound. (Some suspect this might be a copycat attempt to emulate Jesus' resurrection.)

Yet it's clear from his job description that the beast is up to no good. He slanders and blasphemes God. He beats up "saints" (believers in Jesus). He solicits literal worship from people. And on top of everything else, he is motivated by pride. This may sound like your current boss, yet the Antichrist will also appear to be all-powerful. In fact, since people are asking, "Who can make war against him?" it might indicate that he takes over without a fight. (Other world leaders can't exactly be happy that the masses are so enamored with someone else.)

Clanging Symbols

You might have noticed the brief reference to the "book of life" belonging to the Lamb. It was also mentioned in Revelation 3:5, and will come up again later in Revelation. This is assumed to be a literal book, a heavenly ledger. Yet it lists (and therefore symbolizes) all believers. Two primary schools of thought exist for how the Lamb keeps his books. One is that as each person becomes a Christian, his or her name is written in the book. The other is that everyone's name is in the book to begin with, but is removed if the person doesn't become a Christian.

Because of the figurative language used in Revelation, some people throughout history have tried to associate this beast with every wicked or unpopular leader who has come along. Since John's writing was fresh at the end of the first century, a lot of Roman emperors were suspected of being the Antichrist. Later nominations included Emperor Frederick II, William II (of Germany), Napoleon Bonaparte, and a number of popes. And when Hitler, Mussolini, and Stalin came along, they had a lot of people wondering as well. A bit later, when we get to the "number" of the person, some additional names will come up.

Some people continue to attempt to match history with this description in Revelation. Others don't bother, convinced that the Antichrist is closely tied to the tribulation expected to take place in the last days. Again in this passage we find a mention of 42 months (three and a half years)—a period very important to those who take a future-oriented outlook of Revelation rather than a historical one.

Immediately following the graphic description of the Antichrist is a warning about captivity and death by sword, which probably connects with the previous mention of the beast's propensity to make war against and conquer the believers of the time. It seems that while one group of humanity is worshiping and wondering at the amazing colossal power of the beast, others who aren't so enamored with him will be persecuted.

A Bright Spot

We've gotten to another portion of Revelation where the bright spots aren't frequent—and they're not all that bright! Yet even with everything that is described going on in connection with the beast/Antichrist, no cause is given for pessimism or hopelessness. Instead, the "saints" are challenged to maintain an outlook of patient endurance and faithfulness.

Two Beasts Are Far Worse Than One

Then I saw another beast, coming out of the earth. He had two horns like a lamb, but he spoke like a dragon. He exercised all the authority of the first beast on his behalf, and made the earth and its inhabitants worship the first beast, whose fatal wound had been healed. And he performed great and miraculous signs, even causing fire to come down from heaven to earth in full view of men. Because of the signs he was given power to do on behalf of the first beast, he deceived the inhabitants of the earth. He ordered them to set up an image in honor of the beast who was wounded by the sword and yet lived.

He was given power to give breath to the image of the first beast, so that it could speak and cause all who refused to worship the image to be killed. He also forced everyone, small and great, rich and poor, free and slave, to receive a mark on his right hand or on his forehead, so that no one could buy or sell unless he had the mark, which is the name of the beast or the number of his name.

This calls for wisdom. If anyone has insight, let him calculate the number of the beast, for it is man's number. His number is 666 (Revelation 13:11–18).

No sooner does the first beast come on the scene than he is followed by a second one—a clone, a disciple, a groupie. They are definitely two different characters, yet are completely united in purpose and strategy.

The first beast had come "out of the sea." Some people consider this to mean the Mediterranean and attempt to pinpoint a geographic location, and others feel the phrase indicates the "sea of humanity" and suggests he is a Gentile. Regardless of the particular interpretation, it is noteworthy to see that the second beast comes "out of the earth." So they are both beasts, but are not the same beast.

Later references in Revelation speak of "the beast and the false prophet," so the "false prophet" is almost certainly a reference to this second beast. For our purposes, rather than the potential confusion of continually referring to Beast #1 and Beast #2, let's call these two troublemakers the Antichrist and false prophet.

A Dragon in Lamb's Clothing

The very description of the false prophet alerts us to his true nature. He appears to be a cute little lamb, but when he speaks he has the voice of a dragon (and we all remember who the dragon represents). The primary function of this false prophet seems to be to promote the Antichrist. The power of this second figure seems to be every bit as impressive as that of the first one—if not more so. Yet while the Antichrist uses his power to solicit the worship of the people, the false prophet seems to seek no personal glory and uses his power to direct others to the Antichrist as well.

And amazing power it is! Human beings throughout history have been suckers for signs and miracles. In a culture where headline news is made when the image of Jesus or the Virgin Mary supposedly appears on washed-out walls of ramshackle shacks, and even the face of Mother Teresa is thought to be seen in Tennessee cinnamon rolls, just think what would happen if someone came along who could make fire fall from the sky while everyone stood around looking! Based on the eagerness of the general population to put faith in anything extraordinary, it wouldn't take long for such a figure to accumulate a large following.

Apoca-Lips Now

"Woe to him ... who has no court of appeal against the world's judgment."

—Thomas Carlyle

In addition to his fire-from-the-sky trick, he is able to build a statue of the Antichrist that appears to come to life—not only speaking, but killing those who refuse to bow before it. Yet with all his incredible power, he has ulterior motives. We are told that with his wondrous signs, "he deceived the inhabitants of the earth."

Pleased to Meet You. Won't You Guess My Name?

Before long, worship of the Antichrist ceases to be voluntary. Thanks to the obsessive work of the false prophet as PR manager for the beast, he quickly comes up with a plan to enforce loyalty to his evil peer. People are required to receive a "mark" on their right hands or foreheads that "is the name of the beast or the number of his name." Without such a mark, they are refused privileges to buy or sell. And if the famines, earthquakes, and other natural disasters of Revelation are literal, it's going to be unlikely that people can last long without certain trade privileges. Almost certainly, there will be great pressure to receive the "mark of the beast," like it or not.

Perhaps the most pondered mystery in the Book of Revelation is the significance of the number 666, which John records as "the number of the beast" with the clue that, "it is man's number." In addition, he almost dares us to figure it out if we're smart enough: "This calls for wisdom. If anyone has insight, let him calculate the number."

Apoca-Lips Now

"Blasted be the bones of those who calculate the end, for when the calculated time comes and Messiah does not appear, people despair of his ever coming."

—Rabbi Jonathan

The authors, regretfully, cannot profess to having such wisdom. We might have benefited more from a physical description rather than a numerical one. Had the Antichrist been described as 6 feet tall, with brown eyes, salt-and-pepper hair, a dimpled chin, and left-handed, we might quickly accumulate a list of suspects. But the single number 666 doesn't mean much to us—at least, not yet.

Still, people throughout history have taken on this passage as a personal challenge. And once you start fooling around with numbers (as many rabbis and scholars loved to do during this time, assigning numeric values to alphabetic letters), you can make them come out most any way you want. Consequently, a list of nominations for the identity of the Antichrist, based on numerical manipulations of their names to arrive at 666, have included Nero Caesar, Hadrian, Trajan, Caligula, Diocletian, Julian the Apostate, Luther, Mohammed, and many more. And if you really want to crawl out on the limb of speculation, some people have even tried to associate 666 with "www." If the Internet is the Antichrist, a lot of us are going to be in deep trouble.

A completely different way to look at this passage, however, isn't quite as prophetic (and perhaps not as much fun). Another train of thought is to see 666 not as six hundred sixty-six, but merely as three sixes side by side. We have said that the numeral seven is perceived to be the number of perfection and completeness. Therefore, six would be the number that doesn't quite stack up.

Couple this thought with the fact that basic to Christian faith is the belief in the Holy Trinity—Father, Son, and Holy Spirit. Many commentators like to point to the three figures in this passage of Revelation as a kind of *unholy* trinity. The dragon (Satan) imitates God, but doesn't quite have his power, since the dragon lost the war in heaven. The first beast (Antichrist) is empowered by the dragon and does his bidding, just as Jesus came to earth to fulfill God's will and redeem people for the Father. And the second beast (false prophet) supports the work of the Antichrist just as the Holy Spirit is actively involved in continuing the work of Jesus Christ.

Satan, Antichrist, and false prophet … side by side … 666. It's a theory. Take it or leave it.

And the Beast Goes On

We haven't seen yet what happens as a result of getting (or not getting) the mark of the beast, but future chapters will follow up on this passage. Most commentators believe this section of Revelation is parenthetical to the chronological portions, so there is much diversity in the perspectives of how and when the Antichrist becomes influential, and which of the other signs of the end times are taking place as he enjoys a rise to power.

And while the actual word *Antichrist* isn't to be found in most versions of the Book of Revelation, the figure we know by that title is certainly there. Our society's fascination with this being is certain to continue, and esoteric scholars will go on assigning numbers to the Greek, Hebrew, English, and other alphabets to try to determine if any up-and-coming world leaders have names that somehow equate to 666. In the meantime, keep in mind that any fictional portrayal of such a being will almost surely contain a good deal of literary license.

In Chapter 10, "Where the Grapes of Wrath Are Stored," we will move on from the dragon and the two beasts into some of the best and worst that the Book of Revelation has to offer.

Apoca-Lips Now

"Good luck lies in odd numbers …. They say, there is divinity in odd numbers, either in nativity, chance or death."

—William Shakespeare

Clanging Symbols

If you're trying to keep up with the various "sevens" in Revelation, bear in mind that Revelation 12–13 contained seven key figures: (1) the woman; (2) the red dragon; (3) the male child; (4) Michael the archangel; (5) the persecuted offspring of the woman; (6) the beast from the sea; and (7) the beast from the earth.

The Least You Need to Know

➤ As the seventh trumpet sounds, a sense of finality is expressed from those in heaven.

➤ In what appears to be a timeout in the ongoing action, we are introduced to a woman, a child, a dragon, and two beasts.

➤ The "beast," or Antichrist, is portrayed as a supernaturally powerful figure, empowered by Satan and supported by another figure known as the false prophet.

➤ At some point, people will be expected to receive the "mark of the beast"— either his name or his number (666).

Chapter 10

Where the Grapes of Wrath Are Stored

In This Chapter

➤ A look at Revelation 14

➤ The return of the Lamb and the 144,000

➤ Three angels make some announcements

➤ The earth is "harvested"

So far we have seen certain groups of people in Revelation challenge God for not being firm enough in dealing with the injustices of humankind (6:9–11), and we've seen other groups repeatedly act in defiance of what they know to be God's wishes (9:20–21). We've also seen from John's behind-the-scenes heavenly perspective that God appears to be on a timetable people know little about. He is aware of, but not at the mercy of, both the accusations of being too soft on crime and the assumptions that he is unwilling to step in and reprimand blatant rebellion.

But we are nearing the time in the Book of Revelation when, in spite of all of God's love, patience, grace, and mercy, he is at last going to take action on those who refuse to acknowledge him. This is no longer merely a disciplinary action, because we are told that God disciplines people he loves for their own good and spiritual growth (Hebrews 12:4–11). We have seen that the heavenly Father ensures that each of his "children" is provided for. Some receive "seals" and appear to be immune to harm; others are persecuted and/or put to death, yet are richly rewarded in the afterlife. But those who have nothing to do with God are about to discover his wrath—the worst that can happen when they don't do anything to reel in their inappropriate behavior and attitudes.

That's It! You're Grounded

Most parents quickly learn to tolerate a lot of less-than-desirable behavior from their kids before taking drastic action. A child's first offense might be met with a joking threat. The next one might draw a fixed stare. Later the verbal warnings might get louder and more serious. Only if the child continues to intensify inappropriate behavior will he or she receive the full force of the parent's disciplinary tactics.

With a little experience, most children know approximately where the final line is drawn between pushing Mom or Dad right up to the limit and going just a little too far. Wise children back off before crossing that line. And of course, parents have good and bad days, affecting their tolerance when dealing with irascible moods and defiant behavior.

If we perceive God as a parent, as more of a literal "heavenly Father" than a figurative one, we might see certain similarities. This isn't to suggest that he has bad days where he irrationally takes out his own problems on someone else. But we might consider that it is possible for humankind to cross a barrier where we push the limits of his grace and mercy too far. All parents know: When being nice doesn't work, sometimes other tactics are called for.

Apoca-Lips Now

"Dios tarda pero no olvida" [God delays but doesn't forget].

—Spanish proverb

A Thousand Gross Believers

Then I looked, and there before me was the Lamb, standing on Mount Zion, and with him 144,000 who had his name and his Father's name written on their foreheads. And I heard a sound from heaven like the roar of rushing waters and like a loud peal of thunder. The sound I heard was like that of harpists playing their harps. And they sang a new song before the throne and before the four living creatures and the elders. No one could learn the song except the 144,000 who had been redeemed from the earth. These are those who did not defile themselves with women, for they kept themselves pure. They follow the Lamb wherever he goes. They were purchased from among men and offered as firstfruits to God and the Lamb. No lie was found in their mouths; they are blameless (Revelation 14:1–5).

In the Book of Revelation the shift from the last verse of chapter 13 and the first verse of chapter 14 reveals a graphic contrast that gets diluted a bit because we have begun a new chapter in this *Complete Idiot's Guide.* The very last statement of Revelation 13 is, "His number is 666." You might remember that we left off with the mark of the beast, present on the right hands or foreheads of all those who pledged loyalty to the Antichrist.

Yet the very next thing witnessed by John was the Lamb again, this time standing with a group of 144,000. They, too, bear a mark on their foreheads, but it is definitely not the same symbol. No beastly tattoos on *their* hands or heads—rather, they displayed the Lamb's name and his Father's name. And they appear to be glad about it. They are singing "a new song"—a special song that no one else could learn. The sound is something like rushing water and thunder, yet also like harpists playing their instruments.

A Bright Spot

In spite of all the terrible things that have taken place since we last saw our group of 144,000, they seem to be still standing, still singing, and still going strong.

It's usually assumed that this is the same group first seen in Revelation 7 because both were groups of a thousand gross believers ("gross" in terms of *number*, not appearance!). And just as parents write their children's names on lunches and clothes to keep them from being mixed up with those of other schoolchildren, God appears to have written his name on these people to make it impossible for anyone else to mark them, or for them to get mixed up with the majority of humankind quick to pledge loyalty to the Antichrist.

Clanging Symbols

When it comes to religious faithfulness, a recurring analogy throughout the Bible is of Jesus as a bridegroom and the church (the group of believers—both male and female) as the bride. Paul had written to the church at Corinth: "I promised you to one husband, to Christ, so that I might present you as a pure virgin to him" (2 Corinthians 11:2). In this and other cases, references to virginity, marriage, and such frequently have less to do with literal gender than symbolic spiritual purity.

This group is identified more by their behavior than by their appearance. We are told, "These are those who did not defile themselves with women, for they kept themselves pure." Many people consider this a symbolic statement. To begin with, this is not a clear indication that only males will be among the group. In addition, the focus is more on the spiritual aspects of the group than the physical. So the "women" who defile others might be a reference to the seductive religions being promoted by the Antichrist and others during this time.

This possibility is also supported by the observation that the group of 144,000 was blameless, with no lie found in their mouths. This is a rather remarkable statement in the context of their surroundings. Whether symbolic or literal, the earthly scene described by John is one of lies, deception, and manipulation. What must it take to respond not in kind, but with exactly the opposite qualities? Many would say this is the challenge to the church of any age, yet during these end times, the ability to remain absolutely truthful and blameless is especially noteworthy.

Flashback

The group of 144,000 is referred to as the *firstfruits* to God and the Lamb. The term is strange to most of us, but would have been meaningful to the Jews of the first century. Their perception was that, "The earth is the Lord's, and everything in it, the world, and all who live in it" (Psalm 24:1). So as the crops came in each year, the tradition was to offer back to God a portion of those that ripened first (see Leviticus 23:9–14). In this example in Revelation, the group marked by God seems to represent a token first wave of people to be redeemed by God during the turbulent end times.

And what John records next seems to indicate that the 144,000 were on the right track.

Just Call Them Angels of the Mourning

Then I saw another angel flying in midair, and he had the eternal gospel to proclaim to those who live on the earth—to every nation, tribe, language and people. He said in a loud voice, "Fear God and give him glory, because the hour of his judgment has come. Worship him who made the heavens, the earth, the sea and the springs of water."

A second angel followed and said, "Fallen! Fallen is Babylon the Great, which made all the nations drink the maddening wine of her adulteries."

A third angel followed them and said in a loud voice: "If anyone worships the beast and his image and receives his mark on the forehead or on the hand, he, too, will drink of the wine of God's fury, which has been poured full strength into the cup of his wrath. He will be tormented with burning sulfur in the presence of the holy angels and of the Lamb. And the smoke of their torment rises for ever and ever. There is no rest day or night for those who worship the beast and his image, or for anyone who receives the mark of his name." This calls for patient endurance on the part of the saints who obey God's commandments and remain faithful to Jesus.

Then I heard a voice from heaven say, "Write: Blessed are the dead who die in the Lord from now on."

"Yes," says the Spirit, "they will rest from their labor, for their deeds will follow them" (Revelation 14:6–13).

Yet another procession of angels is recorded, this time in a series of three. The first announced the hour of God's judgment, with clear instructions to "Fear God and give him glory …. Worship him who made the heavens, the earth, the sea and the springs of water."

Clanging Symbols

Babylon started as a literal place—one of the world's oldest cities, as a matter of fact, as well as the country in which the city was located. Once a place of grandeur and prominence, it eventually fell, but remained a symbol both of the secular world as a whole, and more specifically of the depravity inherent in secular culture throughout the ages. Some people feel that Babylon will one day be rebuilt and restored as a literal city, only to be destroyed again in fulfillment of the end-times prophecies.

From what we've seen taking place with the activity of the dragon, the Antichrist, and the false prophet, we might not expect much of a response to this message (and we would be right). Numerous commentators feel that the "eternal gospel" proclaimed by the angel is no longer a call to salvation. Rather, in the context of what's happening, the eternal aspect of this message is one of judgment. This interpretation seems to be supported by the angels that follow.

The second angel, for example, announces the fall of "Babylon the Great, which made all the nations drink the maddening wine of her adulteries." We're going to get a clasp picture of Babylon, drinking, and adultery when we get to Revelation 17–18. Here, however, little more is said.

The third angel is more talkative, addressing in detail what will happen to those who ally with the beast (Antichrist). It's one of those passages in the Bible that can cause discomfort among Christians as well as nonbelievers. Eternal judgment is not a pretty picture however you approach it.

This third angel warns that the Antichrist's supporters will "drink of the wine of God's fury, which has been poured full strength into the cup of his wrath." It boggles the mind for someone pondering an omnipotent God to consider his full-strength fury added to his wrath. Those who rebel against this almighty God by supporting the Antichrist find themselves tormented in burning sulfur (a more recent translation of the old "fire and brimstone") as "the smoke of their torment rises for ever and ever."

These days tattoos can be removed almost as easily as they are applied. But you get the sense that the mark of the beast has a permanence that cannot be erased when God begins meting out judgment. Like it or not, this portion of the Book of Revelation clearly indicates eternal pain and punishment for certain people, at least, who boldly defy God.

And from this perspective, the next statement in Revelation makes sense. Not only do the few faithful believers need "patient endurance," but during these end times death for them will be preferable (in the context of eternity, at least) than life with the mark of the beast. The "saints" will rest from their labor—but only after they are dead.

And the bleakness of the picture continues as additional angels just keep appearing.

Apoca-Lips Now

"Antichrist is so proud as to go before Christ; so humble as to pretend to come after him; and so audacious as to say that himself is he."

—John Bunyan

Apoca-Lips Now

"The Lord gets his best soldiers out of the highlands of affliction."

—Charles Haddon Spurgeon

It's Enough to Make You Sickle

I looked, and there before me was a white cloud, and seated on the cloud was one "like a son of man" with a crown of gold on his head and a sharp sickle in his hand. Then another angel came out of the temple and called in a loud voice to him who was sitting on the cloud, "Take your sickle and reap, because the time to reap has come, for the harvest of the earth is ripe." So he who was seated on the cloud swung his sickle over the earth, and the earth was harvested.

Another angel came out of the temple in heaven, and he too had a sharp sickle. Still another angel, who had charge of the fire, came from the altar and called in a loud voice to him who had the sharp sickle, "Take your sharp sickle and gather the clusters of grapes from the earth's vine, because its grapes are ripe." The angel swung his sickle on the earth, gathered its grapes and threw them into the great winepress of God's wrath. They were trampled in the winepress outside the city, and blood flowed out of the press, rising as high as the horses' bridles for a distance of 1,600 stadia (Revelation 14:14–20).

No sooner had the three angels flown by making their announcements like heavenly town criers than John's attention was directed to another heavenly figure. It was someone sitting on a cloud, wearing a crown, and holding a sharp sickle. The figure is described as "one like a son of man."

Perhaps this is yet another angel, because the context mentions at least three more in addition to the previous three. Another possibility is that this is a different manifestation of Jesus. He had recently appeared as "the Lamb" (Revelation 14:1), but "son of man" was one of Jesus' favorite titles for himself while he was teaching on earth. It was also the term John used in his initial description of Jesus at the beginning of Revelation (1:13). Either way, this figure on the cloud is a powerful figure who, based on what happens next, represents judgment.

Flashback

The connection between Jesus and the title "Son of Man" can be traced to the Old Testament. Daniel described a figure "like a son of man" approaching a powerful heavenly figure called "the Ancient of Days." Of the "son of man" in this particular vision, it is said: "He was given authority, glory and sovereign power; all peoples, nations and men of every language worshiped him. His dominion is an everlasting dominion that will not pass away, and his kingdom is one that will never be destroyed" (Daniel 7:13–14). This was clearly a messianic prophecy.

The figure on the cloud, in response to a cue from an angel in the heavenly temple, swung his sickle. And immediately "the earth was harvested." The impact of this event is surely of great import, yet the laconic simplicity of the statement is equally noteworthy. Four words equate to the final judgment of the population of an entire planet.

Flashback

Sowing and reaping were prominent themes in Jesus' teaching. Some of his parables used images similar to the harvesting image in Revelation:

➤ "A seed grows day and night, producing grain. When the time is right, the owner puts a sickle to it and harvests it" (Mark 4:26–29).

➤ "A man's enemy sowed weeds into his good crops. The decision was made to let the good plants and weeds grow together, and the weeds would be separated, bundled, and burned after the harvest" (Matthew 13:24–30, 36–43).

Other of his parables used different symbols to make similar points of how God will separate the sinful people from the righteous at a future time (sheep and goats [Matthew 25:31–46], fish caught in a net [Matthew 13:47–52], and so on).

We recently saw the first fruits of a crop offered to God. But while the initial first-fruits referred to those with whom God was pleased, and suggests that other faithful people are to follow, this particular harvest doesn't appear to be a positive thing at all.

The so-called grapes that were harvested are said to be "ripe," but the original word suggests a state of being *overripe,* and perhaps even beginning to wither. Consequently, some interpreters see the "grapes" not as good people being gathered to return to God, but the baddies who have been getting away with too much for too long. What follows seems to confirm such an outlook.

After the first mighty swing of the sickle, another angel follows up with a more concentrated cleanup of

Apoca-Lips Now

"Man proposes, but God disposes."

—Thomas à Kempis

the "harvest." The grapes that are gathered are then thrown "into the great winepress of God's wrath." The imagery is not very pleasant. Grapes would only be tossed into a winepress to have all the living juices squeezed out of them. In the picture presented in this portion of Revelation, however, the fluid produced by these grapes is not juice, but blood. And quite an abundant harvest it is!

A stadium (sometimes translated "furlong") was a distance of about 606 feet, so the distance of "1,600 stadia" equates to roughly 180 miles. It was this distance that blood is described rising "as high as the horses' bridles." The mention of blood and horses suggests a battle, though no other clues are given at this point. Later we will come across the name of a famous battle which many people couple with the events described in this passage.

It is unlikely that the scene witnessed by John was one of horses actually standing in blood up to their bridles, though such hyperbole (extreme exaggeration) may be used in apocalyptic literature. Others explain this image as blood *spatter* that streaks as high as horses' bridles. Either image is one of great violence, and if it spans 180 miles, it seems that such a battle is unprecedented in human history.

A Topic We'd Wrath-er Avoid

The argument is frequently made that a loving and merciful God would surely never condemn people to hell—much less for eternity. Some people assume that on the off chance there *is* substance to Christianity, and if it turns out that there *is* an afterlife, that God is going to buckle under and let them slide regardless of their prior offenses and misdeeds. Others point out that such reasoning uses faulty logic.

What the Judge Said: The Judgment

The latter group suggests we need only to look at our own judicial systems. Nothing raises the ire of a community more than a judge who doesn't do his job. It's one thing if he or she takes it easy on youthful offenders and gives youngsters a second chance. But if the judge begins to release murderers on technicalities, sets sex offenders free to return to local neighborhoods, and lets other criminals off just so he or she won't be perceived as a mean person, the community is outraged.

It is the job of a judge to make hard decisions that the rest of us don't like to make—and to do so impartially. Some people point out that God is not only described in Scripture as a loving Father, a

Apoca-Lips Now

"The final chapter of human history is solely God's decision, and even now He is everywhere active in grace or judgment. Never in all history have men spoken so much of end-time, yet been so shrouded in ignorance of God's impending doomsday."

—Carl F.H. Henry

wise counselor, and a gentle shepherd, but also a fair judge. Sometimes a judge must mete out life sentences or even execution. Doing so does not reflect in the least whether or not the judge is a loving father, compassionate friend, or anything else; it only has to do with the fact that the offender breached an established system of justice.

The judge may or may not be personally outraged at the severity of the crime. His or her emotional state is not supposed to affect the decision. Whether the judge has the personality of Mister Rogers or Mr. T, he should reach the same conclusion based on the law. The sentence passed has nothing to do with the personal character of the judge.

Based on much of what we've seen in the Book of Revelation, we should not be surprised if the heavenly gavel falls and certain hardhearted people find themselves facing harsh sentences. Eternal judgment is not what God desires for anyone (2 Peter 3:9). He does not pass this harsh sentence because he is angry (although he happens to be); he does it because he is fair.

Judgment Requires a Battle Hymn

Past generations weren't so quick to shy away from considering the wrath of God. One of the classic songs of American history references the very portion of Revelation we've covered in this chapter. Consider the words of the "Battle Hymn of the Republic," written by Julia Ward Howe around 1862:

> Mine eyes have seen the glory of the coming of the Lord;
> He is trampling out the vintage where the grapes of wrath are stored.
> He hath loosed the fateful lightning of His terrible swift sword.
> His truth is marching on.

> I have seen Him in the watchfires of a hundred circling camps.
> They have builded Him an altar in the evening dews and damps.
> I can read His righteous sentence by the dim and flaring lamps.
> His day is marching on.

> He has sounded forth the trumpet that shall never sound retreat.
> He is sifting out the hearts of men before His judgment seat.
> O be swift, my soul, to answer Him! Be jubilant, my feet!
> Our God is marching on.

> In the beauty of the lilies, Christ was born across the sea
> With a glory in His bosom that transfigures you and me.
> As He died to make men holy, let us live to make men free
> While God is marching on.

> [Refrain] Glory! Glory, hallelujah!
> Glory! Glory, hallelujah!
> Glory! Glory, hallelujah! Our God is marching on.

120

In these politically correct times we don't hear much about God's wrath—not in our songs, and not even in most of our churches. The Book of Revelation, however, doesn't shy away from it, so we're trying not to in this book, either. Most Christians are quite convinced that God is unwilling (and even incapable) of playing favorites, making a mistake, or doing anything else that is in the least unfair. If anything, God might be accused of being much too lenient in the grace and mercy he extends to humankind.

One theological position is that God has nothing to gain or lose by receiving people into heaven—or dooming them to hell, for that matter. God is complete, with or without our company. According to this line of reasoning, we have the opportunity to share in his splendor if we wish to do so.

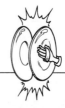

Clanging Symbols

The imagery from the Book of Revelation used in this song, reflecting God's pending judgment as a call to action, has been used as a rallying cry in previous wars. At one time, our society expected judgment and justice to walk hand in hand.

We see in the Book of Revelation that God has his limits. The day will come when the clock runs down and the heavenly Father puts on his robe to act with finality as the heavenly Judge.

Give the matter a little thought here, but you need not reach any hasty conclusions. As we go through the next chapters in the Book of Revelation, the issue of God's wrath will come up again. In fact, we're about to see seven heaping bowls of it as we get back to the events following the sounding of the seventh trumpet. (Maybe you'd like to take a break at this point to go see a romantic comedy or read some light fiction!)

The Least You Need to Know

➤ No fewer than 144,000 people have endured the nasty end times up till this point.

➤ Angels remain active in announcing ongoing events—most of which continue to be unpleasant.

➤ The judgment of those who oppose God in this account is said to be both painful and eternal.

➤ As the text begins to describe the wrath of God, the earth is "harvested" like grain falling before a sharp sickle.

Chapter 11

The Bowled and the Beautiful

In This Chapter

➤ A look at Revelation 15–16

➤ Seven angels, seven plagues, seven bowls of God's wrath

➤ The devastation of the earth intensifies

➤ War at Armageddon

Why do bad things happen? It's an age-old question with numerous books written in answer. But a twenty-first century twist on this question—one that is likely to pop up at this portion of Revelation if it hasn't already come to mind—is "Whom can I blame when bad things happen to *me?*" As we're going to see, there may be several reasons why bad things happen. So when the bad times come, perhaps we shouldn't be too quick to blame the first person who comes to mind.

God catches a lot of blame for bad things. Some say he is apathetic and doesn't care much what happens down here. Some say he is impotent and can't prevent bad events from taking place. Some suggest he is passive-aggressive, and depending on his current whim, bestows either blessings or curses. What most people *don't* say in response is, "We were doing some really bad stuff we shouldn't have been doing, and we suffered the consequences of our actions."

Just the Blame Old Story

For example, when little Billy runs in crying and covered with hornet stings, and you ask what happened, he tells you, "I was just playing and the stupid bees attacked me." When his sister comes in with her eyewitness account, however, she might add that Billy's "playing" had involved repeatedly poking the wasps' nest with a stick.

When Clem gets laid off at work he tells his wife it's because of a massive downsizing plan. What he doesn't tell her is that the boss had already warned him a couple of times about his three-hour lunches and poor performance before he came in today, late again and with scotch on his breath.

Perhaps this all started when little Cain started asking Adam and Eve why they got kicked out of the Garden of Eden. Maybe they told him that God got mad at them for no reason, conveniently leaving out the part about the forbidden fruit, the serpent, and the fig leaves.

Apoca-Lips Now

"There's folks [who would] stand on their heads and then say the fault was [in] their boots."

—George Eliot

Apoca-Lips Now

"Although the world is full of suffering, it is full also of the overcoming of it."

—Helen Keller

When God comes into the picture as we try to figure out his connection to bad things, it's amazing how desperately we want him to be one-dimensional. We want to figure him out. Is he loving or vengeful? Is he patient or a take-charge kind of God? Does he care about our pain, or expect us to suck it up?

It's tricky to glean insight on spiritual relationships based on human ones without occasionally coming to some false conclusions. But consider your own life. On an average day of going to work, it might be perfectly normal for you to passionately kiss your spouse, playfully hug your kids, casually acknowledge your neighbor, swear at the jerk who cuts you off in traffic, fear how your boss will respond to your only half-completed presentation, and rejoice with a coworker who has just had her first baby. You are only one person, but look at that wide range of emotions!

Why then are so many of us surprised that God might have an even wider range of emotions? Why shouldn't his responses differ depending on the situation and the person(s) with whom he is relating? Do we think he can't be loving and judgmental at the same time? Is he not capable of smiling down on children playing in the schoolyard even as he scowls at the adults lurking in the shadows, also watching the children, yet with horrendously perverted thoughts and intentions? If he treats you with compassion and someone else with harshness, does that mean he likes you better—or might it mean the other person was repeatedly attempting, in a figurative sense, to poke him with a stick?

The perspective of the Book of Revelation indicates that God ought not be the target of blame for all the bad stuff going on. We've seen a dragon and a couple of beasties working together to generate all kinds of chaos and pandemonium. Why should God be blamed for what *they've* been doing?

Similarly, when bad things happen today, why is God the first choice to receive our scorn? We're quick to accuse *him,* yet we just ignore that his evil counterpart might be responsible. If anything, the Book of Revelation has shown us to this point that bad things might happen because bad forces are at work.

And then again, sometimes bad things might happen because God is displeased and ready to take action. We saw in Chapter 10, "Where the Grapes of Wrath Are Stored," that God is ready to express wrath that, to this point, he has held in check. Most Christians would say that God's wrath is not directed so much at people as at rampant sin. Yet if the people doing the rampant sinning don't make any attempt to reconcile with God, they will eventually pay the consequences. And regardless of the shameful, violent, or otherwise abhorrent behavior of such people, no doubt God is going to be blamed whenever he steps in to address the situation.

> **Apoca-Lips Now**
>
> "Believing as I do that man in the distant future will be a far more perfect creature than he now is, it is an intolerable thought that he and all other sentient beings are doomed to complete annihilation after such long-continued slow progress. To those who fully admit the immortality of the human soul, the destruction of our world will not appear so dreadful."
>
> —Charles Darwin

Last Is Hardly Least

So far in the Book of Revelation, the seven seals and seven trumpets have been an expression of God's wrath toward a predominantly sinful world. And still, God remains in control of to what extent he expresses his anger. We have seen some devastating things, to be sure, yet the world goes on—apparently as wicked as ever, if not more so. In this chapter, however, we're planning to move ahead into a final series of judgments after which "God's wrath is completed" (Revelation 15:1).

But if we consider that God may indeed be capable of more than one emotion, as are we who are created in his image, we need to realize that he can direct his wrath toward one group of people while maintaining love and compassion for another. We have seen this borne out throughout the Book of Revelation, and will see it yet again in this chapter.

I saw in heaven another great and marvelous sign: seven angels with the seven last plagues—last, because with them God's wrath is completed. And I saw what looked like a sea of glass mixed with fire and, standing beside the sea, those who had been victorious over the beast and his image and over the number of his name. They held harps given them by God and sang the song of Moses the servant of God and the song of the Lamb: "Great and marvelous are your deeds, Lord God Almighty. Just and true are your ways, King of the ages. Who will not fear you, O Lord, and bring glory to your name? For you alone are holy. All nations will come and worship before you, for your righteous acts have been revealed."

After this I looked and in heaven the temple, that is, the tabernacle of the Testimony, was opened. Out of the temple came the seven angels with the seven plagues. They were dressed in clean, shining linen and wore golden sashes around their chests. Then one of the four living creatures gave to the seven angels seven golden bowls filled with the wrath of God, who lives for ever and ever. And the temple was filled with smoke from the glory of God and from his power, and no one could enter the temple until the seven plagues of the seven angels were completed (Revelation 15:1–8).

Flashback

Awareness of the wrath of God against sin was a powerful influence on believers throughout the Bible. It was motivation for a healthy "fear of the Lord" and was by no means new to the Book of Revelation. This is why repentance is such a big deal for those in the Judeo-Christian camp. They believe repentance brings God's forgiveness and restoration of the previously broken relationship. Otherwise, God is expected to judge and punish sin. Consider these thoughts from Hebrews 10:30–31, for example: "For we know him who said, 'It is mine to avenge; I will repay,' and again, 'The Lord will judge his people.' It is a dreadful thing to fall into the hands of the living God."

Human beings know little about righteous anger. We get mad for a number of reasons—many of them quite petty and/or selfish. To attribute such motivation to the holy God described in the Book of Revelation might lead to some unfounded conclusions. God's wrath about to be poured out on the earth in this passage is just his taking care of unfinished business. From the perspective of the righteous people both in Revelation (6:9–10) and those in the contemporary Christian church, God never gets angry without reason. His full wrath, therefore, will be in direct response to specific actions that have had painful and wicked results. And after being expressed, according to this passage, God's wrath will be over and done with.

In fact, as the apostle John continues to record what he sees, he begins with a crowd of people standing beside a "sea of glass" who all seem to be quite pleased that God is about to complete his judgment of the world. We previously saw a sea of glass spreading out before God's throne (Revelation 4:6). And we previously saw a similar (if not the same) group standing before God's throne in Revelation 7:9–17. They are again clearly identified: "those who had been victorious over the beast and his image and over the number of his name."

Since this group is no longer on earth but in heaven strongly suggests that they died at the hands of the Antichrist and his minions. Yet what surely had been perceived as their defeat on earth resulted in their being described as "victorious" in heaven. And they celebrated their victory with a big sing-along—the song of Moses … and the song of the Lamb.

A Bright Spot

Here again we see the joyful people in heaven contrasted with all the other harsh events being described. Harps had been handed out to them, and they were singing up a storm. And they weren't blaming God for the bad stuff that had happened. Just the opposite. They sang, "Just and true are your ways, … For you alone are holy … your righteous acts have been revealed."

Flashback

Singing to celebrate victory was a common practice during the time of Moses and throughout the Old Testament. Biblical songs are recorded after the crossing of the Red Sea (Exodus 15:1–21), after victories during the times of the judges (Judges 5), and in other places (not least among them, the Book of Psalms). The fact that the heavenly choir sang "the song of Moses … and the song of the Lamb" suggests that they might have added some refrains in honor of Jesus to accompany the ones traditionally praising God the Father.

In contrast to this happy scene is a lineup of seven angels "with the seven last plagues." John is privileged to see what is taking place both in heaven and on earth, so he sees this Magnificent Seven being prepared prior to actually going into action. They came out of the heavenly temple dressed in dazzling white linen and golden sashes. One of the four living creatures (first seen in Revelation 4:6) handed out "golden bowls filled with the wrath of God." Each of the seven angels received a bowl.

At this time, the heavenly temple fills with smoke, representing "the glory of God." No one enters or leaves the temple from this moment until the seven plagues of the seven angels are completed. From the perspective of those in heaven, the smoke-filled temple indicated that the pouring out of the final wrath of God would be a holy moment.

Clanging Symbols

Smoke had long symbolized the somber presence of God witnessed by onlookers. When God descended to meet Moses atop Mount Sinai, the smoke billowed up from the mountain like smoke from a furnace (Exodus 19:18). At other times in the history of Israel, the earthly Tabernacle/Temple had been so filled with God's smoky presence that no one could enter—not even Moses (Exodus 40:34–35) or the priests of King Solomon's court (1 Kings 8:10–11).

Down to the Last Seven Super Bowls

After a brief diversion taken by the Book of Revelation to describe a few key symbols and events, it is at this point where we return to what happens following the sounding of the seventh trumpet. Just as the seventh seal revealed the seven trumpet judgments, the seventh trumpet has sounded and is now about to initiate the seven bowl judgments.

Then I heard a loud voice from the temple saying to the seven angels, "Go, pour out the seven bowls of God's wrath on the earth."

The first angel went and poured out his bowl on the land, and ugly and painful sores broke out on the people who had the mark of the beast and worshiped his image.

The second angel poured out his bowl on the sea, and it turned into blood like that of a dead man, and every living thing in the sea died.

The third angel poured out his bowl on the rivers and springs of water, and they became blood. Then I heard the angel in charge of the waters say: "You are just in these judgments, you who are and who were, the Holy One, because you have so judged; for they have shed the blood of your saints and prophets, and you have given them blood to drink as they deserve." And I heard the altar respond: "Yes, Lord God Almighty, true and just are your judgments."

The fourth angel poured out his bowl on the sun, and the sun was given power to scorch people with fire. They were seared by the intense heat and they cursed the name of God, who had control over these plagues, but they refused to repent and glorify him.

The fifth angel poured out his bowl on the throne of the beast, and his kingdom was plunged into darkness. Men gnawed their tongues in agony and cursed the God of heaven because of their pains and their sores, but they refused to repent of what they had done (Revelation 16:1–11).

No time frame is given for how far apart the angels' actions are spaced, yet from all appearances it seems that this final series of judgments comes as a rapid-fire blast from heaven. And if things have seemed bad up till now, these bowls of God's wrath trump everything that has gone before.

The first one is a divine smart bomb, targeting only people with the mark of the beast. Those who had been smitten with the Antichrist enough to worship him are now smitten with not only painful sores, but ugly ones as well. Why do we need to know that the sores are ugly? Perhaps this is a subtle commentary on the pride inherent in society during the last days.

The second bowl of wrath was poured into the sea, turning it to blood (probably figuratively) and killing everything in it. You may recall from previous judgments that a significant portion of sea life had already died. This time, however, nothing is left alive. Those familiar with "red tides" know how annoying it can be when tiny protozoans overpopulate and produce enough toxins to kill fish and contaminate shellfish in a localized area. Standing beside an entire lifeless, red ocean won't be a day at the beach.

The third angel poured out his bowl on the earth's fresh water, which also became bloodlike. Nothing is said about killing off the sources of food as had been done in the oceans, but the effect on drinking water is emphasized instead. It was an intentionally ironic judgment. If the people of the time so enjoyed shedding the blood of the few people who continued to believe in God, then God would give them "blood" to drink. And although few of the people on earth are going to be happy about what's going on, a voice from the heavenly altar sounds at this point to confirm that God's judgments are "true and just."

The fourth angel poured his bowl on the sun, seeming to fuel it with extraordinary heat. The sunshine became so intense as to "scorch people with fire." Apparently no existing SPF level was adequate to protect against this divinely inspired sunburn. The lack of pure water probably added to the problem, and was surely a factor in the people's response at this point: "They cursed the name of God."

The fifth angel in the series poured his bowl of God's wrath "on the throne of the beast"—probably a poetic reference to the earth, or perhaps a more specific geographic area. The earth, in response, was "plunged into darkness." And the nature of people being what it is, the very ones who were complaining about the heat

yesterday are today sitting in the cool dark, cursing God. The cumulative effect of the bowl judgments has left them with painful sores, crisis-level sunburn, and no doubt a wicked thirst so that they are gnawing on their tongues.

Even though it seems the people were aware that they really ought to repent of their evil ways, they refused to do so. Incidentally, this is the last outright statement in the Book of Revelation that people refused to repent, but it seems clear from here onward that such a fact is taken for granted.

Apoca-Lips Now

"If God has spoken, why is the universe not convinced?"

—Percy Bysshe Shelley

Flashback

Consider what the earth must look like after all the events that have been taking place. The world as "the throne of the beast" is a far different place than the world that had been created. The creation story (Genesis 1–2) describes a world created from God's loving labor, with lush trees, pure rivers, underground springs, animals, people, and no shame. And just as humankind "lost their lease" on paradise by defying God, the Book of Revelation indicates that the attitude of defiance continues until the very end of the world.

A Call to Armageddon

The sixth angel poured out his bowl on the great river Euphrates, and its water was dried up to prepare the way for the kings from the East. Then I saw three evil spirits that looked like frogs; they came out of the mouth of the dragon, out of the mouth of the beast and out of the mouth of the false prophet. They are spirits of demons performing miraculous signs, and they go out to the kings of the whole world, to gather them for the battle on the great day of God Almighty.

"Behold, I come like a thief! Blessed is he who stays awake and keeps his clothes with him, so that he may not go naked and be shamefully exposed."

Then they gathered the kings together to the place that in Hebrew is called Armageddon (Revelation 6:12–16).

In pouring out his bowl, the sixth angel targeted the Euphrates River, causing it to dry up. Apparently this newly drained riverbed will provide easy access for "kings from the East" to gather for a massive war. Few commentators seem to agree on exactly who these "kings" will be, so we won't attempt to speculate. Yet the kings assemble at a place called Armageddon—a Hebrew word that identifies the location as Mount Megiddo. (Keep in mind, however, that those not seeking a literal interpretation of Revelation do not see this as a literal place either, but rather a symbolic representation of the final clash between good and evil.)

Flashback

At the foot of Mount Megiddo (in the northern portion of Israel) lies a large plain and the Valley of Jezreel where several biblical battles were fought. Deborah, the warrior woman during the time of the judges, won a victory there. So did Gideon (Judges 5:19–20; 6:33). King Saul, who had gone his own way rather than listen to God, lost his life in battle there (1 Samuel 31; 2 Samuel 4:4), as did two lesser-known kings: Ahaziah and Josiah (2 Kings 9:27; 23:29–30). Egyptian pharaohs had fought there almost fifteen centuries before Christ, and as recently as 1917 the British won a decisive battle over the Turks in the same location.

You would think with the current widespread use of the term Armageddon (either in reference to history's final and most intense war, or more generally to describe large-scale violent conflict of any kind) that the Book of Revelation would have a lot to say about it. This, however, is the only place the specific word is used in the entire Bible. Yet as we will see when we get to the interpretations of Revelation, the bloody battle described in the previous chapter (Revelation 14:19–20) is frequently associated with this massive gathering of armies at Armageddon, as are certain events yet to follow. Again, many of the conclusions you reach will depend on which interpretations you prefer.

But in connection with the "kings of the East" assembling to do battle is another little kicker which John records for us in describing this sixth bowl judgment. He again

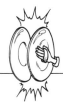

Clanging Symbols

The mention of the return of Jesus "as a thief" had been a recurring New Testament symbol. Jesus had told parables that called for the watchfulness of his disciples, using the illustration of a thief as a teaching analogy (Luke 12:35–40). And Paul was even more direct, clearly stating that "the day of the Lord will come like a thief in the night" (1 Thessalonians 5:2).

sees the dragon (Satan), the beast (Antichrist), and the false prophet. From the mouth of each of these characters comes a froglike figure that John describes as "spirits of demons performing miraculous signs." It is these froggy critters that are credited with bringing together the parties who will eventually go at each other with unprecedented intensity.

We have seen in Revelation that certain demons were previously released from their prison Abyss (9:1–11) to torment people. In this case, they go out to goad huge numbers of people into war and slaughter. While people speak of the *battle* of Armageddon, some commentators prefer to call it a *war*, expecting the fighting to take place over a significant length of time.

And while John reveals to his readers the behind-the-scenes activity of these "three evil spirits," he also drops in a quote, apparently from Jesus, about the certainty of his return. Many pounce on this clue in making a direct connection between the war taking place at Armageddon and the second return of Jesus (which is still ahead of us in the Book of Revelation).

Come Hail and High Richter

The seventh angel poured out his bowl into the air, and out of the temple came a loud voice from the throne, saying, "It is done!" Then there came flashes of lightning, rumblings, peals of thunder and a severe earthquake. No earthquake like it has ever occurred since man has been on earth, so tremendous was the quake. The great city split into three parts, and the cities of the nations collapsed. God remembered Babylon the Great and gave her the cup filled with the wine of the fury of his wrath. Every island fled away and the mountains could not be found. From the sky huge hailstones of about a hundred pounds each fell upon men. And they cursed God on account of the plague of hail, because the plague was so terrible (Revelation 16:17–21).

After seven seals, seven trumpets, and six bowls of wrath, we get to this final bowl and the acknowledgement that, "It is done!" God's wrath hits as a storm on the remaining people who have been defiant to the end. Devastation comes from both the earth and the sky.

While the earthquakes measured by the Richter scale usually range between 1 and 9, the scale has no upper limit. Each number represents an increase of 32 times the released energy of the previous number, which is why we don't see many higher numbers. If the Book of Revelation is to be believed, however, this final earthquake will set a new record as the earth shudders like never before. The "great city," identified as Babylon, will unwillingly form subdivisions, and the surrounding cities will crumble and fall. Mountains will flatten and islands will disappear. (Whether "Babylon" is the literal city in Mesopotamia, or a symbolic reference to Jerusalem or someplace else, is debated. Chapter 12, "The Elaborately Dressed, Blood-Drinking, Scarlet-Beast-Riding Prostitute," will go into more detail concerning the final fall of Babylon.)

Flashback

The Book of Job tells of a man who was hit with some of the worst that Satan could dish out: the loss of his herds, the deaths of his children, and personal affliction that left him in constant pain. Several people gave him advice as he tried to understand God's part in all the terrible things that had happened to him. The best advice his loving wife could offer was, "Curse God and die" (Job 1:1–2:10). This seems to be the attitude of the remaining few during the final bowl judgment.

From the sky will come lightning, rumblings, and peals of thunder. In addition, 100-pound hailstones will barrage the people who have survived everything else. These days we gaze in wonder on golf-ball-sized hail as we see what kind of damage it can do. It's hard to imagine what effect hail the size of Old English sheepdogs will have. We do know from the account that people will be not only blaming God for all that is happening, but cursing him as well.

Cursing God at a moment of imminent death may seem like getting in the last word, if you're unable to do anything else. But as the Book of Revelation continues, we shall see that God will take another opportunity to address the rebellious remnant of humanity and will, in fact, have the final word.

Here we see how the people feel about God. In Chapter 12, we will get a better look at how God perceives the lifestyles of these remaining people.

Apoca-Lips Now

"Man is neither angel nor beast; and the misfortune is that he who would act the angel acts the beast."

—Blaise Pascal

It will explain more clearly many of the things we have been taking for granted about the behavior and attitudes of the people.

Why do bad things happen? Perhaps Satan is hard at work, creating pain and trouble we don't deserve. Maybe we *do* deserve it, and are merely reaping what we have sown. And according to the Book of Revelation, some day *really* bad things are going to happen when God is no longer willing to hold his anger and we discover that justice is more severe than we ever imagined.

The Least You Need to Know

➤ People killed by satanic forces during the end times are described as still waiting for justice.

➤ The last of the seven trumpets initiates seven "bowl judgments," bringing about the worst suffering described so far.

➤ God's wrath is completed with this final series of judgments.

➤ A terrible final war is set to occur at a place called Armageddon.

Chapter 12

The Elaborately Dressed, Blood-Drinking, Scarlet-Beast-Riding Prostitute

---

In This Chapter

➤ A look at Revelation 17–18

➤ John is invited to witness an orgy of sorts

➤ More clues for those seeking interpretations for the Book of Revelation

➤ The dramatic fall of "Babylon the Great"

The past couple of chapters have touched on the wrath of God, and it hasn't been a pretty sight. But as we continue we need to keep a couple of things in mind: (1) What we're seeing in the Book of Revelation is the *culmination* of God's wrath after millennia of love, mercy, grace, and forgiveness; and (2) As the narrative of Revelation rolls along in this chapter, we're going to get a view of the world the way God sees it.

God May Not Be Quick to Judge—But We Are

Human nature being what it is, most of us don't need much information to form opinions about other people. When a protective mother shows up for her son's first Little League game and sees the coach screaming at her kid (and others), she immediately pegs him as unstable. Had she gotten there earlier, she might have seen that all the boys had been exceptionally inattentive, disobedient, and hyperactive (as young boys are known to be on warm summer days). The coach, after numerous "nice" approaches, had finally resorted to his most fearsome and attention-getting voice. But no matter how justifiable his actions, the mom is likely to form an erroneous opinion about him because she witnessed a single, overly gruff example, out of context.

At the end-of-the-year office party, everyone praises Steve for being a popular, money-earning go-getter who was primarily responsible for their large holiday bonuses. Meanwhile, his wife sits quietly in a corner, the only one with any clue that Steve is also an alcoholic and abusive. The partygoers gossip about ol' outgoing Steverino, wondering how he could be attracted to someone so ... different.

What you know about other people influences your attitudes and actions toward them. Some people pride themselves on being able to quickly assess another's character. Yet if you know more than others, and don't necessarily want to share potentially embarrassing or unpleasant knowledge, perhaps *you're* the one who is perceived as abnormal.

From a biblical perspective, the Jesus of Revelation is the same Jesus who came to earth, attended parties with prostitutes and sinners, hugged lepers, shushed his disciples' complaints on occasion when he wanted to play with some kids, and treated everyone with the utmost of love and acceptance. And he did these things, among other reasons, to show people what God is like. So if God appears to be harsh in his dealings with people during the last days, perhaps it will help to get his perspective on what is going on. Maybe, just maybe, he has a reason.

Flashback

Jesus made it clear to his disciples that his actions and behavior were indicative of God himself: "Anyone who has seen me has seen the Father. How can you say, 'Show us the Father'? Don't you believe that I am in the Father, and that the Father is in me? The words I say to you are not just my own. Rather, it is the Father, living in me, who is doing his work. Believe me when I say that I am in the Father and the Father is in me; or at least believe on the evidence of the miracles themselves" (John 14:9–11).

Ride 'Em, Call Girl

While recording the things he was seeing and hearing, John received an interesting invitation.

One of the seven angels who had the seven bowls came and said to me, "Come, I will show you the punishment of the great prostitute, who sits on many waters. With her the kings of the earth committed adultery and the inhabitants of the earth were intoxicated with the wine of her adulteries."

Then the angel carried me away in the Spirit into a desert. There I saw a woman sitting on a scarlet beast that was covered with blasphemous names and had seven heads and ten horns. The woman was dressed in purple and scarlet, and was glittering with gold, precious stones and pearls. She held a golden cup in her hand, filled with abominable things and the filth of her adulteries. This title was written on her forehead:

MYSTERY

BABYLON THE GREAT

THE MOTHER OF PROSTITUTES

AND OF THE ABOMINATIONS OF THE EARTH.

I saw that the woman was drunk with the blood of the saints, the blood of those who bore testimony to Jesus. When I saw her, I was greatly astonished (Revelation 17:1–6).

Somehow you might think that heaven would be the last place someone would walk up and say, "Hey, you wanna go look at a prostitute?" Yet since this invitation was extended by one of the angels who had just poured out a bowl of God's wrath on the earth, John went along to see what he would be shown.

No Good to the Last Drop

John was transported "in the Spirit" (probably in a vision) to a desert setting, even though he had been told that the prostitute "sits on many waters." While there are other biblical references to "the waters of Babylon," the waters referred to in this passage are later identified specifically as "peoples, multitudes, nations and languages" (Revelation 17:15).

John had also been told to expect a "great prostitute." What he was expecting is not known, but today we might be looking for the common stereotype of a woman with too much makeup, wearing short-shorts and fishnet hose. This woman, however, was dressed elaborately in purple and scarlet. She wore gold, pearls, and other precious stones.

Clanging Symbols

The Antichrist/beast we saw in Revelation 13:1, coming out of the sea, had 7 heads and 10 horns—just like this one hanging around with the great prostitute. Coincidence?

She might have been an impressive figure, but her classy wardrobe and accessories lost much of their allure in light of her behavior: drinking blood and riding around on a scarlet beast!

This is one of those passages in Revelation that essentially everyone considers symbolic, yet the narrative also provides insight into what many of these symbols mean. Based on the name written on her forehead, the woman represents Babylon, "the mother of prostitutes." She had previously committed adultery with "the kings of the earth," and her current paramour was a scarlet beast with seven heads and 10 horns. She held a golden cup, but it was filled with "abominable things and the filth of her adulteries." In addition, she was drunk "with the blood of the saints, the blood of those who bore testimony to Jesus."

Babylon, as we have previously noted, has had a long and sordid history. But perhaps we need to go into greater detail at this point.

You've Come a Long Way, Babylon

Babylon, which was located about 50 miles south of modern Baghdad, has been around so long that no one knows for sure when it was founded. Guesstimates put the date at 3000 B.C.E. or earlier. Babylonia and Assyria competed for top position throughout the centuries, sometimes being mutually impressive nations, and other times with one power subduing the other. Much of the time, however, Babylon was the big dog in Mesopotamia.

Flashback

The Old Testament Israelites had run-ins with Babylon, as did most of the other nations of their time. Eventually the Israelites were defeated by the Assyrians and Babylonians, and many were taken into captivity for a while. One biblical account of their defeat and the fall of Jerusalem is found in 2 Kings 24–25, and several of the Old Testament prophets describe life during captivity. In addition are some of the mournful refrains from the psalms: "By the rivers of Babylon we sat and wept when we remembered Zion. There on the poplars we hung our harps, for there our captors asked us for songs, our tormentors demanded songs of joy" (Psalm 137:1–3).

Under Hammurabi (1704–1662 B.C.E.), the ruler known for his organized and detailed legal code, the Babylonian Empire was a presence extending from the Persian Gulf to the upper Tigris and middle Euphrates River regions. Later defeated and sacked, Babylon rose again to a glorious empire under Nebuchadnezzar (605–562 B.C.E.), at which time it was probably the world's greatest city in terms of both size and splendor. Nebuchadnezzar's hanging gardens, said to be his attempt to please a new wife who hailed from a mountainous country, were one of the seven wonders of the ancient world. According to Herodotus, a noted historian, the city during this time spread out across 200 square miles. At times, Babylon contained 50 or more temples that were devoted to various gods and goddesses.

Eventually the Persians conquered the Babylonians (539 B.C.E.). But it wasn't until the Greeks in turn defeated the Persians (330 B.C.E.) that the city of Babylon was destroyed. In its long life, Babylon had hosted numerous religions. It attempted to build towers to heaven for gods to descend. It built temples to honor the goddess of the underworld. It was world-renowned for its astrologers. Its leaders had worn fish-head-shaped crowns to honor their fish god. And Babylon had pursued idolatrous practices too numerous to detail here. Suffice it to say that the history books are correct in remembering Babylon as a great and glorious metropolis. But from a spiritual perspective, the city was a prostitute—associating with any and every religion that came along.

To us, Babylon is ancient history. But as John described this prostitute identified as "Babylon," she was "drunk with the blood of the saints, the blood of those who bore testimony to Jesus." So whether this suggests an uprising of the old Babylon, or is a symbolic reference to a new, Babylon-like power who will persecute believers in God, it appears that a new-if-not-improved Babylon will be a presence in the end times described in the Book of Revelation. Not surprisingly, John was "greatly astonished" to see such a figure. (Speculating futurist Revelation interpreters like to point out that Saddam Hussein began rebuilding Babylon on its original foundations in 1979, and now holds an annual Babylon Festival.)

Clanging Symbols

As John gazes on this "prostitute," it is no real surprise that she is keeping company with a beast covered with blasphemous names. Over the centuries, Babylon had come to symbolize "anti-God." The woman's promiscuity and the beast's blasphemy went hand in hand.

Here It Is—The Full Explanation!

Then the angel said to me: "Why are you astonished? I will explain to you the mystery of the woman and of the beast she rides, which has the seven heads and ten horns. The beast, which you saw, once was, now is not, and will come up out of the Abyss and go to his destruction. The inhabitants of the earth whose names have not been written in the book of life from the creation of the world will be astonished when they see the beast, because he once was, now is not, and yet will come.

"This calls for a mind with wisdom. The seven heads are seven hills on which the woman sits. They are also seven kings. Five have fallen, one is, the other has not yet come; but when he does come, he must remain for a little while. The beast who once was, and now is not, is an eighth king. He belongs to the seven and is going to his destruction.

"The ten horns you saw are ten kings who have not yet received a kingdom, but who for one hour will receive authority as kings along with the beast. They have one purpose and will give their power and authority to the beast. They will make war against the Lamb, but the Lamb will overcome them because he is Lord of lords and King of kings—and with him will be his called, chosen and faithful followers."

Then the angel said to me, "The waters you saw, where the prostitute sits, are peoples, multitudes, nations and languages. The beast and the ten horns you saw will hate the prostitute. They will bring her to ruin and leave her naked; they will eat her flesh and burn her with fire. For God has put it into their hearts to accomplish his purpose by agreeing to give the beast their power to rule, until God's words are fulfilled. The woman you saw is the great city that rules over the kings of the earth" (Revelation 17:7–18).

John's heavenly tour guide had pulled him aside and explained to him "the mystery of the woman and of the beast she rides," and John faithfully recorded what he heard. But it must have seemed something like a fourth-grader trying to absorb Stephen Hawking's thoughts on quantum physics. Again, we might have benefited more from names and dates, but instead we get a rather cryptic description of kings, past and future.

However, these clues can be helpful for those who have "a mind with wisdom." The passage isn't easy to understand, yet it does provide a few helpful notations.

We have previously seen that the beast (Antichrist) is in league with the dragon (Satan), based on Revelation 13:1–4. Here we see that the beast "will come up out of the Abyss and go to his destruction." It confirms what we have already learned about his dark associations, but adds new information about his future. It also confirms what John has already recorded—that the people will be astonished at how the beast operates.

But then the angel's description of things to come gets more specific, even though we may not be able to figure out the significance. Here are our clues:

Apoca-Lips Now

"A wise man sees as much as he ought, not as much as he can."

—Michel de Montaigne

➤ The beast's seven heads represent seven hills, and also seven kings.

➤ The beast will be a king, somehow connected to those who have come before.

➤ The beast's 10 horns symbolize 10 kings who have not yet come to power.

➤ The waters where the prostitute sits, as we have said, are "peoples, multitudes, nations and languages."

➤ The woman (prostitute) is "the great city that rules over the kings of the earth."

Clanging Symbols

In spite of the more precise explanations of these symbols, it is still not a simple matter to overlay the Book of Revelation onto human history and have everything make sense. For example, the reference to the seven hills was naturally thought by early readers of this message to indicate Rome—"the city on seven hills." More recent interpreters, however, have emphasized the second part of the explanation that says the seven heads are *also* seven kings—five past, one present, and one future. This slant on the interpretation seems to indicate a historical progression, not simply a geographic identity.

Bible scholars have not reached a consensus about who the seven kings might be. Are they a series of specific Roman emperors? An allusion to the Roman Empire as a whole? A different progression of powers? A case can be made for each theory.

Yet what comes through clearly in this passage, in contrast to the hazy comprehension of what all the horns and heads represent, is the politicking and jostling for position that seem to be taking place. More alliances seem to be made in this brief section of the Book of Revelation than you'd expect to see in an entire season of the TV show *Survivor*.

One minute the prostitute is riding around on the beast like a drunken cowgirl at a rodeo. The next, we learn that the beast and his allies "will bring her to ruin and leave her naked; they will eat her flesh and burn her with fire."

We see the beast allying with the kings who are represented by his seven heads. As a matter of fact, he will appear to be the eighth king in the series. And his 10 horns that also represent kings "who have not yet received a kingdom" are closely allied with the beast, supporting him with their full power and authority.

And beneath all this positioning and strategizing is an even more basic unifying cause—defiance of God. The beast has a connection with the Abyss, and the other cast of characters (whoever they are) have given their loyalty to the beast. The prostitute was "drunk with the blood of the saints," yet even those who bring her to ruin are united to "make war against the Lamb." In spite of any other disagreements and conflicts, it seems that most people are united in their opposition to God and his people during this time.

A Bright Spot

In spite of the anti-God movement on earth and the outright "war" planned against him, the forecast is made that "the Lamb" will ultimately be victorious because "he is Lord of lords and King of kings." In addition, his "faithful followers" are promised to share in his victory.

The Bigger They Are ...

Revelation 18 is a eulogy of sorts for "Babylon the Great." It begins a series of harsh demises that will continue into the next chapter of this book.

> After this I saw another angel coming down from heaven. He had great authority, and the earth was illuminated by his splendor. With a mighty voice he shouted: "Fallen! Fallen is Babylon the Great! She has become a home for demons and a haunt for every evil spirit, a haunt for every unclean and detestable bird. For all the nations have drunk the maddening wine of her adulteries. The kings of the earth committed adultery with her, and the merchants of the earth grew rich from her excessive luxuries."

> Then I heard another voice from heaven say: "Come out of her, my people, so that you will not share in her sins, so that you will not receive any of her plagues; for her sins are piled up to heaven, and God has remembered her crimes. Give back to her as she has given; pay her back double for what she has done. Mix her a double portion from her own cup. Give her as much torture and grief as the glory and luxury she gave herself. In her heart she boasts, 'I sit as queen; I am not a widow, and I will never mourn.' Therefore in one day her plagues will overtake her: death, mourning and famine. She will be consumed by fire, for mighty is the Lord God who judges her" (Revelation 18:1–8).

Again, we get a heavenly perspective that is quite different from the earthly one. Here we see the angelic commentary on the fall of Babylon, which will be followed by the contrasting response of those watching on earth.

It isn't simply Babylon who is being eulogized here, it is "Babylon the Great." The very lack of humility that would drive someone to add "the Great" to his or her name seems to underlie many of the other complaints lodged against Babylon. First among those complaints is the association of the great city with demons and unclean spirits. It is no wonder this is the city representing opposition to God in the last days—whether literal or symbolic.

Following quickly are other observations about Babylon—adulterous affairs, crimes, pride, excessive luxury, and "sins piled up to heaven." The fact that Babylon is portrayed in the role of a promiscuous woman who dallies with political powers, rather than being included *among* the political powers, has caused some to see this as symbolic of a religious system. The bright-colored clothing and ornate jewelry of the woman suggest to some the robes and icons of a ritualistic church. But when the imagery of the woman is left behind, the fall of Babylon is addressed very much like a literal city—again leaving room for various speculations and interpretations.

The commentary about the fall of Babylon was begun by "another angel" with "great authority," who illuminated the earth with his splendor and spoke with a mighty voice. But he had hardly begun when yet another voice from heaven interrupted and became more specific. God's people were called to get out of Babylon to avoid the coming plagues, torture, grief, death, mourning, famine, and fire.

The second voice describes what's happening to Babylon as a form of divine retribution, and you know what they say about payback. According to this continued commentary, God has not forgotten any of the devious things Babylon thinks it has gotten away with, and is now ready to "pay her back double." The city will be forced to drink "from her own cup"—and getting a taste of your own medicine can be quite distasteful when that cup is filled with "abominable things and the filth of her adulteries" (Revelation 17:4).

Flashback

While Christians are called to minister to others and extend God's love to people who don't know him, they are also cautioned to be careful about getting too involved with secular practices and lifestyles. From a spiritual point of view, they are to "come out from them and be separate" (2 Corinthians 6:11–18). Some groups of Christians (such as the Amish) take this command more literally than others.

A Bright Spot

For those who may have suffered at the hands of Babylon comes a reminder that "God has remembered her crimes," and "mighty is the Lord God who judges her" (Revelation 18:5, 8).

So while the "tribute" to Babylon initially sounds like a eulogy, it soon becomes more like a brief statement read by a judge prior to passing sentence. The great city had already done a magnificent job of building itself up. Now, in stark contrast, comes serious commentary in regard to the tearing down of the city.

Aye, Captain, Thar She Blows ... Up

And after a brief description of how God sees the fall of Babylon, we are shown the same scene from a human point of view. This is a continuation of the commentary provided by the voice in heaven:

> *"When the kings of the earth who committed adultery with her and shared her luxury see the smoke of her burning, they will weep and mourn over her. Terrified at her torment, they will stand far off and cry: 'Woe! Woe, O great city, O Babylon, city of power! In one hour your doom has come!'*

> *"The merchants of the earth will weep and mourn over her because no one buys their cargoes any more—cargoes of gold, silver, precious stones and pearls; fine linen, purple, silk and scarlet cloth; every sort of citron wood, and articles of every kind made of ivory, costly wood, bronze, iron and marble; cargoes of cinnamon and spice, of incense, myrrh and frankincense, of wine and olive oil, of fine flour and wheat; cattle and sheep; horses and carriages; and bodies and souls of men.*

> *"They will say, 'The fruit you longed for is gone from you. All your riches and splendor have vanished, never to be recovered.' The merchants who sold these things and gained their wealth from her will stand far off, terrified at her torment. They will weep and mourn and cry out: 'Woe! Woe, O great city, dressed in fine linen, purple and scarlet, and glittering with gold, precious stones and pearls! In one hour such great wealth has been brought to ruin!' Every sea captain, and all who travel by ship, the sailors, and all who earn their living from the sea, will stand far off. When they see the smoke of her burning, they will exclaim, 'Was there ever a city like this great city?' They will throw dust on their heads, and with weeping and mourning cry out: 'Woe! Woe, O great city, where all who had ships on the sea became rich through her wealth! In one hour she has been brought to ruin! Rejoice over her, O heaven! Rejoice, saints and apostles and prophets! God has judged her for the way she treated you'"* (Revelation 18:9–20).

The fall of Babylon triggers a wave of mourning and regret among the people who witness it. It's natural to pause for a moment in somber contemplation whenever news is delivered of a great catastrophe, even if we have nothing in common with the people who are suffering. News of floods, famines, earthquakes, and other tragedies sometimes stops us in our tracks as we almost allow ourselves to think, *that could have been me.*

But on closer inspection, we see that much of the mourning being done is not so much a result of sincere pity going out to Babylon, but rather a contemplation of selfish self-interests. The onlooking merchants weep and mourn, but it is because they have lost a major distribution center for their merchandise. The sea captains and sailors watch from afar and cry because they just lost a favorite port that made them all rich every time they were in the neighborhood. Babylon may have been a prostitute, but she was *their* prostitute.

Clanging Symbols

The description provided for the city of Babylon is remarkably similar to the previous description of the "great prostitute" John saw. The woman is described in Revelation 17:4; the city is described in Revelation 18:16. Both are said to be dressed in fine linen, purple and scarlet, and glittering with gold, precious stones, and pearls.

Yet in spite of these similarities, some commentators are reluctant to believe this is exactly the same account. As we have said, the woman is obviously a symbolic representation of Babylon while the city is more literal. In addition, the portrayal of Babylon the woman seems to dwell more on her religious indiscretions. The description of Babylon the city, on the other hand, focuses more on its economic/political reputation. And while many people hold vigils for the loss of Babylon in the second account, no such mourning is detected in the first one.

The two descriptions of Babylon—both as "great prostitute" and as great city—may or may not overlap. One may follow the other. Again, much leeway is provided for various interpretations.

But one thing is clear. Even though people are crying over the city, it was no paragon of virtue. If you read closely among the shopping lists of Babylon, you'll find a lot you might expect: gold, silver, gems, spices, food, animals, and so forth. But right alongside these other tantalizing treats on the inventory list is an attention-getting item on the bottom line: "the bodies and souls of men" (Revelation 18:13). In the whirlwind of selling and trading taking place, people are simply one more commodity to add to the list. Not only are they offering their bodies, they are selling their souls as well.

So after a reputation that goes back thousands of years, Babylon (or whatever it symbolizes) will hit the skids "in one hour" (Revelation 18:19). You might recall that the last time we saw Babylon in the Book of Revelation, it had been the epicenter of the *Guinness Book of Records* biggest earthquake ever (Revelation 16:17–21). The city had been ripped apart, physically, into thirds. Many people naturally assume that the Revelation 18 narrative of the demise of Babylon is a more detailed account of the aftereffects of what is described in Revelation 16.

> **Flashback**
>
> In a series of prophecies against numerous nations, Isaiah had written centuries before, "Look, here comes a man in a chariot with a team of horses. And he gives back the answer: 'Babylon has fallen, has fallen! All the images of its gods lie shattered on the ground!'" (Isaiah 21:9). Babylon had fallen in 689 B.C.E., and again in 539 C.E. But from all accounts, the Book of Revelation describes its *final* fall.

Is That Angel Doing an End Zone Dance?

The possible connection between Babylon being hit by an earthquake and its final destruction in this account seems strengthened by what happens next.

Then a mighty angel picked up a boulder the size of a large millstone and threw it into the sea, and said: "With such violence the great city of Babylon will be thrown down, never to be found again. The music of harpists and musicians, flute players and trumpeters, will never be heard in you again. No workman of any trade will ever be found in you again. The sound of a millstone will never be heard in you again. The light of a lamp will never shine in you again. The voice of bridegroom and bride will never be heard in you again. Your merchants were the world's great men. By your magic spell all the nations were led astray. In her was found the blood of prophets and of the saints, and of all who have been killed on the earth" (Revelation 18:21–24).

The description of the boulder being slammed into the sea certainly jibes with an earthquake striking. Like a running back who crosses the end zone and slams down the football in triumph, the angel's "spike" will bring the final end to Babylon. No more music, work, light, or weddings. No more nothing!

And the final observation returns to a somewhat spiritual aspect. It is essentially the official heavenly "cause of death" for the city of Babylon: "By your magic spell all the nations were led astray." And as a result of this spiritual slide, "In her was found the blood of prophets and of the saints, and of all who have been killed on the earth." This was no small offense in the eyes of God.

The very fact that so much time is allotted to this "eulogy" for Babylon suggests it is important. The Book of Revelation has been rushing toward the big finish. But here we have seen both the heavenly and earthly perspectives of the final fall of one of the earth's great cities (whether literally Babylon, or symbolic of Rome or somewhere else). It will be an emotional moment, for both the good guys and the bad guys. And it is certainly a sobering moment for those who witness what is going on.

But enough time spent in contemplation. If you think what happened to Babylon is bad, just wait till Chapter 13, "All Bad Things Must Come to an End." We're about to see some *real* suffering and destruction.

Apoca-Lips Now

"All that has achieved existence deserves to be destroyed."

—Johann Wolfgang von Goethe

The Least You Need to Know

➤ John sees a "great prostitute," identified as Babylon, destroyed by the beast.

➤ John also sees the city of Babylon destroyed.

➤ As people on earth mourn, those in heaven see this destruction as payback and justice for long years of abuse of God's people.

➤ In a more detailed description of the beast, numbers of kings and other clues are provided which some people use to attempt to connect the Book of Revelation with human history.

Part 3

High Noon at the End Times Corral

By this point in the Book of Revelation, you've probably come to think of yourself as the Grim Reader. The events being described do not make a pretty picture. And to be honest, things get worse before they improve. But they are going to improve.

We previously said that reading the first portion of Revelation is like watching storm clouds roll in. If so, then this section will be the height of the thunder, lightning, hail, and worse. But we've learned to look for silver linings in dark clouds, and Revelation goes us one better. Those who overcome this storm are rewarded with a heavenly city with streets of gold and gates of pearl.

So keep reading. By the time you finish this section, you may discover you have become the Gleeful Reader as you get to some of the most promising and rewarding sections of Scripture you'll ever hope to find.

Chapter 13

All Bad Things Must Come to an End

In This Chapter

➤ A look at Revelation 19–20

➤ The second coming of Jesus and a 1,000-year reign

➤ The ultimate end of the beast, the false prophet, and the devil

➤ A final judgment before a great white throne

In June 1947, the *Bulletin of the Atomic Scientists* was published with a clock on its cover. The time was seven minutes before midnight. The artistic portrayal had been designed to symbolize the urgency the editors were feeling in regard to the nuclear state of affairs in the world. Now known as the Doomsday Clock, and still being monitored by the atomic scientists, it has become a cultural reminder that we live in constant peril—to greater or lesser degrees. The minute hand is moved occasionally to adjust to changing times, but only 16 times since the clock was originated. In 1953 the clock "ticked down" to two minutes before midnight, but things were much better in 1991 when the Strategic Arms Reduction Treaty pushed the minute hand all the way back to 17 minutes before the hour. Still, we're never really very far away from experiencing "the worst that could happen."

Whether we realize it or not, the Book of Revelation countdown clock is fast approaching its own midnight. But in visualizing this clock, it might be helpful to think of the traditional image of an hourglass. In this chapter, we're about to see the final grains of sand tumble through the funnel—for some people, at least. But we're also going to see that the hourglass is flipped over, beginning a new span of time for certain others before the ultimate end of the earth.

Confused? We can't blame you, but just read on.

A Hallelujah Chorus

After this I heard what sounded like the roar of a great multitude in heaven shouting: "Hallelujah! Salvation and glory and power belong to our God, for true and just are his judgments. He has condemned the great prostitute who corrupted the earth by her adulteries. He has avenged on her the blood of his servants."

And again they shouted: "Hallelujah! The smoke from her goes up for ever and ever."

The twenty-four elders and the four living creatures fell down and worshiped God, who was seated on the throne. And they cried: "Amen, Hallelujah!"

Then a voice came from the throne, saying: "Praise our God, all you his servants, you who fear him, both small and great!"

Then I heard what sounded like a great multitude, like the roar of rushing waters and like loud peals of thunder, shouting: "Hallelujah! For our Lord God Almighty reigns. Let us rejoice and be glad and give him glory! For the wedding of the Lamb has come, and his bride has made herself ready. Fine linen, bright and clean, was given her to wear." (Fine linen stands for the righteous acts of the saints.)

Then the angel said to me, "Write: 'Blessed are those who are invited to the wedding supper of the Lamb!'" And he added, "These are the true words of God."

At this I fell at his feet to worship him. But he said to me, "Do not do it! I am a fellow servant with you and with your brothers who hold to the testimony of Jesus. Worship God! For the testimony of Jesus is the spirit of prophecy" (Revelation 19:1–10).

A Bright Spot

This portion of the Book of Revelation kicks off on a bright note—at least from the heavenly onlookers who see what's been going on. The elegy of "woes" on earth is drowned out by the high-decibel "Hallelujahs" coming from this heavenly chorus.

Sometimes you get the idea that poor John's head must have been snapping back and forth like a spectator at Wimbledon as his attention was directed back and forth between the events taking place on earth and everything going on in heaven. But he's still being observant and taking good notes. And he may not know it, but he's almost finished.

Some of the most recent earth-based sights and sounds he had recorded were the fall of Babylon and the many "Woes" that arose from the people looking on. But "after this," a loud noise from heaven captured his attention. He heard what he supposed to be "a great multitude" who had apparently witnessed the same events, but they were not mournful in the least.

Flashback

While we may tend to use "hallelujah" as a synonym for "yippee," the word would have meant more to those attuned to biblical history. From the Hebrew words, *Hallelu Yah*, the literal meaning is "Praise Jehovah." These days believers more commonly use the slight variation, "Praise the Lord." Several of the psalms are classified as hallelujah psalms. The last five, for example, both begin and end with this expression of praise (Psalms 146–150). But this occasion in the Book of Revelation is the only place the word is used in the New Testament (Revelation 19:1, 3, 4, 6).

The rejoicing wasn't merely because Babylon had fallen. While the event was certainly noteworthy in itself, its significance went far beyond the destruction of a city. If someone lights a torch for light or heat, it's not a big deal. But if it happens to be the Olympic torch that denotes the opening of the international games, you can expect a rousing cheer that lasts a long while. In a similar way, the fall of Babylon was a signal—an opening ceremony, of sorts. It was a turning point that signified something of utmost importance about to occur, and it was enough to generate an entire series of heavenly hallelujahs.

The heavenly observers seem to equate Babylon the woman/prostitute with Babylon the city. They note that, "God … has condemned the great prostitute," and, "the smoke from her goes up for ever and ever." The use of symbolic language can be tricky to follow as different symbols might be used for the same thing, and as the focus shifts from one symbol to the other.

Apoca-Lips Now

"The unleashed power of the atom has changed everything save our modes of thinking, and we thus drift toward unparalleled catastrophes."

—Albert Einstein

It seems that, again, everyone in heaven is falling down and shouting praise to God. But in the midst of this worship and devotion, an angel turned his focus on John instead, and said something to the effect of, "You'd better get this down." So John was sure to record, "Blessed are those who are invited to the wedding supper of the Lamb." John got the quote, and he noted the angel's editorial comment as well: "These are the true words of God."

Clanging Symbols

In the case of "the wedding of the Lamb" and his "bride," the "Lamb" is still Jesus and the "bride" represents the group of people who have put their faith in him. The required clothing is "righteous acts" rather than literal "fine linen."

Proper attire was expected at weddings during New Testament times. The honored couple would host a celebratory party that could carry on for a week or so, to which friends and family were invited. It was the epitome of bad taste to crash such a party, or to show up in the first-century equivalent of sweat pants rather than formal clothes.

And while the union of Jesus with all his followers had been repeatedly predicted in Scripture, John was witnessing the point at which "the wedding of the Lamb has come." The heavenly celebration wasn't so much a sadistic putdown of Babylon, but more of a rehearsal dinner in preparation for a big wedding.

Flashback

Jesus used similar images of weddings and/or banquets in several of his parables:

➤ Matthew 22:2–14: What happens when people ignore the king's invitation or don't wear proper wedding clothes

➤ Matthew 25:1–13: How lack of preparation can cause some people to miss God's big celebrations

➤ Luke 14:7–14: The importance of humility in regard to others

➤ Luke 14:16–24: How mundane activities prevent people from witnessing really special events

When John realized what he was seeing, he fell at the feet of the nearest heavenly figure, who happened to be an angel. The angel quickly corrected him and clarified that the two of them were "fellow servants" of the same master. Any worshipping to be done should be directed to God and Jesus. That point was about to become quite clear.

Look ... Up in the Sky ... It's a Horse!?

I saw heaven standing open and there before me was a white horse, whose rider is called Faithful and True. With justice he judges and makes war. His eyes are like blazing fire, and on his head are many crowns. He has a name written on him that no one knows but he himself. He is dressed in a robe dipped in blood, and his name is the Word of God. The armies of heaven were following him, riding on white horses and dressed in fine linen, white and clean. Out of his mouth comes a sharp sword with which to strike down the nations. "He will rule them with an iron scepter." He treads the winepress of the fury of the wrath of God Almighty. On his robe and on his thigh he has this name written: KING OF KINGS AND LORD OF LORDS (Revelation 19:11–17).

Up till this point, it appears that most of God's judgment on the earth was in the form of natural (or, to be more precise, *supernatural*) disasters. People assumed the earthquakes, water pollution, ugly sores, and such were a sign of divine displeasure, yet God remained unseen. John was privy to what was taking place in the heavens, but humankind as a whole remained in the dark (sometimes literally).

Clanging Symbols

The blood-dipped robe of the figure on the white horse might represent the warfare he is involved in. Or assuming this is a portrayal of Jesus, it might be representative of the blood he shed on behalf of humankind. The blood from animals offered at the Tabernacle or Temple symbolized sacrificial atonement, which may also be the case in this instance. And the white horse itself would have symbolized victory for those familiar with triumphal parades sponsored by the Roman Empire.

Now, however, a face is being assigned to this final deployment of God's justice—and what a face it is! A figure comes riding out of heaven on a charging white horse. His eyes are like blazing fire, and he wears a number of crowns. His robe appears to have been dipped in blood.

There is little doubt that this is an image of Jesus. The names used to describe him are big clues: "Faithful and True," "the Word of God," "King of kings and Lord of lords," and yet another one that only he knows. It is also clear that he represents God, and he leads the armies of heaven, also riding white horses and dressed in fine, white linen.

By this time the symbolism has shifted from that of "Lamb" to that of mighty warrior. A sharp sword comes out of his mouth "with which to strike down the nations." Yet it is clearly stated that he judges and makes war "with justice." He is bringing to bear the final phase of the "fury of the wrath of God," so be warned: The job he has to do contains graphic violence.

Carrion, My Wayward Sons

> *And I saw an angel standing in the sun, who cried in a loud voice to all the birds flying in midair, "Come, gather together for the great supper of God, so that you may eat the flesh of kings, generals, and mighty men, of horses and their riders, and the flesh of all people, free and slave, small and great."*
>
> *Then I saw the beast and the kings of the earth and their armies gathered together to make war against the rider on the horse and his army. But the beast was captured, and with him the false prophet who had performed the miraculous signs on his behalf. With these signs he had deluded those who had received the mark of the beast and worshiped his image. The two of them were thrown alive into the fiery lake of burning sulfur. The rest of them were killed with the sword that came out of the mouth of the rider on the horse, and all the birds gorged themselves on their flesh* (Revelation 19:17–21).

We've followed several threads through the Book of Revelation so far in this *Complete Idiot's Guide*. But here, it seems, a lot of those threads lead to the same place and time. The beast and false prophet have been hard at work, persecuting believers in God and creating chaos in general. A number of kings had marched across the dry bed of the Euphrates River. An army of 200 million soldiers had assembled. A horribly bloody battle was set to take place at a location called Armageddon. Resurrected martyred people were crying for justice in heaven. And the heavenly Lamb had been working his way through the seals, trumpets, and bowls revealed in the scroll he held.

This may not be the ultimate alignment of all these events, though some people suggest so. However, it seems that at least some of these threads are interwoven in this passage.

Certainly the scene will be one of unimaginable blood and death. The call goes out to the birds of the world to assemble and gorge themselves on kings, generals, slaves, horses—by the time this battle is over, monarchs and peasants are all going to look pretty much the same. To the human soldiers, this looks like a big war. To the birds, it's going to be "the great supper of God"—a big steaming pile of carrion.

The beast and false prophet are spotted on the scene as well, aligned with the kings of the earth to oppose the heavenly rider and his army. But just as we get ready for a lot of details—casualty counts, gory injuries, battle strategies, and such—the war is over, essentially as soon as it is begun. To many, this event is seen as the "second coming" of Jesus, an event promised in numerous prophecies.

Apoca-Lips Now

"Alas, regardless of their doom,
    the little victims play!
No sense have they of ills to
    come, nor care beyond today."

—Thomas Gray

Flashback

In Jesus' teachings about the end times, he first spoke of many natural disasters to take place, and then added, "At that time the sign of the Son of Man will appear in the sky, and all the nations of the earth will mourn. They will see the Son of Man coming on the clouds of the sky, with power and great glory. And he will send his angels with a loud trumpet call, and they will gather his elect from the four winds, from one end of the heavens to the other" (Matthew 24:29–31).

The beast and false prophet who are most responsible for war crimes are punished immediately and severely. They are "thrown alive into the lake of burning sulfur." Details for this process are not provided. We don't know if they are dragged, kicking and screaming, by mighty angels, of if they are dispatched to their final destination by a flick of a divine finger. Nor do we know the details of what happened to all of their supporters, other than their being killed "with the sword that came out of the mouth of the rider on the horse."

But we do receive confirmation that the birds don't go home hungry. Those who say God's judgment is for the birds may just be right.

Today's Forecast: 1,000 Years of Reign

And I saw an angel coming down out of heaven, having the key to the Abyss and holding in his hand a great chain. He seized the dragon, that ancient serpent, who is the devil, or Satan, and bound him for a thousand years. He threw him into the Abyss, and locked and sealed it over him, to keep him from deceiving the nations anymore until the thousand years were ended. After that, he must be set free for a short time.

I saw thrones on which were seated those who had been given authority to judge. And I saw the souls of those who had been beheaded because of their testimony for Jesus and because of the word of God. They had not worshiped the beast or his image and had not received his mark on their foreheads or their hands. They came to life and reigned with Christ a thousand years. (The rest of the dead did not come to life until the thousand years were ended.) This is the first resurrection. Blessed and holy are those who

A Bright Spot

The group resurrected at this point are pronounced "blessed and holy," and are promised jobs as priests of God and of Christ, reigning with him for the next thousand years.

have part in the first resurrection. The second death has no power over them, but they will be priests of God and of Christ and will reign with him for a thousand years (Revelation 20:1–6).

After the beast and the false prophet were disposed of, another angel descended with a chain to tie up another loose end—Satan. In fact, the devil would be tied up, tossed into the Abyss, and locked up tight for a thousand years.

And in contrast to all the deaths and gory things that had been taking place, another bunch of people came back to life. Resurrected at this point are the ones who had been killed because they refused the mark of the beast and would not waver in regard to their faith in Jesus. We also get another clue here to the brutality of their deaths—many had been beheaded.

A number of thrones are also set up, though many commentators express doubt that it is the martyrs who sit on the thrones. Regardless, they are people "who had been given authority to judge." With Satan bound and Jesus ruling, this kingdom would be far different from anything the world had seen lately.

This is another good place for a reminder that in spite of the construction of the story told in the Book of Revelation and any continuity and specifics provided, lots of people believe it to be only symbolic (and to different degrees). The 1,000-year period (millennium) described in this section is the source of much disagreement.

Flashback

Some suggest that the people ruling with Jesus during this period of time might be those of his original disciples who had remained faithful. He had once told them, "You are those who have stood by me in my trials. And I confer on you a kingdom, just as my Father conferred one on me, so that you may eat and drink at my table in my kingdom and sit on thrones, judging the twelve tribes of Israel" (Luke 22:28–30).

Some people believe this is a literal length of time, just as they believe most of what can be understood about Revelation is literal. This group of interpreters likes to point out that John was writing not only what he saw, but what he heard. He certainly couldn't have known that a thousand years would pass unless he learned that fact from a reliable source. And he makes six separate and specific references to that length of time.

Other people prefer to think that the thousand years is a symbolic period, and could be more or less than a literal millennium as we know it. Still others are convinced the entirety of Revelation is symbolic, and this mention of a span of time is not all that significant. We will get more involved with these interpretations in Chapters 16–19.

After All These Centuries, the Devil Gets Fired

When the thousand years are over, Satan will be released from his prison and will go out to deceive the nations in the four corners of the earth—Gog and Magog—to gather them for battle. In number they are like the sand on the seashore. They marched across the breadth of the earth and surrounded the camp of God's people, the city he loves. But fire came down from heaven and devoured them. And the devil, who deceived them, was thrown into the lake of burning sulfur, where the beast and the false prophet had been thrown. They will be tormented day and night for ever and ever (Revelation 20:7–10).

Perhaps one reason there's so much confusion about this 1,000-year period is because the Book of Revelation doesn't provide much detail about it. You might think that if Jesus were indeed ruling, more would be said about it.

Perhaps after seeing how he is portrayed in heaven, his leadership over a still-not-perfect world wouldn't provide the same degree of glory and interest. Maybe John wasn't shown much about this time period to record. Maybe John was eager to propel his readers to what is coming next. We just don't know.

However, the Old Testament makes a number of references to this peaceful kingdom. Perhaps you've seen artistic portrayals where a lion is lying beside a lamb, with no glimmer of danger or fear from either. Many Old Testament believers in God were looking forward to a time when he would get personally involved with the leadership of the world. This reign in the Book of Revelation seems to fulfill most of those prophecies.

Flashback

"The wolf will live with the lamb, the leopard will lie down with the goat, the calf and the lion and the yearling together; and a little child will lead them. The cow will feed with the bear, their young will lie down together, and the lion will eat straw like the ox. The infant will play near the hole of the cobra, and the young child put his hand into the viper's nest. They will neither harm nor destroy on all my holy mountain, for the earth will be full of the knowledge of the Lord as the waters cover the sea" (Isaiah 11:6–9).

Another head-scratcher from this section is why Satan will be bound for the thousand years, then released, and *then* disposed with. It would seem to be much more expedient to do away with him before he can cause further trouble. Why release him after you had him locked up?

Those who view this portion of Scripture literally often suggest that the people Jesus rules during the millennium are those who made it through all the awful events of the tribulation. If so, for a thousand years people will continue "regular" life—marriages, births, deaths, and such. With the Antichrist and false prophet gone, and Satan bound, life should be sweet. But as it was in the Garden of Eden, God will not manipulate people into obedience by removing all other options. If we consider that the forbidden fruit was in Eden not to tempt Adam and Eve, but to give them a

Apoca-Lips Now

"And the lion and the calf shall lie down together, but the calf won't get much sleep."

—Woody Allen

choice of whether or not to follow God, we see a similar situation here in Revelation. Generations raised under the leadership of Jesus would certainly have a religious slant in one direction. So, theoretically, perhaps Satan is unbound to allow them a choice of whether or not to go along with what they had been told.

This is more speculation than we like to consider, yet it is a frequent explanation for this section. What we *are* told is that as soon as Satan is unbound, it's right back to business for him. He has no trouble finding a following. He deceives and collects recruits "in the four corners of the earth" to oppose God's people. But in the great heavenly hourglass, he can kiss his last grain of sand goodbye. His time has run out. No war is fought. No struggle is experienced. Instead, fire falls from heaven on all those who support him.

Flashback

The mention of "Gog and Magog" in this section is something of a puzzler. If we flash back to Ezekiel 38, a battle is described where Gog (the leader) and Magog (a group of people and/or the "land of Gog") plan to attack a peaceful and unsuspecting city. In response, God sends a great earthquake and "will pour down torrents of rain, hailstones, and burning sulfur on him and on his troops and on the many nations with him" (vv. 18–22). This is the only place besides Revelation where Gog is mentioned, and his identity in history is unclear. And while the setting described in Ezekiel is similar to that in Revelation, it is not usually assumed that the two passages refer to the same event.

The devil is then personally thrown into the "lake of burning sulfur, where the beast and the false prophet had been thrown." Those two characters are apparently still there after a thousand years, and the additional commentary tells us, "They will be tormented day and night for ever and ever."

It seems clear from this passage that our legends of Satan as the sneering overlord of the underworld are not in the least biblical. He's not shown as a ruler of hell—just another tormented inmate. In fact, Jesus had once mentioned, while telling a parable, that the eternal fire was "prepared for the devil and his angels" (Matthew 25:41). The biblical perspective is that from Lucifer's original defiance of God onward, his retirement plan was fixed. It would be only a matter of time until he was sentenced to his final resting place in the fiery lake. Over that time, however, it seems that he has recruited a lot of company.

Flashback

In a couple of instances in the Old Testament, we hear about people going to heaven without dying physically. One example is a guy named Enoch who "walked with God; then he was no more, because God took him away" (Genesis 5:24). More clear is the case of Elijah, who was carried alive into heaven on a fiery chariot in the presence of a witness (2 Kings 2:11–12). In Revelation, however, we see three figures who apparently bypass the usual death/resurrection/judgment process and go to hell, go directly to hell, do not pass go, do not collect $200. The beast and false prophet are thrown alive into the fiery lake of burning sulfur (Revelation 19:20), and Satan follows a thousand years or so afterward (Revelation 20:10).

No Place to Run, No Place to Hide

> *Then I saw a great white throne and him who was seated on it. Earth and sky fled from his presence, and there was no place for them. And I saw the dead, great and small, standing before the throne, and books were opened. Another book was opened, which is the book of life. The dead were judged according to what they had done as recorded in the books. The sea gave up the dead that were in it, and death and Hades gave up the dead that were in them, and each person was judged according to what he had done. Then death and Hades were thrown into the lake of fire. The lake of fire is the second death. If anyone's name was not found written in the book of life, he was thrown into the lake of fire (Revelation 20:11–15).*

Perhaps you've been noticing clues about the afterlife as we've been going through the Book of Revelation. For example, we've seen souls of people in heaven—martyrs at the hands of the Antichrist—who are actively praising God and are conscious at some level (7:9–17; 15:2–4). Yet it appears to be somewhat later when we are told, "They came to life and reigned with Christ a thousand years" (20:4). And other people who were dead "did not come to life until the thousand years were ended" (20:5).

Without getting into all the explanations and theories about what happens when we die, let's simply note at this point that …

1. There appear to be different stages of existence after death, a spiritual state at first, followed by a bodily resurrection.

2. It appears that not all the resurrections of the dead take place at the same time.

These observations will further complicate the process of interpreting Revelation and coming up with a timetable that makes sense to everyone.

Yet in this passage we see another group of people resurrected to stand before God and be judged. Many commentators suggest that all of the people who profess faith in Jesus will have already been resurrected at this point, so to them the image of the "great white throne judgment" is somber and final, with only punishment and no rewards.

No one escapes this judgment—those from the sea, and death, and Hades are called before the great white throne. Hades (or Sheol, the Old Testament equivalent) is thought to be some sort of "holding cell" for souls awaiting resurrection, much as we saw the martyrs in heaven waiting for theirs. It seems to be a place of conscious punishment, but not the eternal destination of those souls.

In any event, the "dead" before the throne are judged according to "what they had done as recorded in the books." The book of life is consulted, as are others of which we know little about. All the jokes told about our "permanent records" might not be so funny for those people standing before this large white throne, hearing the divine judge read from books containing the deeds of their past. Those whose names aren't found in the book of life (which some people assume is the entire lot at the great white throne judgment) find themselves in the company of the devil, the Antichrist, and false prophet in the lake of fire.

Apoca-Lips Now

"Nobody can have the consolations of religion or philosophy unless he has first experienced their desolations."

—Aldous Huxley

This is known as "the second death." Just as believers are sometimes called "born again" because they expect a new, spiritual life after death, the parallel teaching in the Book of Revelation is that other people will find themselves "dead again." In both cases, the second version is much more intense and eternal than the first.

So in this portion of the Book of Revelation, a lot of old accounts are settled. As we have

Apoca-Lips Now

"Justice is the virtue that assigns to every man his due."

—St. Augustine

previously noted, the Bible may not explain to our satisfaction why bad things are allowed to happen. But it certainly makes it clear that intentional evil will not go unpunished forever. And for those who take Revelation literally, evildoers will be punished forever.

And thankfully, now that we've seen the worst of what can happen, we get to turn our attention to the best that can happen. With two chapters left in the Book of Revelation, there's still plenty of time for a happy ending.

The Least You Need to Know

➤ At long last, Jesus and the armies of heaven ride out of the sky to put an end to the Antichrist and his followers.

➤ Satan is bound for 1,000 years while Jesus rules, apparently on earth.

➤ Various groups of people are resurrected to receive either rewards or punishment.

➤ The devil, the Antichrist, the false prophet, and their supporters wind up in a fiery lake of burning sulfur, where they are said to be tormented forever.

Chapter 14

Imagine There's a Heaven

In This Chapter

➤ A look at Revelation 21–22:6

➤ A new heaven, a new earth, a new Jerusalem

➤ John is given a tour of a heavenly city

➤ People relate to God in a whole new way

The past few chapters of Revelation have been generally unpleasant and quite grim in places. But don't despair. In this chapter, things are going to start looking up— way up.

The topic is heaven. Since the beginning of time, people have stared into the heavens with a sense of wonder, and we still don't know a whole lot about what's up there. The celestial heavens are too marvelous to comprehend. And the biblical concept of heaven … well, that's another source of awe. According to the Book of Revelation, heaven is more than simply a backdrop for God's throne. It's more than a vast expanse of the universe. It's a very real piece of real estate—a paradise with no rent and plenty of availability for anyone interested in spending an eternity there.

Above Us Only Sky?

Of course, we've been asked to "imagine there's no heaven." This is the opening line of what is perhaps John Lennon's best-known song as a solo artist. Set to a simple and beautiful melody, Lennon's lyrics were a bold challenge for people to stop using religion, national pride, personal wealth, or anything else to generate unnecessary dissension.

"Imagine" became an instant classic, though it wasn't particularly well-received by the Christian community as a whole. Some, of course, had a knee-jerk reaction to the opening line and probably never got around to understanding what Lennon was trying to say. Others, however, had deeper concerns.

Many Christians fully supported Lennon's dream of more closeness among the citizens of the world, yet the reality of their personal experience wouldn't allow them to dream quite so big. Some people discover that no matter how hard *they* work toward unity, they're always at the mercy of others who aren't going to respond as they hope. Christians are notorious for being nice to others, extending third and fourth chances, supporting needy people financially—and being taken by every scam artist that comes down the pike.

And for many of them, that's okay. They do what they feel is the right thing to do, and their conscience is clear. However, after being taken for chumps three or four times, they begin to doubt that they'll ever see a "brotherhood of man" where "the world will be as one." Sorry, John.

As we have seen, those who take the Bible literally must come to grips with (or make some explanation for) what is described as a literal hell. It's a difficult and unpleasant concept to acknowledge. And the only way it makes sense for most people is to also put faith in what the Bible describes as a literal heaven. If we imagine there's no heaven or hell, life boils down to good people vs. bad people—and the odds are always with the bad guys.

But the hope of heaven changes those odds. So what if the bad guys win? So what if some unscrupulous con man bilks granddad out of his life savings? So what if someone dies for what she believes? If we imagine there's a heaven, we can believe that it's never too late for God to make things right. *That's* why lots of Christians were so disconcerted upon hearing "Imagine" for the first time. Too many people have seen with certainty that they will never find justice and peace during their lifetimes, and they're banking on eternity.

Apoca-Lips Now

"The trouble with kingdoms of heaven on earth is that they're liable to come to pass, and then their fraudulence is apparent for all to see. We need a Kingdom of Heaven in Heaven, if only because it can't be 'realized.'"

—Malcolm Muggeridge

Flashback

The Apostle Paul made it clear Christians shouldn't expect much justice and equality during their lifetimes. He wrote: "If only for this life we have hope in Christ, we are to be pitied more than all men" (1 Corinthians 15:19).

No "New"s Is Bad News

In Chapter 13, "All Bad Things Must Come to an End," we saw a portion of Revelation that was stark, dark, and downright horrid in places. Symbolic or not, the thought of people being flung alive into a lake of burning sulfur to suffer forever is unsettling. Even if they are getting the justice they rightly deserve, such judgment is still beyond the understanding of many people.

But my, what a difference we're about to see! As extreme as the occasional horror and violence have been up to this point, the pendulum swing is going to be just as extreme in the other direction. According to the Book of Revelation, God's wrath against sin is intense, but no more so than his eagerness to reward faithfulness.

> Then I saw a new heaven and a new earth, for the first heaven and the first earth had passed away, and there was no longer any sea. I saw the Holy City, the new Jerusalem, coming down out of heaven from God, prepared as a bride beautifully dressed for her husband. And I heard a loud voice from the throne saying, "Now the dwelling of God is with men, and he will live with them. They will be his people, and God himself will be with them and be their God. He will wipe every tear from their eyes. There will be no more death or mourning or crying or pain, for the old order of things has passed away."
>
> He who was seated on the throne said, "I am making everything new!" Then he said, "Write this down, for these words are trustworthy and true."
>
> He said to me: "It is done. I am the Alpha and the Omega, the Beginning and the End. To him who is thirsty I will give to drink without cost from the spring of the water of life. He who overcomes will inherit all this, and I will be his God and he will be my son. But the cowardly, the unbelieving, the vile, the murderers, the sexually immoral, those who practice magic arts, the idolaters and all liars—their place will be in the fiery lake of burning sulfur. This is the second death" (Revelation 21:1–8).

A Bright Spot

For once, essentially *everything* in this portion of Revelation is a bright spot, but dwell for a moment on the newness described here. Think of the emotions that traditionally accompany a "new" item of some importance—a new car, a new house, a new baby, a new job, or whatever. These are rare occurrences for most of us, and usually evoke a sense of hope, wonder, and a fresh break from the past.

While we usually expect to pay a large price or make a firm commitment to leave something behind in order to acquire something new, it seems that *everything* is new in this section—from heaven and earth itself, to humankind's relationship with

God. In Chapter 13 we were told that, "Earth and sky fled from [God's] presence, and there was no place for them" (Revelation 20:11). Here we see that the first heaven and the first earth have "passed away" and have been replaced with new versions. Oddly (to us, at least), the new model has no sea.

Clanging Symbols

Jerusalem had always been a special city throughout the Bible, both literally and symbolically. Yet not so long ago we saw that the "old" Jerusalem had deteriorated to the point of being compared to Sodom (Revelation 11:8)—not exactly a compliment. So Jerusalem had not only regained its status as a city of God, but the city had also been made new, symbolized as "a bride beautifully dressed for her husband."

Apoca-Lips Now

"This world is only the vestibule to another; you must prepare yourself in the vestibule so that you may enter the banquet hall."

—Talmud

In addition is a new Jerusalem "coming down out of heaven." Jerusalem had long been considered the "Holy City," but never before was the title so accurate. The significance of this event is quickly made clear. God is now able and ready to live among his people. *That's* certainly new.

Just as a caterpillar spins a cocoon and emerges as a butterfly, in this portion of the Book of Revelation old familiar things morph into new, perfected versions of themselves. They are still somewhat familiar, yet so improved as to be essentially unrecognizable.

And perhaps it will be the new relationship with God that seems strangest of all. In essentially every biblical account about an encounter with God (or heavenly beings), the human involved falls flat in utter fear. Even though such people usually had great faith and devotion to God, they were still sinful human beings, and sin separates people from God.

Not so in this "new" setup, however. God isn't popping out from behind clouds and shouting "Boo!" just to get a reaction. Instead, he is portrayed as walking among his people, wiping every tear from their eyes, having eliminated all sources of death, mourning, crying, and pain. He is providing for every need "without cost." He is not only the "Alpha," preexisting the beginning of human existence as we know it, but also the "Omega," showing up to see us beyond what we usually consider the end. According to the Book of Revelation, the "end of the world" as we define it is actually just the starting point for something completely new and better.

But a point of clarity is made at this point in the Revelation narrative. Not everyone makes the cut. Those who are "thirsty" and who "overcome" will receive the best of what God can conceive to provide. Those who continually rebel, however, receive not new life, but new death in the lake of fire. A few specific sins are listed here: cowardice, unbelief, vile behavior, murder, sexual immorality, occult practices, idolatry, and lies. But having covered such things in the category of "old" news, the topic quickly returns to what's new.

Urban Renewal

Some portions of the Book of Revelation have been a bit frustrating due to their lack of clarity. Not so the description of the heavenly city. Take your time reading this passage, and note the numbers, measurements, colors, and additional details that John provides.

> One of the seven angels who had the seven bowls full of the seven last plagues came and said to me, "Come, I will show you the bride, the wife of the Lamb." And he carried me away in the Spirit to a mountain great and high, and showed me the Holy City, Jerusalem, coming down out of heaven from God. It shone with the glory of God, and its brilliance was like that of a very precious jewel, like a jasper, clear as crystal. It had a great, high wall with twelve gates, and with twelve angels at the gates. On the gates were written the names of the twelve tribes of Israel. There were three gates on the east, three on the north, three on the south and three on the west. The wall of the city had twelve foundations, and on them were the names of the twelve apostles of the Lamb.
>
> The angel who talked with me had a measuring rod of gold to measure the city, its gates and its walls. The city was laid out like a square, as long as it was wide. He measured the city with the rod and found it to be 12,000 stadia in length, and as wide and high as it is long. He measured its wall and it was 144 cubits thick, by man's measurement, which the angel was using. The wall was made of jasper, and the city of pure gold, as pure as glass. The foundations of the city walls were decorated with every kind of precious stone. The first foundation was jasper, the second sapphire, the third chalcedony, the fourth emerald, the fifth sardonyx, the sixth carnelian, the seventh chrysolite, the eighth beryl, the ninth topaz, the tenth chrysoprase, the eleventh jacinth, and the twelfth amethyst. The twelve gates were twelve pearls, each gate made of a single pearl. The great street of the city was of pure gold, like transparent glass.
>
> I did not see a temple in the city, because the Lord God Almighty and the Lamb are its temple. The city does not need the sun or the moon to shine on it, for the glory of God gives it light, and the Lamb is its lamp. The nations will walk by its light, and the kings of the earth will bring their splendor into it. On no day will its gates ever be shut, for there will be no night there. The glory and honor of the nations will be brought into it. Nothing impure will ever enter it, nor will anyone who does what is shameful or deceitful, but only those whose names are written in the Lamb's book of life (Revelation 21:9–27).

This is one of those passages where John must have felt limited by vocabulary and ability to adequately pass along what he was seeing. But at least he tried. (These days, many commentators would simply note, "It was awesome, man" whether referring to a ride on the space shuttle or the most recent Adam Sandler movie.)

The city descended from heaven like a bride coming down the aisle. And just as all eyes are on the bride at such a time, the glittering city seemed to have captured John's full attention. The city was crystal clear and illuminated by the glory of God, creating a degree of brilliance "like that of a very precious jewel, like a jasper."

Clanging Symbols

Here we see the city of New Jerusalem, the new residence of God's people, once again symbolized as a bride. We have no better way to suggest intimacy than a new bride and groom beginning life as a couple. And from this point forward, God's people will be able to relate to him in a much more intimate way than ever before.

It was not only square, but also just as high as it was long and wide—giving rise to debate as to whether the description is of a cube or a pyramid. (The Most Holy Place in a tabernacle or temple was a cube.)

And this is no small-town watering hole we're talking about. John witnessed the measuring of the city by an angel, and recorded each side of it as "12,000 stadia." So even using a conservative measurement in translating, he is describing a city that is approximately 1,400 *miles* long … and wide … and high. (Some estimates put it at closer to 1,500 miles.)

The city was walled, with three gates in each of the four walls and an angel at each gate. Also represented at each gate was the name of one of the 12 tribes of Israel. The city was built upon 12 foundations, and on each foundation was the name of one of Jesus' apostles. So faithful reminders from both Old Testament and New Testament history are evident in places of honor throughout this holy city.

On closer inspection, it was the high wall around the city that was made of clear jasper—over 200 feet *thick*. The city itself and even the streets appeared to be pure gold that John compared to "transparent glass." The city also had pearly gates, which have become legendary, but somehow each gate is made of a single pearl. (Perhaps the oysters in heaven have been super-sized.)

A Bright Spot

The light of God's presence shining through transparent gold and gems makes this city of New Jerusalem not only a symbolic bright spot, but according to John, a literal one as well.

The foundations beneath the walls are not only functional, but remarkable as well. Each layer consists of a different precious stone, which provides a variety of colors—blue, green, red, white, yellow, purple, and probably more. We aren't exactly sure what the first-century equivalent of some of these precious stones were, yet it is clear a great variety existed. (If you care to speculate a bit more than necessary, some people visualize this New Jerusalem as hovering above the new earth, and believe the "foundations" to be stabilizing columns in between to support it.)

Sharp readers may point out the absence of diamonds in the city, but it isn't a significant omission because diamonds weren't known as gems in the first century. In fact, they didn't start popping up in European jewelry until about 1,200 years later.

John pointed out other key omissions. This city had no sun, no moon, and no temple. God fulfills all these roles. He is all the illumination that is needed. And since the temple had been used as a place where people would congregate to get closer to God, it apparently had no further use.

Because God's presence is so central to this heavenly city, others things are absent as well—night, impurity, shame, deceit, and other once-common sources of so much pain and fear on earth.

In addition, it's a city that never closes. The gates never shut because no enemy is present. And wait … there's more!

Talk About a Happy Meal!

Then the angel showed me the river of the water of life, as clear as crystal, flowing from the throne of God and of the Lamb down the middle of the great street of the city.

On each side of the river stood the tree of life, bearing twelve crops of fruit, yielding its fruit every month. And the leaves of the tree are for the healing of the nations. No longer will there be any curse. The throne of God and of the Lamb will be in the city, and his servants will serve him. They will see his face, and his name will be on their foreheads. There will be no more night. They will not need the light of a lamp or the light of the sun, for the Lord God will give them light. And they will reign for ever and ever.

The angel said to me, "These words are trustworthy and true. The Lord, the God of the spirits of the prophets, sent his angel to show his servants the things that must soon take place" (Revelation 22:1–6).

Once inside the walls of this glistening heavenly city, John began to describe "Main Street." In the middle of the central thoroughfare is "the throne of God and of the Lamb." From the throne flowed

Flashback

When Jesus had his conversation with the woman at the well, he offered her "living water" (John 4:10). Later he told a crowd of people, "Whoever believes in me, as the Scripture has said, streams of living water will flow from within him" (John 7:37–39). The explanation given in this latter example defines the "living water" as "the Spirit whom those who believed in him were later to receive."

"water of life," clear as crystal and forming a river right down the street. Again, we come to a passage where both literal and symbolic interpretations can be applied in various degrees.

One reason the symbolism issue comes up at this point is that we are told the tree of life (singular) stands "on each side of the river." This is a perplexing image for those attempting a literal interpretation, if we are to be bound by the current laws of physics. Some suggest the river is more like a creek that flows around the tree on both sides, so that the branches extend to both sides of the river. Some propose that the "tree of life" is more like a *grove* of trees, as a farmer might point out various timber on his land, gesturing to various groups of trees, saying, "There we have cedar, over there maple, and hickory down in the hollow"—singular forms for each thicket.

What we do know is that the tree of life—whether singular or plural, literal or symbolic—is important. You may remember we noted in Chapter 4, "Seven Churches Get a Performance Review," that it once grew in the Garden of Eden (Genesis 2:9) and that those who ate from it would live forever (Genesis 3:22). More recently, Jesus had promised the overcomers in the church at Ephesus "the right to eat from the tree of life, which is in the paradise of God" (Revelation 2:7). The promise seems more concrete in the context of this passage in Revelation 22 where John sees the tree actually growing in such a glorious place.

John also tells us that the tree of life is a fruit-bearing tree—and one unlike any other. It bears 12 crops of fruit, one fresh every month. In addition, its leaves are "for the healing of the nations." Of course, there should be no need for healing in a place with no death, mourning, crying, or pain. So, instead of *healing*, another equally valid translation of the original word (*therapian*) is *health*. Assuming the tree of life is not used for medicinal purposes as such, it is suggested that the fruit and leaves will still be good for those who consume them.

John appears to be so enamored by everything he's seeing that he wants to be sure his readers don't miss anything. He repeats the astounding news about no night and no need for other light sources. He again describes God's throne where his people can finally see his face—and John notes that the people have God's name on their foreheads.

And in a new bit of information, John adds, "No longer will there be any curse." Perhaps most of what we know about curses comes from fairy tales. When a curse is lifted, we expect frogs to revert to handsome princes or Snow White to wake up from a long, long nap. The biblical version of having a curse lifted is much less Disney-esque, but no less wonderful. From essentially the beginning of time as we know it (from the point when Adam and Eve sinned), the earth has

Apoca-Lips Now

"We see but dimly through the mists and vapors;
Amid these earthy damps
What seem to us but sad, funereal tapers
May be heaven's distant lamps."

—Henry Wadsworth Longfellow

been under a curse. As good as things get sometimes, they're never close to the point God intended them to be. But with the fresh start in the holy city, no longer will people have to deal with the curse that has plagued the entire history of humankind.

Flashback

The curse after Adam and Eve intentionally disobeyed God in the Garden of Eden was actually *curses*. The serpent was cursed and condemned to crawl on its belly, eating dust. The woman lost a bit of status in relationship with her husband, and had "greatly increased" pain in regard to childbirth. To get Adam's attention, the very ground was cursed, causing Adam to sweat for his food and endure thorns and thistles while trying to make a living. And of course, all of them lost their immunity to pain and death, and were sentenced to return to the dust from which they had been created (Genesis 3:14–19).

Pie in the Sky When We Die?

Some people don't put much stock in the Book of Revelation as a whole, yet are interested in it as a flight of fancy. Others give it credence as a feasible look into the bleak void of a future for a world that seems determined to plunge itself into annihilation. But as of this chapter, some people begin to write it off as "too good to be true." Anything with such a happy ending must surely be a fairy tale. Not only is the curse lifted, but we all live happily ever after? C'mon! Get real!

Perhaps that's why John gets so repetitive in this final section. Maybe even *he* was having a hard time believing what he was seeing. And perhaps that's why the heavenly beings keep emphasizing that these things are true (19:9; 21:5; 22:6). In fact, John's personal tour guide in this final section of his vision was one of the seven angels who had poured out the wrath of God (21:9), so he should know what he was talking about.

At this point, let's remind ourselves that the Book of Revelation is being addressed to seven churches, and will be spread from those churches to others. So regardless of how *we* might feel about the bad and/or the good of this strange book, we need to try to see things from the point of view of a first-century church.

Apoca-Lips Now

"What is heaven going to be like? Just as there is a mystery to hell, so there is a mystery to heaven. Yet, I believe the Bible teaches that heaven is a literal place. Is it one of the stars? I don't know. I can't even speculate. The Bible doesn't inform us. I believe that out there in space where there are one thousand million galaxies, each a hundred thousand light years or more in diameter, God can find some place to put us in heaven. I'm not worried about where it is. I know it is going to be where Jesus is. Christians don't have to go around discouraged and despondent with their shoulders bent. Think of it—the joy, the peace, the sense of forgiveness that he gives you, and then heaven, too."

—Billy Graham

From their perspective, commitment to God and a high standard of Christian principles wasn't easy. They were suffering, and during such times God may seem remote and uncaring. Still, believers faithfully attempt to realize he is there for them. Those who were willing to seek his help and strength were getting by in spite of their personal struggles. John's angel-guide even referred to "the spirits of the prophets," a reminder that the prophets were almost always minority voices amid a crowd of unbelievers, confirming that God was still well aware of everything that was going on.

A number of Old Testament believers had been told to expect a Messiah/deliverer, but had died before he ever appeared. Many throughout centuries of history had been promised a new and better kingdom, but had faced death under Babylonian, Persian, Greek, or Roman dominance. More recently, some had been personally promised a home with Jesus in heaven, but he had left before honoring his promises. After Jesus ascended, leaving behind his band of followers, many of them had been accused of foolishness, stupidity, naivety, delusion, and worse. And the verbal abuse was nothing compared to the physical persecution.

A Bright Spot

Some people suggest that this portion of the Book of Revelation is as bright as the reader wishes to make it. For believers, it is a refreshingly blinding light of confidence and hope; for others, hardly a blip. In this case, the rheostat is in *your* hand.

Now, at long last, those faithful individuals were being shown the big payoff. From the church members' perspective, they had endured and their names were inked into the "Lamb's book of life." They might have spent a lifetime of hard and intentional work for an unseen boss, but they were finding out that their retirement plan was not only eternal, but absolutely glorious as well. John observed that "they will reign for ever and ever."

And still, almost 2,000 years later, numerous believers turn to this passage during times of stress, confusion, and pain. They resist the pessimistic voices of their peers and squeeze out their last reserves of faith in a desperate attempt to believe that this is true.

A place free from aches, pains, worries, and cares? A place where you can look God in the eye and not fear his wrath or derision? A sparkling world of golden streets, pearly gates, and crystal-clear water? A land where love is the rule and all negative emotions purged for good? And all this for eternity?

Imagine that!

The Least You Need to Know

➤ John was shown a remarkable heavenly city called the New Jerusalem.

➤ Not everyone is allowed into this city. Those who are admitted, however, enjoy the absence of death, pain, and suffering; and they live in the presence of God himself.

➤ Among other special treats, the heavenly city contains the tree of life and the river of life.

➤ Again and again, John is assured that the things he is seeing are real and true.

Chapter 15

A Real Page-Turner Comes to a Close

In This Chapter

➤ A look at Revelation 22:7–21

➤ John, Jesus, and an angel make some closing comments

➤ An invitation and a warning

➤ A final emphasis on the return of Jesus

A primary challenge for authors—particularly fiction writers—is to come up with a satisfying ending for their works. Most people who do a lot of reading have favorite authors, yet many express disappointment that those storytellers don't do a consistently better job of tying up all the loose ends. Many writers are quite good at weaving plots and subplots, setting pace, sustaining suspense, and everything else—except wrapping things up. The endings are either too predictable, too contrived, or simply not up to par with the rest of the story.

If you're still reading at this point (and haven't skipped too much), you've worked almost all the way through the entire Book of Revelation. In fact, there are only 15 verses remaining. No doubt you still have questions and concerns, but we hope you've learned a few things so far. And the logical questions for this chapter are: What's next? How do you end a work like the Book of Revelation? What did the author want to emphasize for his readers?

Revelation: The Epilogue

Whether you view Revelation as a work of fiction or inspired Scripture (or believe, as some do, that perhaps it is *both*), the account has included a number of stunning scenes. We have seen angels and demons, heaven and hell, God and Satan. We have seen triumph and tragedy, terror and thrills. And as we saw in the last chapter, we've already had quite a happy ending. So what else is there to say? Let's find out.

> *"Behold, I am coming soon! Blessed is he who keeps the words of the prophecy in this book."*
>
> *I, John, am the one who heard and saw these things. And when I had heard and seen them, I fell down to worship at the feet of the angel who had been showing them to me. But he said to me, "Do not do it! I am a fellow servant with you and with your brothers the prophets and of all who keep the words of this book. Worship God!"*
>
> *Then he told me, "Do not seal up the words of the prophecy of this book, because the time is near. Let him who does wrong continue to do wrong; let him who is vile continue to be vile; let him who does right continue to do right; and let him who is holy continue to be holy"* (Revelation 22:7–11).

This might be a good place to remind ourselves yet again that the Book of Revelation was originally addressed to *churches*. It was never intended to be a worldwide best-seller. The closing comments assume that many who were doing wrong prior to the writing of Revelation would continue to do so after its publication. Those who were "vile" would not necessarily drop to their knees in terrified repentance. But for the struggling church members who were wondering whether their flagging faith would get them through the next crisis, this message—as strange as it is—would have been just like God speaking directly to them. In their struggle to remain holy, they would have been inspired to stick it out just a bit longer.

A Bright Spot

We're nearing the end, and still the text speaks of blessing. The promise is made both that Jesus is coming soon, and that the time is near.

It helps to have a words-of-Christ-in-red Bible at this point, because in the previous passage Jesus is quoted in places and an angel is quoted in other places—and sometimes the attributions aren't exactly clear. The opening statement from Jesus (v. 7) was both a promise and a challenge. He had previously told his disciples he would return. Now he was making the same promise to the churches. And on his timetable, at least, it would be "soon." In the meantime, his challenge was to "keep the words of the prophecy in this book."

The importance of this promise/challenge was further emphasized by what the angel told John: "Do not seal up the words of the prophecy of this book, because the time is near." So while we may not completely comprehend the apocalyptic, symbolic, cryptic, creepy fullness of the Book of Revelation, it's ours to struggle with. What was kept sealed in Old Testament times is now required reading, leading some people to believe that the deadline for the earth was/is indeed approaching.

As John realized his vision appeared to be coming to an end, he again fell at the feet of the angel who was escorting him—and was again curtly reminded to worship only God (Revelation 19:10; 21:8–9). John also reminds his readers that he personally "heard and saw these things." Perhaps he felt like the stadium commentator in the movie *A League of Their Own* who noted at the close of a spectacular game: "I've seen enough to know I've seen too much!"

In this short passage, both Jesus and the angel place great emphasis on "the words of the prophecy of this book." From its origin onward, John's account of Revelation seemed destined to be a source of authority as well as a regular attention-getter.

Flashback

In a similar setting centuries earlier, Daniel had observed many great secrets similar to what John records in Revelation. But in his case, the time apparently was not yet right for sharing his discoveries with the rest of the world. Daniel had been told: "Go your way ... because the words are closed up and sealed until the time of the end" (Daniel 12:9).

Hold On, I'm Coming

You may also have observed the emphasis on Jesus' statement that "I am coming soon!" (Revelation 22:7). This was a prevalent theme in his opening comments to the individual churches (Revelation 2:16, 25; 3:3, 11). But here at the end of the book, after everything John had seen and heard in the meantime, the possibility of Jesus coming soon takes on a new urgency. And he will make the statement twice more before we get through the last few verses of this final chapter of the Book of Revelation.

Apoca-Lips Now

"Look to the end."

—Chilon (Spartan philosopher, 500s B.C.E.)

In the early portions of Revelation, Jesus was personally dictating what John was to write. Soon, however, John began to write what he was being told and shown by various angels and heavenly beings. Of course, we've seen that Jesus was quite busy during most of those occasions—opening scrolls, consoling beheaded martyrs, charging from heaven to earth on a white horse, consulting his book of life, judging the dead, and performing other chores that needed attending to. But for the big close, Jesus again dictates some final observations and instructions. The following section is a direct quote:

Behold, I am coming soon! My reward is with me, and I will give to everyone according to what he has done. I am the Alpha and the Omega, the First and the Last, the Beginning and the End.

Blessed are those who wash their robes, that they may have the right to the tree of life and may go through the gates into the city. Outside are the dogs, those who practice magic arts, the sexually immoral, the murderers, the idolaters and everyone who loves and practices falsehood.

I, Jesus, have sent my angel to give you this testimony for the churches. I am the Root and the Offspring of David, and the bright Morning Star (Revelation 22:12–16).

Clanging Symbols

Up till now Jesus has been the Alpha, the First, the Beginning. But as he fulfills what is predicted in the Book of Revelation, he becomes the Omega, the Last, the End.

Apoca-Lips Now

"God has decreed that there be sick and poor in this world, but in the next it will be the other way around."

—Napoleon I

As it turns out, not only is Jesus coming soon, but he's also prepared to take care of all unfinished business when he gets here. Numerous titles for him in this section remind us that he came before, and strongly confirm that he will come again. This emphasis is made because (to the church, at least) unless Jesus is everything he claims to be, the Book of Revelation is nothing that it claims to be.

To the believers who will be receiving this Book, the final message of Jesus is a promise of rewards and blessings. It is a call to get ready, like the warning sirens that sound the moment a tornado is spotted. It is a cherished down payment of greater things to come, like an arrangement between two love-struck teenagers to go on a date next Saturday night. And underneath all the rest, it is a reminder that Jesus hasn't forgotten about them. Not only is he aware of their plight, he's also coming back to do something about it.

To others, of course, a 2,000-year-old promise is not much of a promise at all. It's more like a debt carried on the books for so long that it's more worthwhile to write it off rather than plan to collect on it. If there were anything to this Revelation phenomenon, surely Jesus would have acted by now. The reign of Hitler would have been a good time to come plummeting from the sky. Nuclear atrocities, ethnic cleansing, wars in the name of religion, large groups of people starving so a few others can remain wealthy—all these seem like viable catalysts to prompt heavenly action, if indeed Jesus' promise to return is still valid. If nothing else, the Y2K ordeal had many of us nervously awaiting the worst. Jesus would have had our full attention then. Will it take us another thousand years to get to that state of readiness again?

Believers would respond that the events in Revelation aren't scheduled to take place when *we're* ready for them, but whenever God deems it to be the right time. He waited many centuries to fulfill the first wave of messianic prophecies in the Old Testament; why is it odd that he would wait a while (by our calendars) to honor the promises of Jesus' second coming? And as we have said, time is only a human constraint, anyway. In the context of eternity, 2,000 years to God is less than what a nanosecond is to us. So those who believe Jesus is coming again will readily acknowledge that "soon" means different things to different people.

Apoca-Lips Now

"What is a thousand years? Time is short for one who thinks, endless for one who yearns."

—Alain

Famous Last Words

The previous short section of Revelation was attributed as a direct quotation of Jesus. But with the exception of one short phrase, the final verses of Revelation shift back to John's perspective. After everything you've read, here's how the Book of Revelation ends:

> *The Spirit and the bride say, "Come!" And let him who hears say, "Come!" Whoever is thirsty, let him come; and whoever wishes, let him take the free gift of the water of life.*

> *I warn everyone who hears the words of the prophecy of this book: If anyone adds anything to them, God will add to him the plagues described in this book. And if anyone takes words away from this book of prophecy, God will take away from him his share in the tree of life and in the holy city, which are described in this book.*

> *He who testifies to these things says, "Yes, I am coming soon."*

> *Amen. Come, Lord Jesus.*

> *The grace of the Lord Jesus be with God's people. Amen.*

So the closing of the Book of Revelation contains an invitation. The first 20 or so chapters suggest that one of these days, human history will be a "done deal" and God will actively get involved in balancing the books in a fair and final manner. But the last five verses suggest that in the meantime, those who are interested still have time to take action if they wish.

Some offers are "no cost, no obligation." This one is certainly no charge—a "free gift" for any takers. Yet as we have seen in previous chapters of Revelation, getting involved with God cannot be said to be "no obligation." The minority of people who refused the mark of the beast in order to wear God's "brand" found themselves obligated all the way to the guillotine (Revelation 20:4). For them, it was worth it. For others, maybe not.

If any of these final comments have sounded preachy or churchy, please forgive the authors. However, that's the purpose of their placement here at the end of this apocalyptic work of wonder. It might be more prudent to gloss over them here in this *Complete Idiot's Guide*, but we've tried to cover and explain the entire Book of Revelation. A certain amount of biblical background has been necessary to place certain comments or events into perspective, though we've tried to keep it to a minimum.

In fact, all readers of this great book (the Book of Revelation, not this *Complete Idiot's Guide*) are warned against editing out portions they don't particularly care for, or adding to what's there. Adding to these words is grounds for having God "add to him the plagues described in this book." Leaving out portions results in God "[taking] away from him his share in the tree of life and in the holy city." Neither of these options is desired by the authors. So John reported what he saw and heard, and we have tried (to this point) to stick close to what John reported.

Where our explanations are confusing or incomplete, we've provided the text of the Book of Revelation to let you struggle with the original material on your own. And this chapter completes our start-to-finish whirlwind tour through the Book of Revelation. Compared to certain other portions of the Bible, Revelation is a real page-turner. We may not understand what we're reading, but it goes by rather quickly. Now as we move ahead, the following chapters look at various interpretations of what we've seen so far.

But before we move on, not to be missed is one more biblical reminder in the next-to-last verse. We've heard this promise of Jesus several times throughout Revelation, but it makes a great closer.

Flashback

The "free drink" offer in the closing verses of Revelation echoes a much earlier Old Testament invitation: "Come, all you who are thirsty, come to the waters; and you who have no money, come, buy and eat! Come, buy wine and milk without money and without cost .... Give ear and come to me; hear me, that your soul may live. I will make an everlasting covenant with you, my faithful love promised to David" (Isaiah 55:1, 3).

Clanging Symbols

Even the curses in Revelation are fittingly symbolic. You add to what's there? The plagues of the book are added to you. You take away from what's there? God takes away what you're looking forward to receiving.

Flashback

The last recorded words of Jesus prior to Revelation are found in Matthew 28:18–20 and Acts 1:6–8. In both cases, Jesus challenges his followers to be faithful witnesses for him and make new disciples. And in both instances he makes references to the future:

➤ "And surely I am with you always, to the very end of the age" (Matthew 28:20).

➤ "It is not for you to know the times or dates the Father has set by his own authority" (Acts 1:7).

The Book of Revelation adds insight to both of these previous statements.

If you read lists of the "famous last words" of people, most of them are quite disappointing—and it is thought that even then many are more legendary than authentic. Only a small percentage of the people cited are well-known or have anything really clever to say. But here in Revelation, the last words of Jesus are perpetually intriguing to many people: "Yes, I am coming soon."

John responded with a couple of closing Amens. (Amen simply means, "Let it be so.") But as time went by, people began to debate, "What, exactly, did Jesus mean by that?" The conclusions they reach are vastly different, and lead to a number of widely divergent interpretations for the entire Book of Revelation. We now turn our attention to a number of those options.

A Bright Spot

After all is said and done, it should be noted that the Book of Revelation closes on a bright and optimistic note.

The Least You Need to Know

➤ As the Book of Revelation closes, John is instructed *not* to keep secret what he had seen.

➤ A curse is added at the end of the book for anyone attempting to add to or take away from what John wrote.

➤ Three times in the closing section, Jesus is quoted as saying, "I am coming soon."

➤ An open invitation is extended to anyone who wishes to respond to God in light of what he or she has read in the Book of Revelation.

Part 4

Theology Meets Optometry

Now you've finished reading the Book of Revelation. So do you have a satisfying feeling of accomplishment and insight? Not likely. The question now becomes, "What does it all mean?"

Some people say the events of Revelation have already occurred over a compressed time period, and accurate interpretation requires a close-up lens and a certain degree of nearsightedness. Some peer through telescopic lenses far into the future to predict events and prove that Revelation is indeed yet to come. Others keep one lens on a historical timeline and another on Revelation, attempting to bring the two into cohesive focus. And still others say to close your eyes to any literal interpretation of Revelation and open your mind to its allegorical significance. Each of these interpretations has some intriguing selling points, and you need to consider all of them before forming your own opinion.

You may never have 20/20 vision when it comes to understanding Revelation. But it is our hope you will see much more clearly by the time you get to the end of this section.

Chapter 16

Open to Interpretation?

In This Chapter

➤ Is interpreting the Book of Revelation really necessary?

➤ A review of some of the key interpretable elements of Revelation

➤ Why people arrive at different interpretations

➤ Some things to expect as we approach various interpretations

---

Some readers are going to wish we had ended this book with Chapter 15. After all, we have laid out some groundwork and have trudged straight through the Book of Revelation. We saw every word John wrote and discussed much of what he might have meant. Shouldn't we be finished?

At this point, however, we're approaching a number of different ways to interpret the book of Revelation. In doing so, we're likely to dredge up many of those unpleasant memories you thought you'd left behind when you finally finished your high school or college English classes—all that stuff about symbolism, what the author really meant, and so forth. Your teachers probably seemed quite excited about underlying meanings, but many students aren't nearly as thrilled.

Call Me Confused

For example, Herman Melville's *Moby Dick* is considered by many experts to be the greatest American novel ever written. Some people aren't as enamored of it as others, of course, yet the consensus is that it is a masterpiece of writing.

But when you go a little deeper into *why* people are so impressed, the reasons vary. To lots of fans, *Moby Dick* is a spellbinding tale of the sea. Each detail adds to the complexity and enjoyment of the action. The plot builds slowly and purposefully, immersing the readers in various facts about the sea and acquainting them with the foibles of each of the quirky characters aboard the *Pequod.* It's a whale of a story, and at a very basic level, many readers find it immensely satisfying.

Others, however, do much reading both between the lines and far beyond the words printed on the page. To this group, *Moby Dick* is more a grand fable, having less to do with the sea than with broad and universal themes: retribution and revenge, unbridled desire, fatally dysfunctional relationships, man vs. nature, and numerous others.

To this latter group of readers, *Moby Dick* could have been staged in the desert between warring tribes, in the skies between fighter pilots, or in any number of other settings while still dealing with the same themes. They tend to criticize the plodding pace and cite examples such as Chapter 32, which is essentially a scientific treatise on whales.

Apoca-Lips Now

"But when a man's religion becomes really frantic; when it is a positive torment to him; and, in fine, makes this earth of ours an uncomfortable inn to lodge in; then I think it high time to take that individual aside and argue the point with him."

—Herman Melville, from *Moby Dick*

The divergent views about *Moby Dick* create a literary version of the old adage about not being able to see the forest for the trees. Some people see the novel as an enormous collection of "trees"—numerous facts, chapters, threads, and ideas—all of which are significant in their own right as well as within the collective. As they see it, the removal of any of the individual pillars tends to weaken the whole.

The other group, however, sees Melville's work more as a forest. And most forests can survive, if not be strengthened in the long run, by having a number of trees removed so the others become stronger. These readers don't need a whole chapter on types of whales to enhance their understanding that when a man like Captain Ahab offers no concern for the redemption of others, he isn't likely to find any himself.

People will never come to total agreement about all aspects of *Moby Dick*. But then, such disagreements are what make the study of great literature interesting and informative.

The Book of Revelation: Essential or Optional?

As we begin to consider various interpretations of the Book of Revelation, we will see similar disagreements. To some people, the importance of Revelation lies in its broad, but clear, message. Evil resists good, but good wins out in the end. The specifics aren't all that important. Who cares who the Antichrist might be? Or if the people being described are Jews or Gentiles? Or how a timeline might be constructed that would include every detail in an organized chronology?

After all, a complete understanding of the Book of Revelation isn't required for one's faith, salvation, or other day-to-day religious regimen. (If there *is* a pop quiz about the details of Revelation before getting into heaven, a lot of Christians are going to be in trouble!) Revelation is a forest of (largely symbolic) information; the individual "trees" need not be singled out and examined ad infinitum. Some people get into that stuff, but it's not really necessary.

The other line of thinking, however, is that the information in Revelation—cryptic though it is—is there for a purpose. Some of Jesus' parables weren't clear at first hearing—should we just ignore them, too? When basic doctrines of the faith get a little complicated, do we just toss them out? We would do ourselves a huge injustice to ignore so much content just because it's a little hard to make sense of it. A bit of legwork may indeed result in big discoveries for those who, like detectives examining clues, put in the effort.

This way of thinking affirms that, yes, it is important to determine whether the events described in Revelation are past, present, or future. It's the height of futility to sit around anticipating something that has already happened, and just as foolish to think all of the warning signals are behind us if indeed they still lie ahead. If even a small percentage of the events described in Revelation are literal and future, then, in this case, ignorance isn't necessarily bliss.

Clanging Symbols

As we get into the chapters detailing various interpretations of the Book of Revelation, you will see several instances of how vastly different conclusions can be reached when one person sees something literally while someone else considers it symbolic.

Life's a Picnic ... or Should That Be "Panic"?

You might recall the recent Y2K hubbub where what was essentially a programming lapse became a huge scare. What was going to happen? How should people prepare? Everyone interpreted the situation differently and endless predictions were made.

Some individuals felt the proper preparation involved building bunkers and heavily stocking them with supplies. Others literally took to the hills, and in addition to food, stocked guns and ammunition. These people were generally viewed as extremists (these were the people who got the most attention from the television networks and other media).

On the other hand, there were a large number of people who carefully studied the facts. While they could not predict exactly every potential outcome, they were able to develop reasonable scenarios and generate reasonable solutions. As a result, around the world, computer programmers worked diligently to minimize the Y2K problem.

What was the outcome? All hell did not break loose as the extremists warned. But there were a few glitches that surfaced and indicated that had the majority view of "do nothing" prevailed, chaos surely may have ensued.

Be Prepared

Revelation and the other apocalyptic writings of the Bible offer a kind of survivor's preparedness manual for the "glitches" we can expect from daily living. While the specific timing and personalities can't be deduced with any amount of certainty, reasonable scenarios can be generated. From each, we can determine truth and become better prepared to face the future.

Apoca-Lips Now

"Reason is natural revelation, whereby the eternal Father of light, and fountain of all knowledge communicates to mankind that portion of truth which he has laid within the reach of their natural faculties."

–John Locke

In going through the Book of Revelation, we have regularly commented as if what John was seeing was literal. We've addressed the various elements of Revelation as we came to them, and have made little effort to dispute any of the descriptions, to connect them with other events, or to otherwise get ahead of ourselves in attempting to interpret John's narrative. From here on, however, we'll be doing a bit more speculating. Some interpretations require stepping back and viewing Revelation as something of a flight of fancy to highlight a simple story of God's triumph. Others require leaps of faith and numerous "what-ifs" to attempt to incorporate and make sense of every bit of information contained in the Book.

Reviewing the Viewing

So let's first review a number of the symbols and significant events we came across as we went through the Book of Revelation. Most interpretations refer to many of these same things, yet arrive at vastly different conclusions:

➤ **A great tribulation.** This suggests a period of unprecedented suffering. By some accounts, all the traumatic events connected with the seals, trumpets, and bowl judgments combine to create havoc unlike anything the world has ever seen. As we will see, some break this period into two parts.

➤ **The rise of the antichrist.** The Antichrist, a person (or perhaps system of religious beliefs), exerts tremendous power, and believers are persecuted and/or put to death.

➤ **Resurrection of the dead.** Deceased individuals arise and are provided new bodies, and not necessarily at the same time. Some of the following interpretations make clear distinctions as to when various groups of people are resurrected.

➤ **The millennium.** This 1,000-year period (or some approximation) is said to be a period when Satan is bound and certain believers come back to life and reign with Jesus.

➤ **The second coming of Jesus.** This is when Jesus returns to earth to bring justice on sinful people and reestablish things the way they ought to be.

➤ **Judgment before a great white throne.** A great heavenly judge consults the books and sentences a large number of people. Those whose names aren't found in the Book of Life are cast into the lake of fire.

In addition to these symbols and events are a few additional things that will come into play as we examine various interpretations. After going straight through Revelation, perhaps you see the wisdom in seeking clues to interpretation wherever we might find them. Here are some further things to consider as we try to make sense of this Book.

A Bright Spot

Now that you've been through the entire Book of Revelation, you should be somewhat encouraged to realize that in spite of the various interpretations, most versions incorporate the same basics. You've already done the groundwork, and now you are better equipped to understand a number of different slants on the same text.

The "Rapture"

As much as some people talk about the "rapture," you might expect to find long discourses about it scattered throughout Scripture. But don't even go looking for the word in the Bible. You won't find it.

However, the Apostle Paul wrote of a time when Jesus would descend and gather up believers to be with him. The Latin word to describe being "caught up" with God is *rapturo*, and is found in only one place in the entire New Testament. Yet the rapture of believers plays heavily into some of the scenarios that follow.

Flashback

"According to the Lord's own word, we tell you that we who are still alive, who are left till the coming of the Lord, will certainly not precede those who have fallen asleep [died]. For the Lord himself will come down from heaven, with a loud command, with the voice of the archangel and with the trumpet call of God, and the dead in Christ will rise first. After that, we who are still alive and are left will be caught up together with them in the clouds to meet the Lord in the air. And so we will be with the Lord forever" (1 Thessalonians 4:15–17).

Jesus' Predictions About the End of the Age

At one point near the end of his ministry, Jesus foretold the utter destruction of the temple in Jerusalem. Soon afterward, his disciples pulled him aside and asked, "When will this happen, and what will be the sign of your coming and of the end of the age?"

Apoca-Lips Now

"We search the world for truth, we cull
The good, the pure, the beautiful,
From graven stone and written scroll,
From the old flower-fields of the soul,
And, weary seekers for the best,
We come back laden from our quest,
To find that all the sages said
Is in the Book our mothers read."

—John Greenleaf Whittier

They happened to be sitting on the Mount of Olives, so Jesus' response is commonly referred to as the "Olivet Discourse." Three gospels contain his lengthy answer to his disciples' questions: Matthew 24–25; Mark 13; and Luke 21:5–36. Much of what Jesus predicted parallels some of the things we have seen in Revelation, and this discourse is the starting point for some people. After they make certain assumptions about what Jesus said would happen—and when—the Book of Revelation is then interpreted to support their presuppositions. In fact, we will see some drastically different interpretations based on varying opinions of what Jesus meant in his Olivet discourse.

Old Testament Prophecy

Many of the prophets throughout Israel's history foretold the coming of a Messiah/Deliverer. Jesus' birth, life, and death are linked to many such prophecies, but a number of others remain unfulfilled. Those who take Scripture literally don't believe God will leave any of his promises dangling, so the as-yet-unfilled prophecies are treated as clues as to what might yet happen in the future. Several of these will influence various interpretations of the Book of Revelation.

Other Promises

In addition to the prophecies given to the Israelites, Jesus made certain promises to his disciples, and various New Testament writers included a number of bold statements regarding things to come. Bible interpreters are going to expect them to be fulfilled.

As we have said before, Revelation is not a stand-alone book. If it were, we would be at a loss to understand much of what has become clear with the help of other Bible passages. But because it isn't, its interpretation is further complicated. Revelation is enough of a jigsaw puzzle in itself. But in addition to all the pieces we're attempting to fashion into a coherent picture, we discover that additional boxes of puzzle pieces from Old Testament prophecies and New Testament promises have been dumped onto the table as well—and somehow they are *all* supposed to come together and make sense.

Don't worry. You won't have to be a Damascus Roads Scholar to undertake this goal. Just be aware that various interpretations will pull clues out of numerous varied places elsewhere in the Bible.

Flashback

"In my Father's house are many rooms; if it were not so, I would have told you. I am going there to prepare a place for you. And if I go and prepare a place for you, I will come back and take you to be with me that you also may be where I am" (John 14:3).

Apoca-Lips Now

"Arguments about Scripture achieve nothing but a stomach-ache and a headache."

—Tertullian

Also keep in mind that we will be examining only basic generalities of various perspectives. Within each viewpoint are other numerous variances of opinion. When we say that so-and-so believes such-and-such an interpretation, we're speaking only in the broadest of terms. While we don't want to shortchange anyone's strong opinions, we cannot pursue every nuance of every interpretation. Certain people are certain to feel slighted, and the authors apologize in advance.

For What It's Worth ...

The bottom line is that fine, respected Bible scholars have agreed to disagree about the interpretation and significance of the Book of Revelation. We will look at some of their viewpoints in Chapters 17–19.

Most have formed strong opinions that make sense to them, yet readily concede that other points of view also have validity. We won't offer the "single" or "preferable" twist to this fascinating Book. Rather, we'll look at some reasons each group believes as it does.

So Many Different Views

For example, we will see that Martin Luther and other Reformers held to a "historicist" view that interpreted the Antichrist to be the Pope and the Roman church. In reaction to this view, Francisco Ribera, a Spanish Jesuit, interpreted Revelation events as all happening in the future, thus deflecting criticism from the Pope and initiating what has become the "futurist" view. Additionally, another Jesuit scholar and contemporary of Ribera, Luiz de Alcazar, interpreted Revelation 4–11 as representing the church's struggle against Judaism. His ideas were foundational to what has become known as the "preterist" view. Very possibly, the idealist or symbolic view, initiated by the German theologian Karl Auberlen, may have been in reaction to all the others, attempting to spiritualize Revelation so it could be relevant to a broader audience.

Apoca-Lips Now

"When I was young I was sure of everything; in a few years, having been mistaken a thousand times, I was not half so sure of most things as I was before; at present, I am hardly sure of anything but what God has revealed to me."

—John Wesley

The histories of each of these views, which are the subjects of the chapters that follow, are varied and complex. As times change, so do the prominent theories. Still, elements from each persist and often color the currently popular view. Also, just as Democrats and Republicans can jump from one party to the other, proponents of these views occasionally reach different conclusions about how to interpret Revelation.

A number of factors contribute to the changes in thinking. It's not because everyone is just waffling!

New Discoveries

One factor is that biblical scholarship keeps improving in part because of the discovery of new documents and more accurate translation methods. Emerging technology has also helped bring better and different understandings to the fore. The shift of societal attitudes also has an impact.

Finally, every individual goes through a personal evolution of learning and understanding, and evaluates any interpretation according to his or her own multifaceted experiences. Many children want to be cowboys when they're little only to discover that cowboys today aren't the same as the ones they saw in the movies. Therefore, they move on to other options.

Multiple Layers

Another element is that, like many writings, Revelation can legitimately be viewed to contain various levels of interpretation. Robert Frost wrote poetry that is appreciated and loved by a very diverse audience. For some, his poetry is straightforward and simple, evoking clear images of yellow forests and wooded trails. Other readers find his poems are steeped in deeper and more complex meanings which they relish ferreting out.

In some cases, we can examine a particular interpretation simply, without much fuss. In other cases, however, we must contemplate considerably more to adequately understand the thinking behind the interpretation. Just because the authors may say more about certain interpretations than others is not necessarily a personal endorsement of those views. (We might vastly prefer addition to calculus, but in describing the two we would have to devote much more time to calculus.)

Having made all these disclaimers, we now turn our attention to how the great minds of the world have tried to make sense out of the Book of Revelation.

The Least You Need to Know

➤ To say there's more than one way to interpret the Book of Revelation is a big understatement.

➤ The same base of information can lead to widely divergent, yet equally defensible, opinions concerning the interpretation of Revelation.

➤ In addition to what is in the Book of Revelation itself, most interpretations also depend on other biblical prophecies and promises.

➤ Our goal will be to examine a number of different interpretations without endorsing any specific one.

Chapter 17

It's the End of the World and We Missed It?

In This Chapter

➤ Interpreting the Book of Revelation as being primarily in the past (the preterist view)

➤ Tying John's prophecies about the future with some of Jesus'

➤ Where preterists disagree

➤ Was Revelation written earlier than traditionally believed?

Imagine you've traveled cross-country to visit an old friend who moved away. You've never been in this particular geographic area, but you're equipped with detailed maps and a number of specific landmarks your friend told you to look for. You know your friend lives "outside the city a ways," so you're not concerned when you don't immediately find any of the street names you expect. Occasionally you pass a landmark and think, *Maybe that's the barn she mentioned,* or, *That could be the Wal-Mart he told me to look for.* But only when you unexpectedly find yourself at the state line do you realize you've been *driving in the wrong direction.*

This embarrassing discovery is something akin to examining the first interpretation of the Book of Revelation we want to consider. As we've gone through Revelation, we've said on numerous occasions that John was looking into the future and recording the things he saw and heard. One of the first distinctions that separate interpreters into groups is *how far* into the future John was seeing. In this chapter, we'll examine the preterist viewpoint, which postulates that most, if not all, of the events described took place by the end of the first century. (The Latin word *praeteritus* means "gone by" and is the root of the term preterism.)

Certainly John was looking into *his* future, but was he looking into *ours?* The preterists say no. John was looking ahead, but if we want to see what he saw, *we* must look *backward* more than 1,900 years.

When the Temple Topples ...

In Chapter 16, "Open to Interpretation?" we noted that Jesus had predicted the destruction of the temple in Jerusalem, and that in response to his disciples' questions he delivered what is known as the Olivet Discourse. Some people suggest that as soon as Jesus described the end of the temple as they knew it, the minds of the disciples automatically went to the end of the world. They could hardly conceive of a time and place without access to the grand temple that Herod had only recently completed.

Let's look closer at some of the things Jesus told them to expect, taken from Matthew 24:

➤ Deceptive leaders claiming to be Christ (v v. 4–5)

➤ Wars and rumors of wars (v. 6)

➤ Famines and earthquakes (v. 7)

➤ Persecution and death of believers (v. 9)

➤ False prophets and a turning away from genuine faith (v v. 10–13)

➤ The message of the gospel preached to the whole world (v. 14)

➤ An "abomination that causes desolation" in the holy place in the temple (v. 15)

➤ A disturbance in the skies, and a darkening of the sun, moon, and stars (v. 29)

➤ The Son of Man coming on the clouds with power and great glory (v. 30)

➤ A loud trumpet call (by angels) to gather God's people together from around the world (v. 31)

Shortly after mentioning all of these yet-to-come events, Jesus added, "I tell you the truth, this generation will certainly not pass away until all these things have happened" (Matthew 24:34). One definition of a biblical generation is a period of approximately 40 years, so adherents of the preterist viewpoint look within that time frame to make sense of everything. In addition, they point out, are the repeated emphases in the Book of Revelation that Jesus is coming *soon*.

Apoca-Lips Now

"The great thing in this world is not so much where we are but in what direction we are moving."

—Oliver Wendell Holmes

They see three options:

1. Jesus was either mistaken or lying (which is not a popular viewpoint among most Bible scholars).

2. Explanations must be provided to finagle an excuse why "all these things" and/or "soon" and/or "this generation" don't mean what we think they mean.

3. Events occurred exactly as Jesus said they would, and we just need to figure out what he meant.

Essentially, they say, those are our only choices. The one that makes the most sense to preterists is #3. And they feel the fall of the Jewish temple in 70 C.E. is a clue too enormous to be overlooked. It's an event that seems to fit most of the criteria for making sense of the end-times prophecies. They consider this to be a logical leap of reason since comments about the temple were what prompted Jesus' long and detailed discourse to begin with.

> **Apoca-Lips Now**
>
> "The truth that makes men free is for the most part the truth which men prefer not to hear."
>
> —Herbert Sebastian Agar

Revelation Through a Preterist Lens

In Chapter 16, we reviewed some of the key events that are mentioned in Revelation. Let's now take a look at how they might come together from a preterist viewpoint.

> **Clanging Symbols**
>
> To the Jews of the first century, the temple was the equivalent of our Liberty Bell, Declaration of Independence, and favorite church all rolled into one. The temple allowed them freedom of worship, even while under political domination of the Romans. They could offer sacrifices there, as they had done for centuries. It was a gathering place for like-minded people across the nation and from lands far away. And the Most Holy Place within the temple symbolized God's presence there in their midst. Losing the temple was much more devastating to them than, say, the loss of any single church today due to fire, tornado, or something else. Temple standards and procedures were so holy and precise that the worshipers couldn't simply move into another building and continue as before.

The great tribulation is one of the clearest symbols to identify according to this interpretation. Indeed, many preterist concepts hinge on the fall of the temple as being a source of unprecedented emotional and physical pain.

For those of us unaware of life in the first century, however, this might not seem like such a big deal. The temple fell. So what?

The temple fell only because Jerusalem fell. The destruction of the temple and the city was the *culmination* of an ongoing and increasingly problematic confrontation between the militant segment of Judaism and the Roman Empire. Occasional skirmishes had taken place over a number of years, eventually leading to an organized, concentrated siege of Jerusalem. The walls of the great city were closed and barricaded against the invading Roman armies, eventually creating severe famine, desperation, and great fear.

The fall of the temple was the final stroke in a long period of intense tribulation. Roman soldiers finally breached the walls and ransacked the "holy city" and temple. They carried ensigns (banners) with eagles, representing their gods, and offered sacrifices to them after their victory over Jerusalem. This is the preterist interpretation of the "abomination of desolation" predicted by Jesus and Daniel.

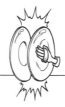

Clanging Symbols

Can it be that eagles are symbolic of Roman soldiers? Jesus had said in his Olivet Discourse: "Wherever there is a carcass, there the vultures will gather" (Matthew 24:28). Some Bible translaters say the original word as "eagles" rather than "vultures." We also know Jesus had mourned over what was about to happen to the city (Matthew 24:37–39). It is sometimes suggested that Jesus was looking into the future and seeing the clusters of pagan Roman soldiers with their eagle banners, having their way with Jerusalem.

Going along with the preterist viewpoint, it is also a cinch to identify the Antichrist. The nomination goes to [*trumpet fanfare*] Lucius Domitius Ahenobarbus. Perhaps you know him better by the name he later adopted: Nero.

Emperor Nero began his reign in 54 C.E. and ruled until he committed suicide in 68 C.E. If you know anything about his personal habits, sexual preferences, and various other perversions, you know he was a beast of a man. Early writers even used the word beast to describe him. He enjoyed being the emperor in a land where emperor worship was becoming popular. And, lo and behold, if you write the Greek form of his name (Neron Caesar) in Hebrew characters, the numerical equivalent comes out to 666.

Where's Jesus?

So the great tribulation and Antichrist are easily identified in preterist thinking. Some of the other symbols in Revelation, however, aren't as apparent. For example, where is Jesus on his white horse, charging down with the armies of heaven behind him?

Preterists suggest that if we consider John's message was that Jesus would return in a judgment role, and that his armies would descend on people who had rejected him, then in a sense the Roman armies could be considered his agents of bringing about judgment. The judgment, therefore, was primarily on the first-century Jewish nation that had met its Messiah, but had rejected him.

While it is true that the Romans were technically the ones who carried out the execution of Jesus, Pontius Pilate had done essentially everything in his power to spare Jesus' life. Jewish representatives had said, "Let his blood be on us and on our children!" (Matthew 27:25). So if the perception is that God's judgment is on the Jews who had rejected Jesus, then the Roman armies carried out his judgment in the same way that the Assyrian and Babylonian armies had done in overpowering apostate Israelites in the Old Testament and carrying them off into captivity.

Continuing this line of thinking, the return of Jesus is an invisible, though no less significant, coming in judgment. The people on earth don't see him in person, yet acknowledge that he is behind the events taking place.

Let's say that you and your neighbor get into a conflict because you accidentally back your car over his prize rosebushes, ruining them. Angry words quickly turn into loud threats. And just before he storms inside, he says, "I'll get you back. Make no mistake. You just wait and see."

When you get up the next morning, every flower in your yard has been clipped to the ground, and in the dirt is written, "I told you so!" Could this have been a freak act of nature or a random act of violence? Not likely! You "see" clearly what happened, even though you didn't *physically* see your neighbor creep over during the night with his hedge clippers.

Flashback

At his trial, Jesus told the high priest and those present: "In the future you will see the Son of Man sitting at the right hand of the Mighty One and coming on the clouds of heaven" (Matthew 26:64). In some preterist thinking, this meant they would literally see divine judgment take place in the destruction of the temple, and would instinctively "see" that Jesus was responsible.

In the way we use language, "You'll see ..." doesn't necessarily require the use of the optic nerve. We sometimes see in other ways. Perhaps this is what Jesus and John were suggesting in some of their prophecies.

If so, then perhaps many of the mentions of "the end of the world" (or more accurately, "the end of the age") are actually references to the end of the *Jewish* age. With the fall of the temple, the Jewish nation lost many of its rights and privileges. And as both Jews and Christians spilled out of Jerusalem under increased Roman persecution, it was the Christians and the spread of the church that took center stage from that point onward. Perhaps, then, the "Millennium" in Revelation (where Jesus rules with his followers) is actually a reference to the church age.

Help from the Historians

Lest anyone accuse preterists of being anti-Semitic, it should be noted that they support much of their hypothesis with the work of Flavius Josephus, a noted Jewish historian of the first century. In his writings, Josephus clearly associated Roman aggression against Jerusalem with God's displeasure. He accused his own generation of being the most wicked ever (which, if you read certain portions of the Old Testament, is saying a lot). And he records a number of supernatural cosmic events that took place during the fall of the city and the temple. He writes of a star resembling a sword that hovered over Jerusalem, and of a comet that lasted for an entire year. (Halley's comet should have appeared in the area in 66 C.E.)

The Roman historian Tacitus also wrote of strange signs in the skies during the turbulent events of the late first century. He strongly believed that the gods were meting out punishment. (Even though the Romans ran rampant through Jerusalem, they were facing defeats on a number of other fronts.)

A Bright Spot

The strange lights in the sky and the glowing altar were perceived to be bright spots by the people of the time. Like many today, they were growing desperate for signs to help them believe during tough circumstances. As it turned out, however, they got just the opposite of what they were hoping for. Even bright signs should be acknowledged with a note of healthy skepticism and not taken out of context.

In addition, Josephus recorded a number of other bizarre and extreme events—so weird, as a matter of fact, that some people have come to question his credentials as a historian. For example, among the events he described just prior to the Roman invasion of Jerusalem was a bright light around the altar in the middle of the night. This took place during a Jewish festival, and later at the same celebration he told of a heifer, just prior to being sacrificed, giving birth to a lamb. Some of these signs, he said, created false hope among the people concerning their future.

But regardless of the effect back then, the significance *now* is that the record of heavenly signs tends to help verify the preterist understanding of the Book of Revelation. By their interpretation, they consider the end of the age to be the end of the *Jewish* age. The Millennium is the church age. The last days are the period between the ministry of John the Baptist and the fall of the temple. The tribulation is the destruction of the holy city. Death and destruction is a historical reality, as is the subsequent forced exile of the people. The return of Jesus is one of judgment rather than physical presence. And the mysterious heavenly happenings and other signs verify that these are indeed first-century fulfillments of both John's and Jesus' former prophecies.

Where Preterists Disagree

Some of the other details of Revelation require additional explanation to fit into the preterist viewpoint, but this will be true of most all interpretations. We won't attempt to go into the fine details of all the various points of all the possible perspectives. We're trying to stick to the broader explanations here.

We do need to point out, however, that preterists disagree as to the extent of how much biblical prophecy has already been fulfilled. And one of the big dividing points is the issue of resurrection.

Some groups (let's call them *full* preterists) believe that *all* the predictions of Jesus in the Olivet Discourse as well as John's visions in Revelation are a done deal. They're history (literally). We need look no further for insight or explanation.

Others (let's call them *partial* preterists, though not everyone agrees to such titles) agree that *most* of these things are past. However, this group believes a few crucial aspects must still be future. For example, how are we to explain the passages that describe the coming back to life of those who were dead so they can rule with Jesus?

Many so-called partial preterists still look to the future for a second coming of Jesus, a resurrection,

Flashback

John the Baptist came with a clarion call to "Repent, for the kingdom of heaven is near" (Matthew 3:1). And while he was preaching this message, Jesus appeared on the scene. So some people who heard John's message initiating the kingdom also saw the ministry of Jesus, and later the fall of the temple. Preterists feel that most biblical end-times prophecies refer to this precise time period.

Apoca-Lips Now

"Knowledge of revelation does not always begin with clarity. It may increase in clarity; it should do so. It may, however, diminish also in clarity. But under all circumstances, it begins with certitude .... Doubt and despair, human unbelief, and even a sea of uncertainties on our part, will not be able to change the certitude of His presence."

—Karl Barth

and a judgment. Indeed, most of the church creeds from the earliest times and throughout the centuries have clearly expressed these beliefs.

When it comes to biblical prophecy, sometimes more than one future event is interpreted to fulfill what was predicted, which may be true in this case as well. So while the fall of Jerusalem was a judgment and a coming of Jesus in a sense, it was primarily limited to the Jewish people. Therefore, isn't it a possibility (and some would say a *necessity*) that we should expect another, more widespread, coming of Jesus and a judgment for the rest of the world?

A Bright Spot

If the preterists are right, then most of the nasty stuff Revelation speaks of is behind us. We need not wince or fear as we look to the future—at least, not in dread of a prophesied great tribulation or Antichrist.

Full preterists resist such thinking, but are then required to speak in terms of resurrection being spiritual rather than bodily. Partial preterists feel this distorts the clear teachings of other biblical passages. Each group feels the other borders on heresy, though both are simply trying to hold fast to what they believe to be biblical truth without having to stretch it too much to make sense of prophecy.

Just keep in mind that we're not trying to prove one group right over the other, but simply to present the concerns and beliefs of most key groups. And indeed, this is only the first of four main ways to view the Book of Revelation. These are just the preterists, and even they have some vastly different interpretations.

Going on a Bad Date?

Before we move on to other interpretations, however, we need to make one more crucial observation about the preterist viewpoint. If the fulfillment of John's prophecies occurred in 70 C.E., he wouldn't have been much of a visionary if he had predicted them *after* they happened.

We originally said that the traditional date of writing assigned to the the writing of Book of Revelation was around 95 C.E. We know it was during a time of intense persecution, and most people have assumed this was during the reign of Domitian (81–96 C.E.).

So those with preterist viewpoints say we are going on a bad date if we think Revelation was written late in the first century, and they are currently trying to get their peers to reconsider. They point out that another primary period of persecution was during Nero's leadership (54–68 C.E.). This is the period that makes more sense to preterists for the writing of Revelation—and in fact is necessary in order for the writer to predict the events of 70 C.E., which is a historical certainty. Recent preterists have made strong and persuasive arguments for consideration of an earlier date for the writing of Revelation.

Case Closed?

The preterists make a convincing argument. But then, we haven't considered a lot of the rebuttal that would certainly come up in a debate on the subject. Rather than bring up such arguments here, we'll simply present other perspectives when we get to the respective viewpoints. As you will see, other opinions may sound equally convincing.

Rarely will you find any serious student of the Book of Revelation go on record as promoting absolute certainty of truth. Many scholars struggle with all of the possibilities until they come up with something that makes a lot of sense to them, and may hold strongly to their opinions. Yet most will readily agree that it *does* come down to a matter of opinion rather than indisputable certainty. They may think they know what to expect, and a few are quite dogmatic. Yet most are open to other input and possibilities.

It has been almost 2,000 years since the Book of Revelation was written, and the wisest among us are still trying to reveal the significance of what's there. Maybe the preterists are right, and most of the fuss is behind us. Then again, maybe not.

Apoca-Lips Now

"Time discovers truth."
—Seneca

"Time reveals all."
—Tertullian

The Least You Need to Know

➤ The preterist interpretation of Revelation is that most, if not all, of the events described have already been fulfilled.

➤ The events surrounding the destruction of the Jewish temple in 70 C.E. were, from a preterist perspective, the great tribulation of the last days.

➤ Preterists disagree as to whether further fulfillment of Revelation's prophecies will take place.

➤ The preterist interpretation requires setting an earlier date than has been traditionally accepted for the writing of Revelation.

Chapter 18

Revelation Interpretations: Some Minority Viewpoints

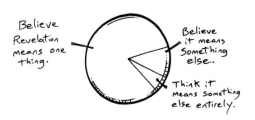

Believe Revelation means one thing.

Believe it means Something else.

Think it means something else entirely.

In This Chapter

➤ Interpreting the Book of Revelation as a chronicle of human history (the historicist view)

➤ Interpreting the Book of Revelation as purely symbolic (the idealist view)

➤ Considering a literary-analytical approach to the Book of Revelation

➤ Approaching the Book of Revelation as grand drama

When it comes to politics, we tend to think of the United States as a two-party nation. The Republicans are continually strategizing and posturing to attempt to gain an upper hand over the Democrats, and the Democrats are doing all within their power to secure more support than the Republicans. And as U.S. citizens approach most elections, the question is usually whether they will vote Republican or Democratic.

Yet if you look at the ballots, there are frequently more than two names there. In presidential elections, especially, the choices usually extend far beyond the top two on the list. You're likely to find candidates representing independents, Socialists, Libertarians, the Green Party, and more. These days, those outside the two main parties don't usually get much press, publicity, or financial support, yet they remain valid choices for those who don't go along with the top two. At times great success has been achieved by the Whig party, the Bull Moose party, and other parties which are no longer in vogue.

We're about to see a parallel as we continue our examination of various interpretations of the Book of Revelation. The preterist interpretation (which we covered in Chapter 17, "It's the End of the World and We Missed It?") is nowhere near as popular as the futurist interpretation (which we will explore in Chapter 19, "Back to the Future"). However, the preterist perspective has recently been growing in popularity and seems to be becoming a respected alternative to the more intriguing futurist viewpoint.

Yet while the preterist and futurist perspectives have the most devotees by far, they have by no means cornered the market on Revelation interpretations. In this chapter, we will look at a few additional options. One of them had quite a following in the past and is still embraced by some today, and some of the others are presented to show both the variety of approaches to the Book of Revelation and the interest generated by the final book of the Bible.

Apoca-Lips Now

"The future you shall know when it has come; before then, forget it."

—Aeschylus

Apoca-Lips Now

"All decisions are made on insufficient evidence."

—Rita Mae Brown

A Roadmap of Human History? (Historicism)

We saw that the preterists attempt to tie up most (if not all) of the contents of Revelation within the same generation that heard Jesus speak of the horrible things that were certain to come. Another group, commonly referred to as the historicists, have quite a different perspective.

Pages of History and Pages of Revelation: One and the Same?

The Book of Revelation begins in the present, with John exiled on the island of Patmos. The Book ends with a wonderful, almost-too-good-to-be-true description of eternal happiness in heaven. Could it be that the sections in between are a continual, connecting line of history describing what will take place between the here and now and humankind's eventual entry into the afterlife? That's what the historicists believed.

For example, not too long after Revelation was written, the western Roman Empire started falling to hoards of Huns and other barbaric tribes. This was almost unthinkable during the Golden Years of Rome. Could this be associated with the seven seals in Revelation 6? Not long afterward, the eastern Roman

Empire was swarmed with Arab soldiers almost like locusts that had been released from a bottomless pit, followed by Turkish armies, stinging and burning like supernatural horses (Revelation 9). Hey, is Revelation trying to tell us something?

Just as the fall of Jerusalem gives clarity to the preterist viewpoint, certain other historical events seem to confirm a historicist perspective. In fact, after Edward Gibbon wrote *The History of the Decline and Fall of the Roman Empire* in the late 1700s, some historicists used it as a companion piece to the Book of Revelation and came up with some rather spectacular comparisons.

Churchistory: An Intersection of Major Concepts

The historicists are the ones who viewed the seven churches as representing seven periods of church history, each bearing characteristics of the original churches. Ephesus is a type of church during the apostolic age. Smyrna is tied to the age of church persecution through about 313 C.E. Pergamus is associated with a compromised church period up until about 500 C.E. Thyatira is viewed as the time of the papacy up until the Reformation. Sardis represents the Reformation age. Philadelphia is connected to the period of increased evangelism and missions. And the Laodicean church is typed to the liberal churches of the present (see Chapter 4, "Seven Churches Get a Performance Review").

An offshoot of the historicist interpretation of Revelation is what is sometimes referred to as the "year for a day principle." The reasoning is that Revelation contains literal information regarding periods of time, but these are disguised in symbolism wherein a day is actually a year. This symbolism was played out by the prophet Ezekiel. He was instructed to lie on his right side for 390 days and then on his left for 40 as part of a prophecy related to Israel and Judah. Respectively, they received 390 years and 40 years of judgment (Ezekiel 4:4–8).

For a long while, historicists thought they were on to something. In the early sixth century, Andreas of Cappadocia had produced a highly regarded Greek commentary. In it he blended the views of a handful of predominant theologians, added some of his own, and included historical interpretations as well as allegorical. This historicist viewpoint of Revelation began to solidify in the 1100s, and by the 1500s had become quite a popular outlook among the Protestant reformers. That's because the "beast" in Revelation 13 was commonly interpreted to be the papacy of the Roman church.

Clanging Symbols

When the Book of Revelation is viewed as a roadmap of sorts for human history, it is tempting to leap to conclusions about the significance of many of its symbols. And indeed, one of the most common complaints about historicism is that different interpreters reach vastly different conclusions.

If it seems the preterist perspective was a little harsh toward the Jewish people, the historicist viewpoint was even more so in regard to the Catholic Church. Few would argue that the church had gone through some terribly low periods during the Middle Ages, but for a while this single point threatened to become the standard by which one's entire religious outlook was measured. If one person believed there was an association between the Catholic Church and the beast in Revelation, and someone else didn't, they hardly needed to discuss other religious matters. If the two couldn't come to terms on this Revelation issue, one wouldn't trust anything else the other had to say. As mentioned in Chapter 16, "Open to Interpretation?" it was in reaction to this antipapacy element of historicism that two Jesuits developed what were the roots of the futurist and preterist views.

A number of prominent people were in the historicist camp. Martin Luther was one, of course. But so were John Wesley, John Wycliffe, William Tyndale, John Calvin, John Knox, Isaac Newton, Charles Finney, C.H. Spurgeon, and numerous others.

Historicism also yielded a few interesting predictions of future events. For example, Robert Fleming accurately predicted the decline of the influence of the Roman church in Europe about 100 years prior to the events. He stated that it would start in 1794, which correlates with the reign of terror of the French Revolution, and it would be completed by around 1848, which was the year that the papacy was forced to leave Rome.

Apoca-Lips Now

"The immutability of God appears in its most perfect beauty when viewed against the mutability of men. In God no change is possible; in men change is impossible to escape. Neither the man is fixed nor his world, and he and it are in constant flux."

—A.W. Tozer

Flashback

Critics of historicism point back to the initial portions of Revelation with its clear address to the seven churches (Revelation 1:11). The geographic location of these seven churches is in *Asia*. Historicists, however, have traditionally tended to limit their interpretations to *European* history, with little if any consideration of what was going on in Asia.

Historicism Loses Ground

As more time (and history) passed, however, this particular interpretation of Revelation began to lose much of its appeal. A number of reasons led to its decline. (We can't quite say demise, because a few contemporary groups still hold to variations of the historicist perspective.) For one, historicists seemed unable to reach a consensus over the significance of many of Revelation's symbols. One person would say one thing, and someone else would promote something else. And, of course, it was usually pretty tough to *prove* one right and the other wrong.

You can understand the difficulty. Let's say it's the happy-go-lucky period of the early 1920s. The Great War is over. The stock market is strong. People are singing "Yes We Have No Bananas" and dancing with abandon. Life is good. Maybe in history we've even reached the Millennium portion of Revelation. It seems the worst is behind us and the future is bright. But fast forward 20 years. After a devastating market crash and subsequent Great Depression, humankind finds itself in yet another World War. Historicist interpreters of Revelation would have to rapidly reconsider biblical significance in light of historical reality.

In addition, the historicist viewpoint was criticized for being too limited in scope. If you wanted to, and if you put a little thought into it, you could probably create a reasonable interpretation of Revelation based entirely on your life and connected to key events that you have personally experienced. Perhaps you've had periods of intense suffering that could relate to some of the biblical prophecies. You may know a "beast" and/or false prophet who tend to make your life miserable. And you may be working toward a retirement that is worry free and spectacularly happy. Some of your life experiences and/or plans are almost certain to jibe with a few symbolic passages if you stretch things a bit. So does that mean the Book of Revelation was written personally for *you?* Let's hope not.

Yet it's this kind of thinking that generates criticism about the historicist interpretation. No matter who's doing the interpreting, the results are almost always too uncertain to be satisfying. If Revelation indeed leads up to the end of humankind as we know it, essentially any local and specific historical application is likely to be shortsighted.

Apoca-Lips Now

"Men spend their lives in anticipations, in determining to be vastly happy at some period or another, when they have time. But the present time has one advantage over every other: it is our time."

—Charles Caleb Colton

Can't You Tell Symbolism When You See It? (Idealism)

While historicists may be accused of trying too hard to tie the writings in the Book of Revelation to specific historic events, the group known as idealists is sometimes accused of not trying hard enough.

Depending on which resources you consult, the idealist approach to Revelation may also be referred to as the allegorical approach, the spiritual approach, the nonliteral approach, or a number of other titles. But whatever you want to call this perspective, the thinking is that the Book of Revelation doesn't match up with human history; it transcends human history.

A Bright Spot

Those with an idealist approach to the Book of Revelation don't look for literal tragedies to come crashing into their future. It's bad enough that Revelation symbolizes the *spiritual* struggles we must endure. But idealists aren't expecting a literal time with all the grand-scale, world-ending earthquakes, wars, cosmic dysfunction, and such described in the Book of Revelation.

Clanging Symbols

Some scholars have noted how easily the idealist/symbolic approach to Revelation blends with other interpretations. For example, the preterist and historicist interpretations, as we have seen, connect certain real-life events with writings in Revelation. The portions that don't exactly seem to match up, however, may be seen as symbolic, which is the idealist approach. So the idealist outlook, to varying extents, is sometimes incorporated into other interpretations.

Dating as early as the third or fourth centuries, the idealist interpretation suggests that few events described in Revelation should be considered literal. (Some people would hold that this is true of the entire Bible—not just the Book of Revelation.) But the reason Revelation is so symbolic, according to this way of thinking, is so each generation of the church can read it and take away something helpful.

If Revelation is perceived as more spiritual than literal, its details of warfare must then refer to *spiritual* warfare. So the beast could represent any evil force prevalent at any given time. The prostitute might be a once-good church that has turned away from God, a seductive secular world system, or some similar threat. The seals, trumpets, and bowls could tie into localized wars, earthquakes, famines, or other disasters. And yet under this approach we need not look too hard for specific correlations.

An overriding principle in Revelation is that good struggles against evil, yet wins out in the end. The idealist view of Revelation says to apply that basic truth as you wish, as it makes sense in your own time and circumstances. This interpretation is freed of trying to link specific symbols with specific events.

The idealists look at the successive events of the scrolls, trumpets, and bowls as recurring times of trouble that increase in intensity. Consistently throughout these times, true Christians increase in their faithfulness to God, while unbelievers grow more unrepentant and defiant.

On the other hand, critics of this approach point out that the stated purpose of Revelation is to reveal "what must soon take place" (Revelation 1:1). Readers are not intended to skim merrily through its pages, but rather "take to heart what is written in it, because the time is near" (1:3). If the message of Revelation is purely spiritual and not in the least literal, it has little to offer that other portions of Scripture haven't already covered.

One other criticism by certain positions is that the idealist approach to Revelation is too liberal. If we're being neither literal nor specific in application, it's easy to spiritualize most of the content to the point of disregarding certain truths that some people consider obvious and essential. While this may be true in cases, a defense can also be made that given the apocalyptic nature of the writing, a spiritual/idealist approach makes a lot of sense.

Other people don't agree. What a surprise!

Other Perspectives

Some people try to get really creative when it comes to the Book of Revelation. While we're on the topic, let's examine two ways of looking at Revelation that aren't so much interpretations of the work as much as *perspectives* on it, one of which is very much like the idealist approach.

Apoca-Lips Now

"Vision encompasses vast vistas outside the realm of the predictable, the safe, the expected."

—Charles Swindoll

The Play's the Thing? (The Dramatic Approach)

A somewhat unusual and imaginative way of viewing the Book of Revelation is by taking the dramatic approach. Somewhat similar to the idealist perspective that the entire book is primarily a symbolic presentation of grand concepts, the dramatic approach goes a bit further. Revelation is seen much like a Greek play, complete with acts and scenes, or even similar to the morality plays of the fifteenth century. The common perspective is that it consists of seven acts, each with seven scenes—the letters, the seals, the trumpets, the plagues, the rise and fall of Babylon, the millennium, and the new creation. (Still can't get away from those sevens!)

Morality plays focused on the struggle of humankind to find salvation. They portrayed the struggle of good and evil, and generally taught one or more specific virtues. The productions were simple and easily carried out under the most austere of circumstances.

Greek plays, on the other hand, were elaborate, carefully staged, and costly. They were often associated with the pagan religion of the day. The tragedies and comedies were written by poets and incorporated solo and choral singing as well as striking and very stylized dancing. There was a lot of graphic action and vivid color. Tragedies had very specific structures with the chorus breaking into song between scenes, very much like the singing that John witnessed in heaven.

Apoca-Lips Now

"For medieval people the stupendous drama of the Last Days was not a fantasy about some remote and indefinite future but a prophecy which was infallible and which at almost any given moment was felt to be on the point of fulfillment."

—Norman Cohn

What You Talkin' About, John? (The Literary-Analytical Approach)

Some people prefer to examine the Book of Revelation much as one would study a work of Shakespeare, with the focus more on the construction of the writing rather than its prophetic significance. This perspective, sometimes called the literary-analytical approach, casts some doubt on John's credentials as an inspired prophet of God. In fact, those with this outlook may be less likely to care *what* John said than to figure out *why* he said it. Their assumption is that Revelation is a compilation of important and fascinating information from a number of sources.

The reason the approach is called literary-analytical is because the goal is to identify each source and better understand its significance. Adherents of this view, therefore, might study Jewish background and culture to more fully explore John's Jewish references and sources. They also believe that Revelation contains a number of Egyptian, Babylonian, and other sources to ferret out and make sense of.

If one begins with the belief that Revelation is a cohesive collection of different sources, it is not such a matter of urgency to determine a single date of writing or even interpretation of prophecy. Satisfaction is achieved not so much by figuring out what John was predicting as much as where he was coming from. But like any other option, of course, adherents of the literary-analytical approach may vary a bit in their opinions and interests.

Apoca-Lips Now

"It's taken me all my life to understand that it is not necessary to understand everything."

—René-Jules-Gustave Coty

The Final Four

Most lists of various interpretations of the Book of Revelation don't include the literary-analytical approach or the dramatic approach. While some people may find fulfillment and even delight in pursuing these perspectives, they don't really lead to the same kind of results as other interpretations.

So when it comes down to the "big four" interpretations, we have ...

1. The preterist interpretation (as we saw in Chapter 17).
2. The historicist interpretation.
3. The idealist (symbolic) interpretation.
4. The futurist interpretation.

Apoca-Lips Now

"The following events will come to pass, as we have learned: Elijah shall come; the Jews shall believe; Antichrist shall persecute; Christ shall judge; the dead shall rise, the good and the wicked shall be separated; the world shall be burned and renewed. All these things, we believe, shall come to pass; but how or in what order, human understanding cannot perfectly teach us, but only the experience of the events themselves. My opinion, however, is that they will happen in the order in which I have related them."

—St. Augustine, early 400s

We'll get to the futurist outlook in Chapter 19. But as you can see, we've already covered quite a few ways of looking at the same body of material. It should already be clear that if three people begin a discussion of the Book of Revelation, and one happens to be a preterist, one a historicist, and the third an idealist, they aren't going to find a lot they can agree on.

But if you think we've already opened too many cans of worms, just wait. The futurist perspective will be an entire Can O' Worms Factory in itself!

The Least You Need to Know

➤ The historicist perspective is that Revelation follows an approximate time line between when it was written and the end of time.

➤ The idealist interpretation views Revelation as being almost entirely symbolic, with no direct tie-ins to any particular era of history.

➤ Other perspectives on Revelation—such as the literary-analytical and dramatic approaches—aren't considered by many to be legitimate interpretations of the work.

➤ The primary interpretations of Revelation have significant distinctions and offer little common ground.

Dispensationalism...
? Rapture... ?
Pretribulation... Amillennial...
? ?

Chapter 19

Back to the Future

In This Chapter

➤ Interpreting the Book of Revelation as still primarily in our future (the futurist view)

➤ A more literal interpretation of the symbols in Revelation

➤ A few (of several) issues that tend to divide futurists

➤ Some alternative views of how the Millennium relates to the prophesied second coming of Jesus

We're getting mighty close to the end of this book, and you may be wondering where all the weird, bizarre, and complicated interpretations of Revelation have gone. No offense to the preterists, historicists, and idealists, but their viewpoints were fairly easy to explain and were somewhat, shall we say, *unspectacular*. Where's all the action that was being suggested as we went through the Book of Revelation—all the teasers about future holocausts, cataclysms, blood-red moons, being raptured off the face of the earth, and all the other good stuff?

Welcome to the futurist interpretation of the Book of Revelation. It's going to be everything you've heard, and probably more. In fact, the dialogues and debates between various futurists are frequently as intense (if not more so) than the ones between futurists and those holding to one of the other interpretations we've already covered.

While the preterists look back into history attempting to identify the symbols in Revelation, and the historicists look at what's happening around them, the futurists ride the ship of time planted firmly on the prow, peering through binoculars toward what's ahead. In 1948, when Israel regained status as an official nation after centuries of being disbanded, many futurists began to suspect that the end-times clock was fast approaching midnight. From that point onward, if we can borrow a phrase from the profound Yogi Berra, "The future ain't what it used to be."

Anticipation, It's Making Me Wait

As we went through the Book of Revelation, chapter by chapter, the authors took something of a futurist outlook for a number of reasons:

1. The futurist interpretation is usually recognized (for now, at least) as the viewpoint held by the most people.

2. This interpretation requires more background and explanation than the others, and we hoped to give you something of a running start.

3. Most of the speculative and spectacular stories based on the Book of Revelation tend to build around a futurist line of thinking. If you want to be able to follow their plot lines, your eyes must be turned to the future rather than the past or present. Masses of people who know little if anything about Revelation assume it has *something* to do with the future.

Apoca-Lips Now

"The doctrine of the Second Coming is deeply uncongenial to the whole evolutionary or developmental character of modern thought. We have been taught to think of the world as something that grows slowly toward perfection, something that 'progresses' or 'evolves.' Christian Apocalyptic offers us no such hope. It does not even foretell ... a gradual decay. It foretells a sudden, violent end imposed from without; an extinguisher popped onto the candle, a brick flung at the gramophone, a curtain rung down on the play—'Halt!'"

—C.S. Lewis

In addition to these things, the futurist perspective takes a much more literal approach to the events in Revelation than most of the interpretations we've seen so far.

While it is next to impossible to avoid *some* symbolic consideration, futurists tend to take much more of Revelation at face value. A thousand years means a thousand years. The return of Jesus is a literal, bodily return. Resurrection, judgment, and other hard-to-comprehend events will take place exactly as Revelation says they will. Yet even after agreeing on many of these basic assumptions, futurists still come to a lot of different conclusions among themselves in regard to what the book is really trying to tell us.

Flashback

A number of prophecies from the Book of Zechariah are frequently cited to suggest that the end times are literal and future. Consider the following passages from Zechariah 14:

➤ Then the Lord will go out and fight against those nations, as he fights in the day of battle. On that day his feet will stand on the Mount of Olives, east of Jerusalem, and the Mount of Olives will be split in two from east to west, forming a great valley, with half of the mountain moving north and half moving south (vv. 3–4).

➤ On that day there will be no light, no cold or frost. It will be a unique day, without daytime or nighttime—a day known to the Lord. When evening comes, there will be light. On that day living water will flow out from Jerusalem, half to the eastern sea and half to the western sea, in summer and winter (vv. 6–8).

➤ This is the plague with which the Lord will strike all the nations that fought against Jerusalem: their flesh will rot while they are still standing on their feet, their eyes will rot in their sockets, and their tongues will rot in their mouths .... A similar plague will strike the horses and mules, the camels and donkeys, and all the animals in those camps (vv. 12–15).

Futurists suggest it is difficult to explain these passages (and numerous others) from any perspective other than expectation of a *future* fulfillment.

It's somewhat ironic that this futurist interpretation has become so widespread. It is believed that the concept was initiated in the sixteenth century when the historicist view was widely popular. Tired of hearing the papal system associated with the beast (Antichrist) of Revelation, a Spanish Jesuit began to teach that the Antichrist would not arise until the "last days." The Protestants of the time were outraged and vehemently opposed this teaching. But by the 1800s, certain Protestant theologians were beginning to incorporate this concept into their belief system. Poor Francisco Ribera, however, would have thought you mad if you had suggested in 1585 that his "new" and despised teaching would become the most accepted interpretation of Revelation in the early twenty-first century!

From a standpoint of intellectual debate, the futurists have it good. It's pretty easy to take potshots and attempt to poke holes in the scenarios presented by preterists and historicists, since we can look to the past to do so. But the reverse is much more difficult. How can someone refute something that hasn't happened yet?

Revelation: Both Sensational and Dispensational?

Keep in mind that this approach to the Book of Revelation will be primarily literal and chronological. Futurists see a clear outline of the entire book presented in Revelation 1:19: "Write, therefore, what you have seen, what is now and what will take place later." The first few verses of Revelation deal with the past ("what you have seen"). Most of the first three chapters speak of the present (or "what is now," from John's point of view). And according to futurists, everything from Revelation 4:1 and onward lies in John's (and our) future.

Clanging Symbols

The seven "dispensations" are defined as follows:

1. Innocence—From creation to the sin of Adam and Eve
2. Conscience—From humankind's expulsion from Eden to the flood
3. Human government—From the flood until the call of Abraham
4. Promise—From Abraham to the Mosaic law
5. Israel/law—From the giving of the law to the coming of Jesus
6. Church/grace—From the first coming of Jesus to the second coming
7. Kingdom—From Jesus' second coming onward

One popular perspective within the futurist camp is known as *dispensational futurism.* Not all futurists are also dispensationalists, but nearly all dispensationalists are futurists. A theological "dispensation" is a religious system or code considered to be divinely revealed. Dispensationalism is credited to John Darby, a leader in the Plymouth Brethren movement during the 1800s. The approach was popularized with the release of the Scofield Reference Bible, which was the first Bible to combine text and commentary. Dispensationalism was also taught in the Bible schools (institutes) of the time. As many prominent seminaries were being accused of not upholding biblical doctrine, more churches turned to the Bible institutes to supply ministers.

New generations of such Bible scholars still believe history can be divided into seven separate dispensations, beginning with creation and concluding with final judgment. These dispensations show how God gradually revealed more and more of himself to his people. This is called progressive revelation.

Think of a loving parent with a brand new baby. As the child grows and matures, the parent relates to him or her in different ways. Pampering works well with newborns, but not so much with teenagers. And no parents interact with an adult child the same way they do with an infant (because those diaper changes can get awfully messy). The maturity of the child has much to do with the parent's approach. If the child responds to one method of motivation, the parent is likely to continue it. But if the child fails to respond after a number of attempts, the parent might take a different approach. This change in style says nothing about the love of the parent, even though one approach might appear more severe than another. From the point of view of the parent, "tough love" is still love, and may be deemed necessary in extreme cases when children become defiant to the point of potentially hurting themselves.

Similarly, as humankind has grown and changed since creation, dispensationalists see various ways God has related to his "children." To suggest that *God* changes is a major heresy in church circles, yet dispensationalists note that it appears he has chosen different ways to interact with humankind throughout our history—not because he changes, but perhaps because *we* do.

Flashback

We have previously cited 1 Thessalonians 4:15–17 as a reference for the so-called "rapture" of Christians. Another clue to its suddenness is found in 1 Corinthians 15:51–53: "Listen, I tell you a mystery: We will not all sleep [die], but we will all be changed—in a flash, in the twinkling of an eye, at the last trumpet. For the trumpet will sound, the dead will be raised imperishable, and we will be changed. For the perishable must clothe itself with the imperishable, and the mortal with immortality."

Here's One Way of Looking at It ...

Some people expect the next big event—the one unmistakable clue that "the end is near"—to be the rapture of the church. This is the scenario traditionally portrayed by Christian fiction writers and the event referenced in those bumper stickers: "In case of rapture, this car will be unmanned."

To be honest, most of us probably know a few Christians we wouldn't mind seeing get an express ticket to heaven. But assuming a full-scale rapture might indeed be on the horizon, a common expectation is that the mass exit of Christians from the world will create more confusion than glee. Worst-case scenarios of a sudden *poof* of Christians predict planes plummeting from the skies as pilots disappear, governments shaken, the remaining populations scrambling for land and assets, and so forth. (Approximately two billion people currently identify themselves as "Christian." Both Africa and Asia now have more Christians than North America, so the effect would be worldwide.)

Clanging Symbols

Lampstands represent churches in Revelation 1 (vv. 12, 20). John first sees them on his island hideaway, but later he sees seven lamps before the throne of God (4:5). Some people see in this symbolism the rapture of the church from earth to heaven.

Flashback

Some people see a foretelling of the rapture in the teachings of Jesus: "No one knows about that day or hour, not even the angels in heaven, nor the Son, but only the Father. As it was in the days of Noah, so it will be at the coming of the Son of Man. For in the days before the flood, people were eating and drinking, marrying and giving in marriage, up to the day Noah entered the ark; and they knew nothing about what would happen until the flood came and took them all away. That is how it will be at the coming of the Son of Man. Two men will be in the field; one will be taken and the other left. Two women will be grinding with a hand mill; one will be taken and the other left. Therefore keep watch, because you do not know on what day your Lord will come" (Matthew 24:36–42).

Those who align themselves with this way of thinking point out that early in the Book of Revelation, John received an invitation to "Come up here" (Revelation 4:1). They suggest that this command will be extended to the entire church to get the ball rolling on end-times events. If so, say many futurists, most of Revelation deals with humankind *after* Christians have been removed from the pack.

But if this is the case, say the critics of dispensational futurism (as well as other groups of futurists), the Book of Revelation is a waste of ink. If its purpose is to address and encourage Christians, why go to such detail about events they won't ever experience?

Gone Today, Here Tomorrow

As a popular hypothesis continues, after the Christians disappear the world would be ripe for a strong and charismatic leader to bring order and peace, all the while gathering personal power and prestige. Before long, however, the dark side of this figure would come to the fore, and the world would be under the reign of the Antichrist.

Flashback

"Know and understand this: From the issuing of the decree to restore and rebuild Jerusalem until the Anointed One, the ruler, comes, there will be seven 'sevens,' and sixty-two 'sevens.' ... After the sixty-two 'sevens,' the Anointed One will be cut off and will have nothing. The people of the ruler who will come will destroy the city and the sanctuary. The end will come like a flood: War will continue until the end, and desolations have been decreed. He will confirm a covenant with many for one 'seven.' In the middle of the 'seven' he will put an end to sacrifice and offering. And on a wing of the temple, he will set up an abomination that causes desolation, until the end that is decreed is poured out on him" (Daniel 9:25–27).

People who at first willingly offer this leader their loyalty soon are *forced* to do so. This is the onset of the great tribulation—the suffering, martyrdom, wars, famine, mark of the beast, natural disturbances, and all the rest. This is where we get back to those time periods presented in the Book of Revelation (and other places in Scripture). Futurists expect the great tribulation to be a period of seven years, in two equal segments of three and a half years each (or 42 months, or 1,260 days, or "a time and times and half a time"). A literal translation of various portions of Revelation determines this time period, as well as the Old Testament writings of Daniel.

Biblical support for a seven-year tribulation is frequently taken from Daniel 9:20–27. Daniel writes of 70 "weeks" (or sets) of "sevens." These are generally interpreted to be "weeks of years." A total of 69 "sevens" is supposed to pass between a decree okaying the rebuilding of Jerusalem and the coming of "the Anointed One" (the Messiah). Here's how some of the futurists do the math:

> 69 "sevens" (weeks of years) = 69 × 7 × 360 (days in a biblical year) = 173,880 days
>
> 173,880 days = 476.38 of our calendar years
>
> King Artaxerxes signs the decree to rebuild Jerusalem 444 B.C.E.
>
> 444 B.C.E. + 476 years = 33 C.E. (because there was no year 0)
>
> Jesus rides into Jerusalem to be crucified 33 C.E.

If we translate a 360-day year that Daniel would have been familiar with into our own 365-day calendar years, and assume that Daniel's 69 "sevens" were 69 weeks of years, then the decree to rebuild Jerusalem until the "cutting off" of Jesus' life was exactly the length of time Daniel predicted. This degree of logic and precision (or perhaps you'd call it "fudging the figures") may be too much for some people to buy into, but it typifies the futurist determination to interpret signs literally whenever possible.

Continuing this train of thought, Daniel was told that a total of 70 "sevens" was decreed "for your people and your holy city" (Daniel 9:24). But since the church age came right on the heels of Jesus' death, it's as if God hit the pause button on his countdown stopwatch at the end of week #69. As long as the church is around, the Gentiles are prominent, so the countdown is still on hold.

But suppose all the Christians were to suddenly disappear due to, say, a rapture into the heavens. Once that stopwatch clicks again, the time remaining is a single "week of years"—or a seven-year period. Many futurists, and especially dispensational futurists, express strong opinions that the Jewish temple will be rebuilt and worship services restored—at least for a portion of the time. They expect the literal Antichrist to commit a literal "abomination that causes desolation" in the literal temple about halfway through the final, literal seven-year period (Daniel 9:27).

Apoca-Lips Now

"The future is called 'perhaps,' which is the only possible thing to call the future. And the only important thing is not to allow that to scare you."

—Tennessee Williams

Flashback

When the Apostle Paul writes of "the coming of our Lord Jesus Christ and our being gathered to him," he predicts the rise of a "man of lawlessness" who is "doomed to destruction." Among his offenses, this figure (whom many interpret to be the Antichrist) "will oppose and will exalt himself over everything that is called God or is worshiped, so that he sets himself up in God's temple, proclaiming himself to be God" (2 Thessalonians 2:1–4).

If Paul is indeed looking into our future, he sees a temple that isn't currently there, so one would have to be constructed between now and then. This is yet another sign many futurists are looking for.

According to some lines of thinking, the two witnesses (Revelation 11:3–14) will appear during the first three and a half years. After they are killed and then rise from the dead, the worst part of the great tribulation (the second three and a half years) will commence.

Good News, Bad News for Jews (So What's New?)

Many futurist interpretations also attempt to provide an (admittedly Christian) explanation for how God might fulfill his Old Testament promises to Abraham, Moses, and the Israelites. If indeed the Christians were to disappear, the church age would end and a new segment of the population would arise as spiritual leaders. Since God has "sealed" 12,000 people from each of the 12 tribes to be protected throughout the tribulation, it seems that he has the Jews clearly in mind (Revelation 7:4–8). In addition, the two heaven-sent witnesses will be presenting a message of truth during this time of great deceit, and who knows how many they will influence during three and a half years of unstoppable ministry? Such a group—even though a minority of

Apoca-Lips Now

"Some religions do not regard our sojourn on earth as true life .... Judaism, on the contrary, teaches that what a man does now and here with holy intent is no less important, no less true ... than life in the world to come."

—Martin Buber

the population—will demonstrate righteousness and offer the opportunity for others to repent and restore their relationship with God.

Christians are sometimes guilty of glibly suggesting that, in a spiritual sense, "Dad [God] likes me better." How must contemporary Jews feel when Christians parade around, accusing them of killing their Messiah and suggesting that their final chance for repentance and restitution is during the great tribulation? *Oy, vey!*

This is not the intention of all futurists, even though some people seem to go to such extremes. But in spite of a few tactless and insensitive Christians, the futurist interpretation of Revelation has a better outcome for the Jews than some of the other interpretations. It is a common conviction of nearly all futurists that God will conclude his business with the Jewish people independent of his interaction with the Christians. His promises are ironclad, and no Antichrist, tribulation, or end of the world is going to prevent him from doing everything he said he would do for his people as he spoke through the lips of numerous Old Testament prophets.

Under some of the preterist viewpoints, the "second coming" of Jesus in 70 C.E. was a visitation of judgment rather than a physical return. Instead of seeing better days of peace and prosperity (as prophesied), the Jews were left much worse off than before. In contrast, many futurists believe that the rapture of the church will zap away all the Christians and conclude what is biblically referred to as "the times of the Gentiles."

A Bright Spot

Many futurists believe the tribulation will be followed immediately by Jesus' 1,000-year reign on earth. If this turns out to be the case, it is expected to be the brightest spot in Jewish history (ironically, from a Christian perspective). The Christian futurists believe this will be the fulfillment of everything the Jewish people have been anticipating for centuries.

The Jews once more will enjoy favored nation status with God. After God pours out his wrath on those who oppose him, he will fulfill every promise made to his faithful people. He will reward perseverance, faithfulness, and righteousness.

Still, the Christian perspective that this future deliverer/Messiah will be Jesus is not a popular concept among contemporary Jews. Even if all the Christians are gone during this period, and the Jewish people are placing their faith in God, this is still the great tribulation—the time so many people who oppose the beast are being martyred. It's expected to be the worst persecution ever known, which is saying a lot—especially if most of the ones persecuted during those days are Jews.

But this time the length of their suffering and struggling will be limited. The great tribulation, as bad as it will be, will last but seven years. For those who endure it, however, the kingdom that follows is 1,000 years … and after that, there's heaven!

What in the Millennium Is Going On Here?

If the natural disasters described in the seals, the trumpets, and the bowl judgments are interpreted literally, the world as a whole is going to be suffering. It's just that those who resist the Antichrist will have additional problems to deal with. While those believers are hiding out or suffering the consequences, this is the period when the armies of the world are gathering for the big war of Armageddon. And according to certain futurist interpretations, this is when Jesus will return to put an end to all the evil nonsense.

At the end of the final "week" as described in Daniel, Jesus comes again, judges the dead, tosses the Antichrist and false prophet alive into the lake of burning sulfur, and confines Satan. Then, for the next 1,000 years, Jesus rules over an earthly kingdom of peace and prosperity. At the end of that thousand years, Satan is released, makes one final defiant act of resistance to God, fails, and is then banished to the fiery lake forever. The earthly kingdom is replaced with new heavens, new earth, and a new Jerusalem. Sin has been abolished and resurrected humankind is able to live in God's presence for eternity.

Essentially, that's the way events are laid out in the Book of Revelation, and certain futurists have no problem going along with the plan as presented. But as we're about to see, few things concerning the Book of Revelation end up being as simple as we hope them to be.

Even if it is agreed that the rapture, the second coming of Jesus, and the millennium will all be literal events, there are still a number of ways to interpret how they will come to pass. Futurists disagree about the chronological order of these events.

Flashback

Those who anticipate a pretribulation rapture frequently cite a defense from the Book of Revelation itself. In the letters to the churches, Jesus told the congregation in Philadelphia, "Since you have kept my command to endure patiently, I will also keep you from the hour of trial that is going to come upon the whole world to test those who live on the earth" (Revelation 3:10). Some see this as a promise that the church will not have to go through the great tribulation along with the rest of the world.

Premillennialism

The previous scenario of end-times events has presented what is commonly referred to as a premillennial position. The "pre" prefix indicates the expectation that Jesus' second coming will occur *prior to* the 1,000-year Millennium.

To further complicate things, you have a choice of when you think the rapture will take place in regard to the tribulation. The opinion that Christians will disappear before any of the serious occurrences of the great tribulation begin is known as the pretribulation rapture view. The mid-tribulation rapture perspective assumes a seven-year tribulation, with the rapture taking place at the three-and-a-half-year midpoint. And the posttribulation rapture assumes Christians will undergo the full force of the entire tribulation, be raptured, and then return immediately with Jesus for the Millennial Kingdom.

Postmillennialism

Dispensational premillennialists get the Christians out of the way first and then have Jesus return for a Jewish-oriented religious/political kingdom for a thousand years. Not surprisingly, postmillennialism has an opposite order. The postmillennialists consider Jesus' *first* coming to be the foundation of the messianic kingdom.

A Bright Spot

Postmillennialists feel the other views of the future are dark and grim. In contrast, they anticipate the world getting better and better, and point to improvements that have already been accomplished—abolition of slavery in many parts of the world, advances in medicine and technology, more concern for the earth and human rights, and so on. Although evil is still with us, it can be diminished as people actively oppose it. If the world keeps moving in this direction, it will eventually be much more the world that God intended it to be in the first place.

Postmillennialists believe that Jesus came, among other reasons, to teach disciples and leave them to carry on after he was gone. Such people consider the follow-up to Jesus' ministry to be the "reign of Christ"—more of a spiritual kingdom than a physical one. During this time period, the world is supposedly becoming a better place, even though it's taking millennia to do so. Spiritual improvements are expected to initiate God's material blessings as well, and eventually fulfill the Old Testament prophecies of a better world. And when he determines the time is right, Jesus will close out this phase of history by returning visibly, at which time he will take care of resurrection, final judgment, and the ushering in of his eternal, heavenly kingdom.

Amillennialism

A less literal, more symbolic approach to the Millennium is provided by amillennialism. This approach tends to see the church as a continuation of God's righteous Old Testament people, so the promises made to Israel are bestowed on Christianity. Since Jesus has come, in a sense Satan is now "bound" because the message of the gospel is being preached throughout the world. Christ rules over his people, but does so in a spiritual sense.

So by this way of thinking, the 1,000-year kingdom period doesn't literally exist. But in contrast to the postmillennialists, the amillennialists believe the world is going to get worse instead of better. It will eventually deteriorate, allowing for the extensive spread of evil, the great tribulation, and a literal Antichrist. After this happens, Jesus will return to resurrect and judge everyone, and will establish his eternal kingdom (which some believe will be heavenly, and others think will be located on a new and refurbished earth).

A Rubik's Cube of Options!

It's not just the futurists who debate the merits and potential drawbacks of premillennialism, postmillennialism, and amillennialism. Preterist interpretations of Revelation can have similar variations. And while the labels help end-times aficionados place themselves into categories that most of *them* understand, all the prefixes can be quite confusing for those of us without a lot of theological background.

We have options as to how the rapture relates to the tribulation. We have options as to how the return of Jesus relates to the Millennium. We have options as to whether we believe these things are essentially literal or figurative. So even after going through this book and having the information fresh on your mind, it can be quite a struggle to differentiate between a postmillennial preterist, an amillennial historicist, a pretribulation premillennial futurist, or any number of other combinations. If the names confuse you more than help you understand, ignore them. Simply be aware that these categories exist, and that some people proudly wave the banners of these labels (usually symbolically rather than literally).

And even the banner wavers aren't always so pure in their views! When examined closely, an argument put forth under a specific label will often have elements of several views intertwined throughout.

One More Issue to Get Crypt Up On

Another key factor that distinguishes certain futurists from the other interpretations is their take on resurrection. A number of people who are inclined to pursue a preterist interpretation of end times continue to struggle with the biblical teaching about bodily resurrection. If most (or all) of the events of the end times are past, the final resurrection of the dead requires more of a spiritualized approach than some people are willing to agree to. And other views seem to consider "the resurrection" as a single event.

Futurists, on the other hand, frequently perceive the resurrection of the dead to take place in a number of stages:

1. Jesus (1 Corinthians 15:20–23)—We have already noted that Jesus was the "firstfruits" of those who have died and come back to life. He is "the firstborn from among the dead" (Colossians 1:18).

2. "Many holy people" (Matthew 27:52–53)—Immediately after the crucifixion of Jesus, a number of known-to-be-dead people came back to life and were seen wandering around Jerusalem.

3. The rapture of the church (1 Thessalonians 4:13–17)—All Christians, dead and alive, are "caught up together … to meet the Lord in the air."

4. The two witnesses of Revelation (Revelation 11:3–12)—As we have seen, the world will be looking on as these two recently deceased figures jolt back to life and go "up to heaven in a cloud."

5. Those who become Christians during the great tribulation (Revelation 7:13–14; 20:4)—This group is portrayed a number of times in Revelation, wearing white robes and worshiping before the throne in heaven.

6. Old Testament saints (Daniel 12:1–2)—Daniel was told of a future resurrection of "your people," both righteous and evil, connected with "a time of distress such as has not happened from the beginning of nations until then."

7. Everyone who is left (Revelation 20:11–15)—If, as it seems, all the righteous people are resurrected first, the only ones left to stand before the great white throne in heaven are those who will be condemned rather than rewarded.

So for futurists, resurrection seems to be a *series* of uprisings at different strategic times rather than a one-time, get-it-over-with event. This isn't to suggest that

Apoca-Lips Now

"Christianity is in its very essence a resurrection religion. The concept of the resurrection lies at its heart. If you remove it, Christianity is destroyed."

—John R. Stott

there are exactly seven specific resurrections, but rather a number of different segments of people whom the Bible says will be resurrected. Some of the previous resurrections may well take place at the same time, though certainly *some* of them will be independent of all the others from a futurist perspective.

Scripture includes all but the final one in what it terms the "first resurrection" (Revelation 20:6). Whenever and however it happens, being resurrected in order to be rewarded by God is a good thing. But those who miss out on that series of reward-oriented resurrections have only the second resurrection and the second death to look forward to. Given the choice, they would avoid resurrection altogether. But according to the Book of Revelation, they aren't given the choice.

Apoca-Lips Now

"The apostolic church thought more about the Second Coming of Jesus Christ than about death and heaven. The early Christians were looking, not for a cleft in the ground called a grave but for a cleavage in the sky called Glory."

—Alexander MacLaren

Authors' Disclaimers

As we have repeatedly said up to this point, it is no small matter to clearly present all the various interpretations of the Book of Revelation. If some people feel their preferred interpretation hasn't been completely represented in the past few chapters, they should take comfort in the fact that those of other persuasions are likely to feel the same way.

Each of the interpretations has a number of adherents, and a number of strong points. Each also has its difficulties in sufficiently explaining certain points of the Revelation text. We have simply taken a look at the broadest, most widespread teachings of each outlook. We could not speculate, as some do, as to all the geographic, biographic, and other aspects of what might be represented by the horns on the beast/Antichrist's head, the reference to Gog and Magog, and numerous other references. For those wishing to pursue any of these things, numerous other resources are available from various perspectives, many of which are included in the appendixes.

Perhaps you haven't found Part 4 of this book, "Theology Meets Optometry," at all helpful. It can certainly be confusing to toss all these possible interpretations into the hopper and try to come up with anything that makes sense. Then again, when you look at the variations one at a time, perhaps they *all* make sense to you, even though they contradict one another.

But don't despair. In Chapter 20, "Putting the Elation Back in Revelation," we'll try to highlight a few things we can know for sure about the Book of Revelation.

The Least You Need to Know

➤ The futurist interpretation of Revelation is more literal and usually more chronological than most other interpretations. This is especially true of dispensational futurists.

➤ Futurists are subdivided into smaller groups, largely due to different understandings of how the second coming of Jesus relates to the Millennium.

➤ A literal tribulation is expected, lasting (by most accounts) seven years.

➤ Futurists generally expect all God's promises to the Jews to be fulfilled, as well as his promises to the church.

Chapter 20

Putting the Elation Back in Revelation

In This Chapter

➤ Why end-times topics are likely to continue to be popular

➤ A few clear lessons among the symbols and confusion of Revelation

➤ Revelation offers hope for everyone, not just the holy rollers of the world

➤ How to respond in light of all we've learned

Sometimes when you take a trip or go on vacation, the pace is such that you don't seem to enjoy it as much as you might like. There's always more to see and do than time allows. So you rush from site to site, cramming as much vacation as you can into the one or two weeks you have. It's only after you get home, sit down with a bowl of popcorn, look at the pictures, and reminisce that you really have time to begin to appreciate many of the terrific sights you've seen.

Perhaps you'll have a similar experience as you reflect on the Book of Revelation. We've taken quite a whirlwind tour—first just to get through the book, and then to whip through a number of popular interpretations. It may have been too much too quickly, creating information overload. But now that you've been immersed in such a wide array of possibilities, maybe you'll go back from time to time and continue to struggle with the symbolism and interpretations until Revelation makes sense to you—a little sense, at least.

When you go to a movie for the first time, you may not catch every piece of action or every phrase of witty dialogue. But when you rent the movie later on video and watch it at home, you pick up on a lot of the details you missed the first time. Similarly, if you come back to Revelation again after reading more of the Bible, you're sure to have a better understanding since you'll be familiar with more of the context.

At this point, however, you may still feel a bit lost and confused about much of Revelation, and that's okay. It's a perfectly normal response considering the depth of the material. But it will be our goal in this chapter to send you away with a few conclusions you can be certain about.

Clanging Symbols

People respond to symbolism in different ways. Some are passionate about it; others resist it with all their being. If you are in the former category, we hope these "Clanging Symbols" sidebars have been helpful. If you're in the latter, we hope they have at least been tolerable. And take heart, because this is the last one!

Flashback

Do you feel at all encouraged about what you've read in Revelation? Many times when the Apostle Paul was writing about the events of the last days, he would add a challenge: "Therefore encourage each other with these words" (1 Thessalonians 4:18; 5:11).

Why Bother?

Interest in the contents of the Book of Revelation, as well as the overall buzz about the future and the end of the world, is likely to be with us until, well, the end of the world. This only makes sense, for a number of reasons.

Revelation is, after all, part of the Bible. For believers, it's just as much Holy Scripture as the gospels about Jesus or Paul's letters that provide the groundwork for most of Christianity's basic doctrines. The fact that Revelation is a bit harder to understand makes it only that much more of a challenge for this group of people.

In addition to the Christian segment of the population, most of the rest have *some* degree of curiosity about the future and how the world might end. Poets, pundits, environmentalists, investment brokers, and numerous other groups look for insight wherever they can get it. The Book of Revelation will continue to be an enlightening and fascinating work even for those who don't perceive it to be a divinely inspired vision of things to come.

Some people theorize that one explanation for the recent popularity of fiction about the end times is because it is "acceptable" horror. Some moms forbid their kids to read Stephen King or Clive Barker, but who's going to disparage Bible-related reading (even if many of the scenes are just as graphic)? The popularity of the horror genre, along with its limited acceptance by Christian and family-oriented markets, may drive the interest in end-times fiction for a while. The Book of Revelation is scary, so the fiction it inspires should continue to sell.

For these and other reasons, various groups of people will continue to read and reread the Book of Revelation, considering various interpretations and looking for insight to get them beyond their initial state of confusion. You're ahead of the pack now, because you've seen exactly what Revelation has to say—even though you're probably still a bit unclear about some parts.

What Do You Know?

While bits and pieces of Revelation are certain to remain obscure, we should not fixate on those segments to the exclusion of what we *can* see clearly. In spite of the symbols, secrets, past-vs.-future controversies, and all the rest, the Book of Revelation contains a wealth of information that shines through all the murky portions. So let's review a few of those points. (You no doubt have your own list of discoveries by this point, which you can add to the following items.)

Keep in mind that the Book of Revelation is addressed to the church, so it isn't surprising that many of the lessons are spiritual. Yet there are other things that speak to a broader reading audience as well.

Apoca-Lips Now

"It ain't those parts of the Bible that I can't understand that bother me, it is the parts that I do understand."

—Mark Twain

The Age-Old Conflict Between Good and Evil Will Continue to the End

Even the interpretations of Revelation that suggest the world will continue to get better do not deny the presence of sin and evil. Various interpretations suggest the scales may tip in one way or the other—whether toward goodness and nobility, or continued degradation—but the tension will last right up to the final moments of life on earth.

No Matter How Grim the Situation Gets, Good Will Triumph

So sin and evil remain strong and powerful, and at times it may even seem useless to resist. If you can't beat 'em, join 'em! Right?

Wrong. Or, so says the Book of Revelation. Sin and evil may indeed win a lot of battles along the way, but they are fighting a losing war. Ultimately, they will fall to the forces of good. Believers reading Revelation prefer to uppercase the G, remove an o, and boldly proclaim that *God* (rather than *good*) will triumph. But regardless of one's spiritual status, the message of Revelation is that sin and evil will someday be done away with—forever and ever.

People Have Choices

When we consider that Revelation was addressed to a bunch of churches, and that it contained such a stark portrayal of things to occur, we see the book as more than simply a peek into the future. The original purpose of the Book of Revelation was to motivate believers to keep making good decisions. They were beginning to experience some relatively intense persecution, and their faith was beginning to waver.

Yet the first-century church was called to make hard choices, and people throughout the centuries have been motivated to choose—one way or the other—after an encounter with the Book of Revelation. Our choices are sometimes very clear, even though much of Revelation remains a mystery to us.

Apoca-Lips Now

"There is a proverb, 'As you have made your bed, so you must lie in it,' which is simply a lie. If I have made my bed uncomfortable, I will make it again."

—G.K. Chesterton

Choices Have Results—Sometimes Eternal Ones

When it gets to the point where everyday occurrences such as buying and selling require a special mark (as in Revelation 13:16–17), who could blame someone for going along with the crowd? What's the big deal?

We rationalize similar decisions every day. We may not necessarily agree with every statement that comes out of our mouths, or with every action we take. Most of us choose to compromise ourselves from time to time due to simple expediency. We say and do whatever it takes to get someone off our backs or get what we want.

Apoca-Lips Now

"When you have to make a choice and don't make it, that is in itself a choice."

—William James

Taken to extremes, however, such as the scenario portrayed in the Book of Revelation, even such logical and expedient choices can become spiritual deal breakers. After casting one's loyalty to the Antichrist—to the point of wearing his label—there's no going back. When Jesus returns, it's too late to change teams. Revelation presents fair warning that our everyday choices of how to interact with God and others may indeed have lasting, eternal consequences.

God Is More Patient Than We Give Him Credit For

Finally, the Book of Revelation provides much insight about God. Is God apathetic, slow to respond, or maybe not even there, as many people attest? Otherwise, he must be infinitely more patient than any of us can comprehend.

Aha! That's exactly the point.

One of the messages of Revelation is that God is indeed slow to anger, waiting and withholding judgment for reasons of his own. Grace and mercy are such rare traits these days that many of us don't even recognize them in the Lord of the Universe. But Christians will attest that hundreds of misguided, messed-up human beings get their acts together every day, and turn their lives around—all because God isn't in a rush to enact his final judgment.

Much of the world is scoffing in derision, not believing for a second that God is alive, aware, or alert. Others cling to God with steadfast faith, yet whine that he isn't acting on their behalf. According to Revelation, all God has to do is hand off a scroll and all the complaints and contempt will end in a short matter of time. But when he does, that's it. No more appeals. No more mercy. No more time. Most of us should be immensely thankful that God doesn't respond immediately to all of our prayers and desires.

Flashback

In a close encounter with Moses, God says of himself that he is a "compassionate and gracious God, slow to anger, abounding in love and faithfulness, maintaining love to thousands, and forgiving wickedness, rebellion and sin" (Exodus 34:6–7).

We Who Are About to Screw Up Salute You!

So these are somewhat spiritual lessons for those who peruse the pages of Revelation. Some are no doubt a bit too churchy for certain readers, and not specific enough for others who take Revelation quite seriously. We saw a number of bright spots as we went through the Book of Revelation, and many people hold those promises dear to their hearts. But the point is that no one should feel left out. If you think God is addressing only the perfect people in this final book of the Bible, you're not looking closely enough.

Think back to the seven churches that were addressed to begin with and ask yourself, why *seven?*

A Bright Spot

We tend to assume that what we don't know about God is probably terrible and terrifying stuff. However, many of Scripture's peeks behind the heavenly curtain describe quite amazing and optimistic encounters with God and/or his messengers.

A couple of those churches were doing very well, thank you. They were steadfast, dedicated, and strong. Why didn't Jesus simply write to those churches that had their spiritual acts together, warning them of things to come and promising them pie in the sky when they die?

Apoca-Lips Now

"God's revelation does not need the light of human genius, the polish and strength of human culture, the brilliancy of human thought, the force of human brains to adorn or enforce it. But it does demand the simplicity, docility, humility, and faith of a child's heart."

—E.M. Bounds

Flashback

Some of those who think they have God all figured out may be quite surprised with the eternal, heavenly structure and those in attendance. One of the common themes of Jesus' teaching was, "Many who are first will be last, and many who are last will be first" (Matthew 19:30 [for one example]).

But no. The Book of Revelation also went out to the church in Ephesus—a group of people who had lost their first love. It went out to Pergamum, where certain church members were both spiritually and sexually promiscuous. It went out to Laodicea, where the spiritual thermometer never showed hot or cold, but only lukewarm.

Revelation may have been addressed to a number of churches, yet its message certainly isn't directed to the goody-goody perfect people of the world. The Book of Revelation isn't a secret message to alert a lot of holier-than-thou people to get ready. It's an open book telling *all* of us to get ready—the lowlier-than-thous, the more-doubtful-than-thous, the unlikelier-than-thous, and all the rest. It doesn't cast aspersions on its readers or rule anyone out who is sincere in faith and seeking eternal truths. In that respect, it's an amazing work.

Stuffy Christians may sometimes give the impression that others aren't worthy of their God. But one of the clear lessons of Revelation is that *no one* is worthy of receiving all God is offering. Still, we see that he welcomes a lot of those undeserving people into his heaven. That final invitation at the end of Revelation 22 (v. 17) seems to suggest that he is eager to increase the population of heaven to include anyone and everyone who wishes to be there.

Revelationmania vs. Revelationphobia

While we're thinking about the churches to whom Revelation was addressed, it's a good time to consider what *our* response should be now that we've had an introduction to end-times events. Much of the world is polarized as to the amount of time they devote to end-times teachings. A significant percentage of them give the Book of Revelation and other prophecies a cursory glance, find them hard to comprehend, and ignore them ever after. Another significant percentage of people seems to contract Last Days Fever, dwelling on those portions of Scripture to the exclusion of everything else. Both of these extremes, though common, can be harmful.

If we ask ourselves *why* Jesus gave this message to the churches, we find a lot of middle ground between panic and apathy. Clearly, he didn't expect Christians to simply ignore this message, because he went to great lengths to provide it. But neither did he suggest they should desert the rest of the world, go climb a mountain, and wait for him in some exclusive and spiritually superior Shangri-la. Instead, he gave rather specific instructions: take care of the problems in your churches, regain your first love, address the heresy that has infiltrated the congregation, get your priorities straight, and either fish for men or cut bait.

Jesus' instructions to the churches, taken as a whole, indicate a regular, ongoing, rather normal day-to-day life. We ought not skip over the complexities of Revelation, because it's really good stuff. But neither should we obsess over it. Perhaps we can make the most of life if we learn to keep a countdown clock ticking in the back of our minds without getting psyched out over the events to come.

Chapter 21, "Epilogue: Biding Your Time, or Timing Your Goodbye?" deals with what can happen when Revelationmania gets out of hand. And if Revelationphobia were a problem, you never would have gotten this far in this *Complete Idiot's Guide*. So perhaps a relevant question at this point is, "Now that you've read all the way through Revelation and considered most of the traditional interpretations, how do you want to respond?"

Now What?

Just as some people read great works of fiction to learn more about the human condition and gain more insight into the complexities of human interactions, others glean similar insights from Revelation. After an encounter with the Book of Revelation, some people have been driven to their knees to "get right with God." Some have been driven to their desks to create heart-wrenching poetry or best-selling novels. Some have been driven to

Apoca-Lips Now

"Today is, for all that we know, the opportunity and occasion of our lives. On what we do or say today may depend the success and completeness of our entire life struggle. It is for us, therefore, to use every moment of today as if our very eternity were dependent on its words and deeds."

—Henry Clay Trumbell

Apoca-Lips Now

"Sometimes those of us who hold that the Lord Jesus Christ is coming again are spoken of as pessimists. I think it can be truly said that we are really the only ones who have any right to be optimistic."

—William Culbertson

artist studios to paint spectacular depictions of how they envision the images described. And some have no doubt been driven to a therapist's office for professional counseling.

Of course, many other people see in Revelation a perfect opportunity to procrastinate. If its message is primarily relevant to the end times, and if the end times aren't bearing down on us right now, well, there's still time to catch another episode of *Who Wants to Be a Millionaire?* Eternity, by definition, will still be there after dinner and a nap. We can think about it then.

However you decide to respond to Revelation—now or later, big or small, public or private—at least you need not respond in fear.

If you learn nothing else from this book, may you always remember that Revelation was written as a "heads up" for spiritually conscientious people. It is not a literary sword of Damocles hanging at the end of the Bible, just waiting to fall on some unsuspecting sucker without warning.

The Book of Revelation, when properly understood and respected, can serve as spiritual embers—like the coals beneath a raging fire that has died down. When spiritual passion wanes and the events of this life have left us emotionally cold, stirring the embers of Revelation can get the fire going again. It reminds us of the inevitability of suffering, but keeps it in its proper context by also reminding us of God's love and power, the certainty of heaven, an expectation of future justice, and an eternity of perfect newness.

According to some people, the heavenly trumpet could sound today and signal a quick end to the world as we know it. According to others, the world might grind merrily on for thousands of years or more. Who is right? Only time will tell.

In the meantime, those who leave God out of the equation aren't going to put much stock in what Revelation has to say in the first place. In contrast, many who read Revelation and want to take him up on his offer are looking forward to much better times ahead.

But in the event that the end of the world comes sooner rather than later, now that you've read the Book of Revelation, at least you can't say you haven't been warned.

The Least You Need to Know

➤ In spite of all the symbolism in Revelation, several truths come through clearly.

➤ A knowledge of Revelation can be useful, because speculation about the future is likely to always be a popular topic of discussion.

➤ The Book of Revelation is especially helpful for believers, yet addresses others as well.

➤ The information in Revelation should motivate people to lead better daily lives, not to ignore the present in lieu of the future.

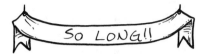

Chapter 21

Epilogue: Biding Your Time, or Timing Your Goodbye?

In This Chapter

➤ The Peoples Temple and Heaven's Gate tragedies

➤ End-time predictions through the ages

➤ A few rules of thumb when dealing with prophecy

Like the minister who, after preaching for an hour, winds down by saying "and in conclusion" four times before he's really done, we're back with just one more chapter. We promise, this is really the end this time! (Unless, of course, you count the appendixes and other helpful material that follows …) Anyway, while we've provided a lot of guidance through the Book of Revelation, we thought it would be a good idea to offer a little bit of caution, too.

In this chapter, we're going to look at some extreme lines of reasoning and the individuals and groups associated with them. We're doing this for two reasons.

First, we'll provide examples of those who have gone off the deep end of the end times. This will give you an idea of what to watch out for when consulting other sources as you continue to read and think about Revelation. Even Jesus warned, "Watch out that no one deceives you. For many will come in my name, claiming, 'I am the Christ,' and will deceive many" (Matthew 24:4–5).

Second, we also will provide some parameters you can use to guide your own thinking of Revelation and help you stay in the bounds of reason and the true intent of the book. It's been said that a little knowledge is a dangerous thing. When it comes to Revelation, this can be true when its message is stretched well beyond its original meanings.

When Faith Becomes Fantastic (and Fatal) Fanaticism

If you own a PC, you probably know at least one person who could be labeled a "quasi-geek." Such people are always talking about the latest computer gadget and offering to help you with any PC troubles you may have. They come over, fiddle around with your PC for several minutes, and say "I know just enough to be dangerous"—just as your monitor goes blank and a little puff of white smoke ascends from the CPU. "Oops," the quasi-geek mutters as he slinks out the door. "I must have miscalculated."

Apoca-Lips Now

"Experience is a costly school, yet some learn no other way."

—Benjamin Franklin

When it comes to eschatology—beliefs or doctrines concerning the end of the world or of humankind—there are lots of quasi-geeks running around who love to make all kinds of predictions and promises. But when it comes to "putting up or shutting up," they usually change their stories or disappear, in one way or another.

You can probably name a few of these people. Some have attained notoriety by not merely developing an extreme end-times philosophy, but turning it into a following that met with a tragic end.

Let's start by looking at two groups where an apparent fascination with future things became twisted and went tragically awry: the Peoples Temple and the Heaven's Gate cult.

Mr. Jones and Me Look into the Future

In 1952, Jim Jones began his ministry career as a student minister in a Methodist church, but soon left the church because it refused to allow blacks to attend. Sometime later, Jones established the Peoples Temple in Indianapolis, Indiana. He preached a social gospel and followed through by providing numerous outreach programs to the poor through the church. In 1965, Jones, his wife, and his followers moved to California. They were in search of a safe haven in the event of a nuclear attack. Again, the ministry was very active in providing outreach to help the needy.

Good Reason to Follow

The shared values of the members of Peoples Temple included a belief in racial justice, the need for redistribution of wealth, and the vital importance of working toward making the world a better place. The group was composed of people of many races and all ages, from all walks of life.

In 1974, a small group from the Peoples Temple went to Guyana, where they established a compound in the jungle. This was known as the Peoples Temple Agricultural Project and, subsequently, Jonestown. By 1977, most of the Peoples Temple followers were relocating to Jonestown, and within a year only a few members remained in California.

Apoca-Lips Now

"Evil is that which God does not will."

—Emil Brunner

A Shift of Emphasis

Mixed in with the social gospel message of Jim Jones was a more sinister message wrapped around the end times and the apocalypse. Further, Jones began to view himself as a God or Christ figure, and even had his adherents refer to him as Dad or Father. He preached that a horrible period of war, suffering, and nuclear holocaust was coming. To be ready for the end, it was necessary to separate from the rest of the world and work to bring about a Utopia on earth, a new Jerusalem of sorts.

On November 18, 1978, U.S. Congressman Leo Ryan visited Jonestown accompanied by media and others who were critical of the ministry. The visit was anything but friendly. Ryan succeeded in convincing a few adherents to leave Jonestown. As Ryan and the others were waiting to board a plane at the Port Kaituma airstrip in Guyana, they were attacked by men sent by Jones. Ryan and three others were killed.

Apoca-Lips Now

"Most people are other people. Their thoughts are someone else's opinions, their lives a mimicry, their passions a quotation."

—Oscar Wilde

Misled to Death

It seems that the Peoples Temple members perceived this visit by Ryan and the others as an attack from their enemies. The perception extended to the feeling that they were about to be invaded and their freedom taken away.

To prevent outsiders from "taking their lives," Jones persuaded his followers to "lay down their lives" and to "cross over to the other side" by committing suicide. That day, about 900 men, women, and children died, either by drinking Kool-Aid laced with cyanide and other drugs or by being killed by other members.

While the message that Jones preached was not *exclusively* related to the end-times, a significant part of it kept people's minds focused on the future. But instead of tempering the message with reason and true spirituality, Jones ignited a firestorm of irrational fear and paranoia. The end was going to come to the Peoples Temple, even if they had to bring it on themselves. If they couldn't create Utopia on earth, then they would leave the earth and find Utopia in death.

As long as Jim Jones focused on present social and political concerns, his accomplishments were mostly beneficial. But when his focus shifted to the future, the scenario he created for his followers was not at all accurate. And he definitely crossed the line when he said he was the Christ. If his followers had been truly familiar with the Bible, they would have seen a huge red warning flag telling them to walk away.

Flashback

Jesus warned: "If anyone says to you, 'Look, here is the Christ!' or, 'There he is!' do not believe it. For false Christs and false prophets will appear and perform great signs and miracles to deceive even the elect—if that were possible. See, I have told you ahead of time" (Matthew 24:23–25).

Gateway to Heaven?

Okay, you're pretty sure you'll never get suckered into joining a suicide cult that lives in a jungle. Good. But there are other groups out there who dress similar beliefs in clothes of a different style. In one case, they wore black clothes and matching running shoes and they came to an end in a mansion.

On March 26, 1997, 39 people died by suicide. They were members of a cult called Heaven's Gate. Their beliefs were a wild mixture of conspiracy theories, biblical end-times doctrines, science fiction, and more. Another crucial element, concern over a "one-world government," is part of many end-times scenarios. Heaven's Gate also incorporated UFOs and comets into its strange mix of beliefs.

Apoca-Lips Now

"Errors to be dangerous must have a great deal of truth mingled with them. It is only from this alliance that they can ever obtain an extensive circulation."

—Sydney Smith

The founders were Marshall Applewhite and his platonic friend, Bonnie Lu Nettles. Nettles was a nurse whom Applewhite met while in the hospital for heart problems. Applewhite, according to his sister, had a near-death experience in the hospital. As a result, Nettles told him that he "could be used mightily" in a group she knew about. She began visiting him regularly. They changed their names, first to Bo and Peep, and later to Ti and Do. The group became the seedbed for Heaven's Gate.

Their common interests included the occult, the apocalypse, UFOs, and more. Eventually, they concocted some really weird ideas about themselves and the world. They believed there was a place called The Evolutionary Level Above Human (TELAH) and that they were possessed by a TELAH alien. Applewhite further believed that this alien had also possessed Christ.

The message that this TELAH alien brought was that a gateway to the Next Level was now open to humans who wanted to cross over. In addition, he said, TELAH was actually another galaxy, more commonly known as heaven. Thus, the name for the cult, Heaven's Gate.

The Two and Their Spaceship

Do and Ti began traveling around the country spreading their otherworldly gospel. They would refer to themselves as "The Two" and claim they were the two witnesses cited in Revelation. Unlike the biblical two witnesses, however, after dying and coming back, Do and Ti planned to be picked up by a spaceship.

Despite their strange claims, they had some sort of spellbinding charisma that entranced people who came to hear them speak. Many followers reported that they thought their ideas were a bit odd, but still found Do and Ti somehow irresistible and compelling.

The group soon grew to around a thousand adherents. Most who joined had abandoned spouses, children, jobs, relatives, and possessions hoping to get a ride on the mother ship that was supposed to arrive in 1975. When it didn't show, hundreds of followers left the group. The remaining members faded from view, but hung together.

A significant part of their teaching involved erasing their humanity and individuality. They abhorred sex and sexuality. They wore unisex clothes and had similar short haircuts. They ate the same foods at the same times and shared the same thoughts and the same opinions. They even took on similar-sounding names that all ended with "ody" (Brnody, Yrrody). This was all part of becoming worthy to move to the true kingdom of God, or the Next Level.

They believed the earth was about to be destroyed and recreated. Much of their philosophy was laced with biblical references that were bent to refer to aliens and spaceships. Instead of a resurrection, there would be a "transformation."

Delusion Goes High-Tech

The group set up a Web design business and spent a lot of time learning the technology of the Internet. This provided income and served as a good distraction from

247

human drives and concerns. Do (Nettles) died in 1985 from cancer. This forced Ti (Applewhite) to reconfigure his teachings about The Two. The members took these changes in stride and maintained their watch for a sign.

In 1996, Chuck Shramek, an amateur astronomer, took a photo of the approaching Hale-Bopp comet. The comet had been discovered in 1995 by Alan Hale and Thomas Bopp. It was estimated to be a thousand times brighter than Haley's comet. Further, rumors had begun to pop up that something seemed to be following the comet. This was Shramek's claim—that his photo showed a large glowing object following behind Hale-Bopp.

Apoca-Lips Now

"Every absurdity has a champion to defend it, for error is always talkative."

—Oliver Goldsmith

Heaven's Gate members presumed this mysterious object to be their long-awaited spacecraft. It was coming to take them home to TELAH. The plan began to form. At the comet's closest proximity to earth between March 21 and 26, each member would shed his or her "container" (what they called their bodies). The TELAH alien inhabiting each would then escort their spirits to the mother ship.

Very much like those from the Peoples Temple, Heaven's Gate members drank a poisonous mixture. Instead of cyanide and Kool-Aid, they chose pheno-barbital and vodka. The group actually died in shifts, with some members helping others die, covering their bodies with triangular purple shrouds.

Wrong Gate, but Too Late

Again, had those who were drawn into this group been more familiar with the Book of Revelation and the rest of the Bible, they would have known that the teachings were way out of line. Individuality is not something God asks anyone to give up. In fact, he is the one who is credited with creating each of us with our own unique characteristics. Further, androgyny is not in any way endorsed by Scripture. Rather, the Bible encourages healthy sexuality and monogamous married relationships among men and women. And those are only a few of the glaring errors with Heaven's Gate thinking.

How were people attracted by such absurdities? Probably partially out of misguided fear and anxiety over the end times and a desire to not be left behind.

Predicting the Future on a Date-to-Date Basis

Jonestown and Heaven's Gate are rather extreme examples. There are others involving attempts to set specific dates for the last days that frequently tend to be more amusing than tragic. Yet they can still lead to harmful results and create undue confusion and doubt.

One day the Disciples asked Jesus when the future things he had predicted were going to happen. They wanted to put it down on their calendar. Jesus answered them very clearly, saying "It is not for you to know the times or dates the Father has set by his own authority" (Acts 1:7).

As you've discovered, Jesus did provide some valuable information as to how they, and we, could know when the last days were approaching. But more important, he also added that the end would come "as a thief in the night," when it was least expected, and we were to "be ready" at any time.

But some people simply aren't content with biding their time until God decides to act. They dwell on prophecy and Scripture, desperately seeking clues and trying to determine a timetable. You can't really put them in the same category as Jim Jones and Marshall Applewhite. But based on their track records, you might want to exert a bit of caution whenever specific dates are mentioned.

Apoca-Lips Now

"The fool has his answer on the edge of his tongue."

—Arabian proverb

Some people might suggest Jesus had meant that just the *disciples* weren't on a need-to-know basis. Or that while we aren't supposed to *just know* the dates and times, maybe we're supposed to try to figure it out.

Doug Clark: Jumpin' Jupiter, the World's Gonna End, Eh!

In 1974, two astrophysicists published a speculative work titled *The Jupiter Effect*. The authors, Stephen Plagemann and John Gribbin, *speculated* that an incongruity in the alignment of certain planets *might* generate tidal effects on the sun causing sunspots. This could *possibly* create further effects that could impact earth's atmosphere to the point that its rotation could *possibly* change, which, *if* that occurred, *could* put undue pressure on the earth's plates and generate earthquakes and other disastrous things. It just so happened that in 1982, all nine planets were supposed to line up.

Even though Plagemann and Gribbin clearly stated that there were "enormous uncertainties" contained in their theories, the public and the prognosticators took the Jupiter Effect to be an absolute. Earthquakes and more were going to happen. This was the end for sure.

Doug Clark, a Canadian teacher of prophecy, leveraged the Jupiter Effect to effectively promote him into the prophetic limelight. In 1976, he began to warn that millions would perish in earthquakes on both the east and west coasts. He urged his listeners to move inland, sell off assets, and keep money out of banks in low-lying areas. He was certain that 1982 would be the year of the rapture and the beginning of the tribulation. Either he was wrong, or a lot of us missed it.

Still, after 1982, he retained a significant following and was even given his own TV show on TBN (Trinity Broadcasting Network) headed by Jan and Paul Crouch called *Shockwaves to Armageddon*. He wrote a book titled *Final Shockwaves to Armageddon* that placed the new kickoff date for the end times in 1988. In 1989, he admitted he had miscalculated and said he wouldn't specify dates anymore. A few weeks later he was back on TBN predicting that World War III would occur in three years and confirming that the tribulation would begin before 2000.

Perhaps Clark should have turned his prophetic skills to his own affairs. It was determined that a side business he ran booking Holy Land trips was a fraud and a warrant was issued for his arrest. Clark fled in 1990 and eluded capture until 1995, when he was discovered in Toronto. He was extradited to the United States, tried and convicted of mail fraud, and went to prison until 1997. No one can predict if he will surface again.

Edgar Whisenant: Rapture Report for Year (Fill in Blank)

Edgar Whisenant retired from his engineering job with NASA and decided to go into prophecy. He wrote two books which were published in 1988 that became his ticket to his 15 minutes of fame. The books, *88 Reasons Why the Rapture Could Be in 1988* and *On Borrowed Time* were clearly written by an engineer, containing a huge assortment of cross-referenced calculations. But people still got the bottom line of his message that sometime between September 11–13, 1988, the rapture would happen and tribulation would begin.

He was absolutely certain about his predictions, claiming that they were wrong only if the Bible was in error. While many dismissed his claims out of hand, he found a few significant supporters.

Jan and Paul Crouch, the heads of TBN, who had supported Doug Clark, also endorsed Whisenant. On the dates he had specified, they even aired instructions for those unbelievers who would be left behind, explaining what to do when loved ones vanished and the tribulation kicked in.

Apoca-Lips Now

"He who wants to know people should study their excuses."

—Friedrich Hebbel

Whisenant's books sold so fast bookstores had a hard time keeping them in stock. Millions of copies were sold and hundreds of thousands were given away to ministers of all denominations.

September 11, 12, and 13 came and went in 1988 with no sign of a rapture or tribulation. No sweat. Whisenant recalculated his calculations and designated September 15 as the date. Then he claimed it was October 3. And then it was clear that it was only a few more weeks.

Oh, hold your horsemen! The Gregorian Calendar threw him off! The end was really coming in 1989, which he explained in a new book, *The Final Shout—Rapture Report 1989!* That was followed by Rapture Report 1990, then 1991, then 1992, and … well, you get the idea.

Harold Camping: Still Ready After All These Years

Harold Camping founded Family Radio and later made a name for himself in the area of prophecy. In 1992, he published a best-selling book titled *1994?* in which he pinpointed September 6, 1994, as the end. Only a year later he published another book, *Are You Ready?* which continued to promote his 1994 deadline for humanity.

He claimed that over his 30 years of studying the Bible he had seen things others had missed. He was positively certain of the date as it was based on what he perceived to be clear evidence in Scripture that allowed for precise calculations.

On September 7, 1994, Camping admitted that he had made a teensy-weensy little error in his precise calculations. The end would come closer to mid September. Then September 29. Then October 2. Then March 31, 1995.

Apoca-Lips Now

"Dishonesty is a scorpion that will sting itself to death."

—Percy Bysshe Shelley

Jack Van Impe: Pushing Back the Deadline

Jack Van Impe made his prophecy debut around 1975 when he published a newsletter with the questions, "Messiah 1975? The Tribulation 1976?" as a headline. He later set dates of 1988 and 1992. In 1995 he made a video that implied the Millennium would begin shortly after 2000. Then, in a book published in 1996, *2001: On the Edge of Eternity,* he pushed the end date back to 2012.

Many Christians object to Impe's reliance on non-biblical occult sources for much of the supporting data for his predictions. He has cited psychics and claimed Nostradamus was a great student of the Bible. However, the Bible clearly forbids followers of God from consulting with anyone or anything related to the occult (Deuteronomy 18:8).

Apoca-Lips Now

"God is the God of promise. He keeps his word, even when that seems impossible; even when the circumstances seem to point to the opposite."

—Colin Urquhart

Hal Lindsey: In a Class of His Own

Hal Lindsey is a really nice guy who has written some very intriguing, best-selling books. These include *The Late Great Planet Earth* (1970), *Satan Is Alive and Well on Planet Earth* (1972), and *The 1980s: Countdown to Armageddon* (1981).

Lindsey believes that the "fig tree" Jesus refers to in Matthew 24:32–33 represents Israel: "Now learn this lesson from the fig tree: As soon as its twigs get tender and its leaves come out, you know that summer is near. Even so, when you see all these things, you know that it is near, right at the door. I tell you the truth, this generation will certainly not pass away until all these things have happened. Heaven and earth will pass away, but my words will never pass away."

He further assumes that "generation" literally means a 40-year biblical generation. (Others suggest that a "generation" could also mean "the whole race," which would render the verse to mean something like "the whole race of Jews will not pass away before these things happen.")

Finally, he asserts that the reestablishment of Israel in 1948 represents the fig tree's leaves coming out. This then led to the prediction that within 40 years or so of 1948, "all these things" would happen. This meant that 1988 would be the end, with the rapture happening seven years earlier in 1981, prior to the tribulation. This formula was also included in his book *The 1980s: Countdown to Armageddon.*

So how has he maintained his credibility? A big difference between Lindsey and the others mentioned in this chapter is that Lindsey tends to avoid actually providing dates. He lays out his reasoning and the evidence, and expresses some strong opinions, yet then leaves it up to his readers to reach their own conclusions.

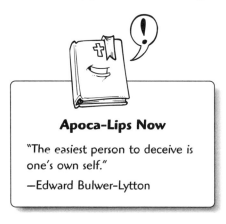

Apoca-Lips Now

"The easiest person to deceive is one's own self."

—Edward Bulwer-Lytton

Since nothing happened in the '80s, Lindsey revised his findings. Instead of 1948, he decided 1967 was a more compelling date based on his reevaluation of Daniel and events involving Israel.

Lindsey continues to write books and attract followers. And to his credit, he is largely responsible for generating mass interest in biblical end-times events. Prior to his writing *The Late Great Planet Earth*, much of society was apathetic and/or confused to the point of ignoring Revelation and related topics. But he made such things approachable, if not fascinating, for his generation and those who followed.

Some Day My Prince of Peace Will Come

If you think that end-times date-setting and bizarre speculations are only recent in nature, you would be wrong. Predicting the unpredictable has been a favorite pastime of people for centuries. Here's a short list of a few predictions predating the examples we've covered so far. The chart lists the year, the originator, and the nature of each prediction.

Year	Who	What
c. 100 C.E.	Clement	God's kingdom was coming "soon and suddenly"
c. 100 C.E.	Ignatius	Wrote that the end "was upon us"
c. 400 C.E.	St. Martin of Tours	Taught that the Antichrist was already born
1000	People in Europe	Most believed the end would come at the turn of their century (Y1K?)
1260	Joachim of Fiore	Proclaimed that the Antichrist would rise in 1260 followed by the end of the world
1533	Melchoir Hoffman	Jesus would come in 1533
1697	Cotton Mather	Predicted the end would come in 1697, then 1716, then 1736
1908	Lee Spangler	Declared the day the world will end with fire
1936	Herbert W. Armstrong	Said the depression will continue until 1936 when the Day of the Lord would come
1938	Orson Welles	Perhaps previous "prophets" led to his fictional broadcast of the "War of the Worlds" being taken as reality
1954	Charles Laughead	Announced that December 20, 1954, would be the last day

We could go on, but we think you've probably gotten the idea by now. Trying to predict the date and time of the end is a fool's game. History has consistently proven wrong everyone who has tried. So if someone tells you he or she knows exactly when the end is going to be, or knows someone else who knows, be on the alert.

Biding our time does not preclude us from being able to be prepared for what lies ahead. As we've seen, the Bible offers plenty of insight as to what we can expect, no matter when it comes to pass. We know, in the end, it's all good!

A Few Rules of Thumb

Discernment regarding prophecies is important. In most instances it's pretty simple to figure out the legitimate from the bogus. It's just a matter of examining what's being presented and determining how it lines up with reputable sources.

But sometimes it can get a little tricky. So the following guidelines we're providing are all based on Scripture. The Bible provides several clear benchmarks for discerning when a message, philosophy, prophecy, or lifestyle is of God or not.

Check the Source

In 1 John 4:1–3, we read:

> Dear friends, do not believe every spirit, but test the spirits to see whether they are from God, because many false prophets have gone out into the world. This is how you can recognize the Spirit of God: Every spirit that acknowledges that Jesus Christ has come in the flesh is from God, but every spirit that does not acknowledge Jesus is not from God. This is the spirit of the antichrist, which you have heard is coming and even now is already in the world.

Whether you believe Jesus is divine is your business. But if a "prophet of God" denies that Jesus Christ was born a man and is the Son of God, he or she is not a biblical prophet. You might want to watch out for such people.

Check the Track Record

In Matthew 7:15–20, Jesus bluntly declared the following:

> Watch out for false prophets. They come to you in sheep's clothing, but inwardly they are ferocious wolves. By their fruit you will recognize them. Do people pick grapes from thornbushes, or figs from thistles? Likewise every good tree bears good fruit, but a bad tree bears bad fruit. A good tree cannot bear bad fruit, and a bad tree cannot bear good fruit. Every tree that does not bear good fruit is cut down and thrown into the fire. Thus, by their fruit you will recognize them. Not everyone who says to me, 'Lord, Lord,' will enter the kingdom of heaven, but only he who does the will of my Father who is in heaven.

By "fruits" Jesus means: What have these people produced? How have they behaved? What have they accomplished? Is their focus on helping and serving others, or are they interested only in attention, lining their own pockets, or asserting their authority?

Essentially, look beyond their sales pitch and determine their character and reputation. If they're not walking in the truth, you should walk away.

Check the Doctrine

In 2 Peter 2:1–3, we read:

> But there were also false prophets among the people, just as there will be false teachers among you. They will secretly introduce destructive heresies, even denying the sovereign Lord who bought them—bringing swift destruction on

themselves. Many will follow their shameful ways and will bring the way of truth into disrepute. In their greed these teachers will exploit you with stories they have made up. Their condemnation has long been hanging over them, and their destruction has not been sleeping.

Jones, Applewhite, and others added "doctrine" that was of their own making and was not based on Scripture. Any "prophecy" or line of reasoning that contradicts Scripture, yet is said to be from God, is a lie. God will never contradict himself.

Any individual or group that says they have discovered a different path to God, such as spaceships or suicide, are terribly misguided. Jesus stated, "I am the way and the truth and the life. No one comes to the Father except through me" (John 14:6). The Jesus we have seen in Revelation backs up this bold claim. Yet we are never expected to give up free will, personality, or individuality in the process.

Check the Numbers

Remember what Jesus told his own disciples? He said very plainly, "It is not for you to know the times or dates the Father has set by his own authority" (Acts 1:7).

He also said, "No one knows about that day or hour, not even the angels in heaven, nor the Son, but only the Father" (Matthew 24:36).

How much clearer could he be? Any man or woman who assigns specific numbers to any of the end-times events is wrong. Jesus made it clear that no one but God knows, and God has not yet made the information public knowledge.

Remain Open to Truth

If after applying the previous standards it appears that a message is legitimate, then treat that person with measured respect. But keep your ears open and never hesitate to question something that sounds a bit off.

In 1 Thessalonians 5:9–22, the Apostle Paul instructed, "Do not put out the Spirit's fire; do not treat prophecies with contempt. Test everything. Hold on to the good. Avoid every kind of evil."

That's good advice!

So don't be fooled. No doubt people will continue guessing, speculating, and assigning specific times for end-times events. Ignore them, and bide your time. One of the clear lessons of Revelation is that God is operating on his timetable, not ours.

And speaking of our time, it's up. We hope you've found this book helpful.

A Bright Spot

Hey! You reached the end of this book with time to spare. Congratulations!

The Least You Need to Know

➤ False prophets can present even the most absurd ideas in a compelling and lucid manner.

➤ If any significant element of someone's teaching clearly contradicts what is taught in the Bible, then all of that person's teaching is suspect.

➤ If someone starts naming specific dates and times that end-times events will take place, you can be certain that person is wrong.

➤ When you encounter a "prophetic" teaching, don't hesitate to question and test its validity. If it's truly "from God" it will line up with God's Word, the Bible.

Interpretation Methods

Futurist View

The initiation of the futurist view is credited to a Spanish Jesuit priest, Francisco Ribera, who developed it as a defense against the historicist views of the Reformers who strongly identified the papacy with the Antichrist.

Characteristics: Refers to the prophetic and apocalyptic elements of Scriptures primarily to an "end time" when all of the events will come to pass. Most of it is still future to us, as it was to those living in biblical times.

Pros: This view allows for a more literal interpretation of the symbols eliminating the need for much conjecture.

Cons: With so much of the Book of Revelation pushed into the future, it would have had little impact on the intended audience of the first-century church.

Historicist View

Martin Luther and the other Reformers were strong advocates of this view.

Characteristics: Sees the apocalyptic as pertaining to events which were still future at the time they were described (for instance, the biblical period) but which have since occurred or are occurring within the life span of the church.

Pros: The view places the message of Revelation in the context of unfolding history, and on many points appears to line up well.

Cons: Those who hold this view fail to agree on which historical events are being represented by the descriptions in Revelation.

Idealist (Symbolic) View

William Milligan, a theologian in the 1800s, is cited by some as a primary proponent and popularizer of the idealist view.

Characteristics: The symbols or events described will not come to pass at some specific point in history, but represent timeless truths concerning the reality of human existence throughout time. Revelation serves as an imaginative inspiration of sorts to encourage suffering Christians to endure to the end.

Pros: Allows for all of Revelation to serve as a source of inspiration and encouragement without getting bound up in specific dates and events.

Cons: With virtually no constraints on how the book is interpreted, the door is left open for very poetic but biblically divergent results.

Preterist View

The initiation of the preterist view is credited to a Jesuit scholar, Luiz de Alcazar, who like his contemporary Francisco Ribera developed the view to deflect the prevailing view that named the papacy as the Antichrist.

Characteristics: Sees the fulfillment of the apocalyptic taking place roughly contemporaneously with the scriptural account of it. Thus the last times would already have arrived when the Scripture writer described them, or shortly thereafter.

Pros: Taking a more literally historical view, the preterists emphasize the importance of relating the book to the times of the author and its original audience.

Cons: This view tends to provide a more subdued hope for Christians. It also places a great deal of importance on Matthew 24:34 which says "this generation will certainly not pass away until all these things have happened." Preterists assume this literally means a 40-year biblical period. However, *generation* could also mean "the whole race." So the verse could also be interpreted to mean "the whole race of Jews will not pass away before these things happen."

Dramatic View

This view is rare and is largely an extreme version of the Idealist view. It takes the book of Revelation merely as a great poem or drama containing the overarching theme of good over evil and the triumph of the church. This view would place Revelation among other literary works such as the *Iliad* and the *Odyssey*.

Literary-Analytical (Critical) View

Another very rare view, this approach believes that Revelation is actually composed from a variety of sources and seeks to identify and analyze those sources. Its focus is on detailed analysis of the source texts and not on other elements.

Millennial Views

The millennium refers to the thousand-year reign of Christ mentioned in Revelation 20. Opinions vary, however, as to whether this period is a literal, approximate, or symbolic period of time.

Amillennial View

Characteristics: There will be no 1,000-year reign of Christ on earth.

The two resurrections mentioned in Revelations 20 occur close together; the first is spiritual, the second is physical.

There will not be a worldwide experience of righteousness, but the world will not necessarily grow more sinful.

The coming of Christ is imminent and could occur at any moment. (Imminence refers to the belief that the return of Christ can and will occur at any time without any other prophetical or historical prerequisites needing to be fulfilled.)

Pros: Recognizes the heavy symbolism of prophetic writings in the Bible which can avoid arbitrary interpretations.

Tends to apply serious exegesis (the act of applying hermeneutics, or the critical analysis of the text) and detailed scrutiny to the Scriptures resulting in a variety of plausible and scholarly meanings.

It recognizes historical trends allowing for the world's improvement or degeneration with neither one conditional to Christ's return.

Cons: The concept of two different resurrections cited in Revelation 20 does not necessarily hold up to rigorous translation.

It can create an ambiguous attitude toward evangelization and missions.

Comments: The 1,000-year reign of Christ is symbolic of perfection or completion. Rather than a literal reign, it represents the fulfillment of Christ's victory over Satan and the glory of heaven for the redeemed.

When it comes to biblical prophecy, the amillennialist generally does not look for actual future fulfillment. Prophecies are viewed as either having relevance only for the time in which they originated or as symbolic or conceptual commentary on current conditions.

Postmillennial View

Characteristics: The kingdom of God is a present reality as the rule of Jesus in our hearts.

All nations will be converted through a supernatural act of the Holy Spirit before Christ's return.

There will be a long period (millennium) of worldwide peace of uncertain duration, but Christ will not be physically present on earth.

The prevalence of God's kingdom will grow gradually leading up to the millennium.

Near the end of the millennium, evil will flare up and rule through the Antichrist.

The millennium will end with the bodily return of Jesus.

At the same time all will be resurrected to judgment and assigned to heaven or hell.

Pros: Emphasizes the present kingdom that exists in the hearts of men who accept Jesus.

Emphasizes activism and encourages believers to be involved in their communities and beyond.

Promotes an optimistic outlook even for our present times.

Points to the reality that the kingdom of God extends beyond the walls of the church.

Cons: The view of the kingdom of God spreading gradually and making the world better and better belies the reality that just the opposite is occurring.

It also neglects Scripture that indicates a worsening of the world in the end times: "Then you will be handed over to be persecuted and put to death, and you will be hated by all nations because of me. At that time many will turn away from the faith and will betray and hate each other, and many false prophets will appear and deceive many people. Because of the increase of wickedness, the love of most will grow cold …" (Matthew 24:9–12).

The emphasis on the kingdom's presence now and its spread through human endeavor tends to minimize the supernatural and can even blur the lines between good and evil. The argument could be made that any agency doing some good is supporting the kingdom, despite that the same agency may be doing many things contradictory to Scripture. In the 1930s some supported Nazism seeing Kaiser Wilhelm's policies as a means of God's grace. Such a view was decried by Karl Barth and others.

Comments: Some adherents of this view have espoused what is known as the Social Gospel. This view believes that the world will be transformed from the outside in through social activism, politics, parachurch efforts, and so on. The feeling is that as Christian ethics, structures, and thinking are more deeply incorporated into the world's structures, the kingdom of Christ will be brought into full reality.

Periods of increased spiritual interest such as the 1950s and today in the United States are seen as supporting the central tenet that the gospel will be successfully preached and received worldwide. The "great commission" of Jesus, "Therefore go and make disciples of all nations, baptizing them in the name of the Father and of the Son and of the Holy Spirit, and teaching them to obey everything I have commanded you. And surely I am with you always, to the very end of the age" (Matthew 28:19–20), is also seen as supporting this view. Among evidences cited that this is taking place is the fact that the Bible and other Christian literature is widely available across the world.

The idea of the kingdom of God being present now as an earthly, and not just spiritual, reality is supported by images and parables from the New Testament. The kingdom is seen as arriving gradually and incrementally. Jesus' image (metaphor) of leaven in a number of his teachings could support this concept. Postmillennialists take the view that as leaven works its way through dough very gradually, but very thoroughly, so is the Word of God slowly transforming the world.

The millennium is not seen as a literal 1,000 years, but rather as symbolic.

Premillennial View

Characteristics: There will be an earthly reign of Christ, who will be physically present for 1,000 years or some other extended period of time.

The millennium reign will come suddenly, supernaturally, and all at once, initiated by the Second Coming of Christ and the binding of Satan. This event will be evident to the entire world.

Society will deteriorate and people will "grow cold" spiritually, with sin greatly intensifying just prior to the Second Coming.

The tribulation will precede the millennium.

Following the millennium, Satan will be unbound for a brief period, and then he and his fallen angels will be finally subdued and sent to eternal and permanent punishment.

Both resurrections mentioned in Revelation 20 are physical. The first involves only believers, and the second will involve "all the rest" who are the unbelievers. This second group will be judged and assigned to hell.

Pros: Premillennialists take matters of eschatology (the study of biblical references to the end times, especially as related to Revelation) very seriously and view them as totally relevant to the Christian today even while asserting that the end times are to take place in the future.

Careful and intense exegesis is applied to Scripture, and the Bible is viewed as totally authoritative.

It can be said that the premillennial interpretation of Revelation 20 answers more questions and leaves fewer problems than the other views.

Cons: Since there are so few biblical references to the millennium, the significance placed on this event by premillennialists can be questioned.

While some interpret Old Testament prophecies, particularly concerning Israel, as figurative rather than literal, premillennialists insist on a more literal approach. However, some prophecies, such as Elijah returning prior to Christ's birth, were not fulfilled literally. Jesus himself made it clear that John the Baptist was the figurative "Elijah" who had preceded him (Matthew 11:11–15).

Comments: Rooted in the apostolic period, this view fell from favor over time. It was considered by many during the Middle Ages and Reformation as being nearly heretical. In the early 1900s, the Scofield Reference Bible, the first of its type including notes and commentary alongside Scripture, strongly supported the premillennial view. Premillennialism has grown in popularity ever since.

Premillennialists tend to take a very literal hermeneutical approach to the Bible, except where to do so would be ridiculous.

Tribulation Views

Jesus and certain Old Testament prophets foretold a coming time of horrible suffering and tremendous distress. Many people associate these prophecies with the "great tribulation" mentioned in Revelation 7:14.

Dispensationalism View

This is a theological and hermeneutical system that can overlay the interpretive and millennial views.

Characteristics: There are seven dispensations, or periods, that comprise all of history, present, and future.

Salvation is by faith exclusively. There is only one way into fellowship with God.

The moral law of God applies to all dispensations equally.

The Bible is to be interpreted as literally as possible.

Israel and the church are separate and distinct entities. Prophecies related to Israel are for Israel and not the "spiritual Israel" of the church.

All open prophecy will be fulfilled during the millennium.

Pros: Dispensationalism is a coherent system for understanding the workings of God in history.

Progressive revelation is validated, recognizing that God has revealed more and more of himself over time to his people.

Dispensationalism views the Bible as totally authoritative and stresses the need to know and understand the entirety of Scripture.

Cons: The sharp distinction insisted upon between Israel and the church is sometimes difficult to maintain consistently.

Dispensationalism, in addition to its literal view of Scripture, also tends to rely heavily on a typological characterization of biblical times, events, elements, and so on. For example, the Song of Songs describes a literal exchange between a lover and his beloved, yet the same imagery can be seen as representing the relationship of Jesus to his church. In some instances of "typing" the added meanings can seem strained.

Comments: Dispensationalism is credited to John Darby in the 1800s. He became a leader in the Plymouth Brethren movement. The approach was readily popularized through the release of the Scofield Reference Bible, which was the first Bible to combine text and commentary. It was also taught heavily in the Bible schools (institutes) of the time. As many prominent seminaries were suspected of departing from biblical doctrine, more churches turned to the Bible institutes to acquire ministers.

Pretribulation View

Characteristics: The severe tribulation will (1) conclude the era of the Gentiles (Luke 21:24) and (2) make ready for the restoration of Israel.

Jesus will come and rapture his bride (the church) out of the world prior to the tribulation. Christians will suddenly disappear from the earth.

The rapture will involve a physical bodily resurrection of the dead and translation of the living to eternal existence.

The coming of Christ is imminent and could occur at any moment.

After the seven years of tribulation, Christ will return to earth again, accompanied by the formerly risen Christians. Those who became Christians and died during the tribulation will also be resurrected to glory. At this time all unbelievers will be caught up for judgment and assignment to hell.

Finally, all resurrected Christians will share in the millennial reign of Christ.

Pros: With their emphasis on the imminent return of Christ, pretribulationists display a marked sense of anticipation and expectancy. This yields a positive forward look and hope, similar to the mindset of the first-century Christians.

Eschatology is a significant part of the overall doctrine of pretribulationists.

The whole Bible is scoured for any and all eschatological implications, with the goal of having a more complete understanding of the Scriptures.

Cons: The sense of imminency derives from the many admonitions of Christ and others to be ready and watchful. However, this emphasis tends to gloss over the fact that some events which have not yet occurred are expected to take place prior to any rapture.

Also, the sense of not knowing the time of the Lord's return does not necessarily imply imminence. Instead, it merely implies that the specific date and time are unknown, but that it will happen in the future after all prophecies required are fulfilled.

Comments: With the strong focus on being ready, adherents of this view tend to actively pursue consistent holiness in their lives, and take comfort in God's never-ending mercy and grace.

Not knowing something often creates an irresistible desire to try to find out. This is true especially within the pretrib circles. Most of the attempts to set dates for the end-time events, or to interpret current events in the context of Christ's return, arise from dispensational pretribulationists. While the intent can be sincere and the results benign, too much speculation generally leads to errors—sometimes public and embarrassing ones.

Posttribulation View

Characteristics: The church will remain on earth through the tribulation.

Following the tribulation, Christ will return. Dead and living Christians will be caught up to meet Christ as he is returning, and will immediately come back to earth to reign with him.

The duration of both the tribulation and the millennium are uncertain.

At the end of the millennium, all who are not Christians will be raised to judgment and assigned to hell.

Pros: This view tends to take in the widest scope of Scripture, avoiding any charge of proof texting. (Proof texting is essentially taking one or a few select verses and interpreting them out of context to support a specific opinion that is often contrary to a biblical position. While single verses can represent larger truths, they do so both within and outside of context.)

Interpretations of texts are viewed to align well with the overall context of the whole Bible, generally avoiding multiple or strained meanings.

Rather than looking forward to escaping future trials, this view prepares believers to endure the end times. Hope is not placed in avoiding the tribulation, but in overcoming it through diligent holiness.

Not having sorted out all the details of the last days, this view tends to preserve some sense of wonder and anticipation about the end times, looking toward the future to see the final working out and clear revelation of God's detailed plan.

Cons: Not having worked through all the specifics of the last days as discussed in Revelation, this view can be said to be vague on certain points. This is true particularly in its uncertainty surrounding the length of time for certain events.

Unless carefully presented, the concept of enduring the tribulation can be viewed as overly negative, eclipsing any message of hope.

There is often less emphasis on precise eschatology due to the tendency to avoid being dogmatic in its stance.

Comments: Posttribulationists generally do not see a sharp distinction between the church and Israel. It is believed that the church has replaced Israel as the covenant people of God.

While believing that the church will endure the tribulation, posttribbers also believe that they will be spared the wrath of God. They point out that the church has consistently endured tribulation of varying degrees throughout time, so this will be, in a sense, nothing new—although probably more intense. The wrath of God, however, is reserved for unbelievers who have rejected God and thus deserve his righteous wrath. Posttribulationists believe when Scripture speaks of deliverance for the saints in regard to end times, it refers to a special measure of grace given by God allowing Christians to endure the difficulties of the tribulation.

Midtribulation View

Characteristics: The church will endure the first part of the tribulation before being removed.

Comments: This view essentially states that while the church will endure a degree of tribulation, theirs will be a light trial ending prior to the outpouring of God's wrath.

Partial-Rapture View

Characteristics: One part of the church is raptured prior to the tribulation and the remaining part is raptured after the tribulation.

Comments: Somewhat tied to the parable of the 10 virgins (Matthew 25:1–13), this view states that faithful and watchful Christians will be the first to be raptured, leaving sleeping Christians behind to endure the tribulation. The tribulation is then a purifying time for those left behind. At the end of the tribulation, Christians who have remained faithful and are now alert will be raptured to be united with the full body.

Additional Reading

Abanes, Richard. *End-Time Visions: The Road to Armageddon?* New York: Four Walls Eight Windows, 1998.

Adams, Jay. *The Time Is at Hand.* Phillipsburg: Presbyterian and Reformed Publishing, 1966.

Alfred, Henry, revised by Harrison, Everett. *The Revelation in the Greek New Testament.* Nashville: Broadman Press, 1972.

Barnhouse, Donald Gray. *Revelation: An Expository Commentary.* Grand Rapids: Zondervan, 1971.

Blaising, Craig A., and Darrell Bock. *Progressive Dispensationalism.* Wheaton: Victor, 1993.

Bultman, Rudolf. *Jesus Christ and Mythology.* New York: Scribner's, 1958.

Caird, G.B. *The Revelation of St. John the Divine.* New York: Harper & Row, 1966.

Clark, David S. *The Message from Patmos: A Postmillenial Commentary on the Book of Revelation.* Grand Rapids: Baker Book House, 1989.

Clouse, Robert G. *The Meaning of the Millenium: Four Views.* Downers Grove: InterVarsity Press, 1977.

Cook, Terry L. *The Mark of the New World Order.* Springdale: Whitaker House, 1996.

Erickson, Millard J. *A Basic Guide to Eschatology: Making Sense of the Millenium.* Grand Rapids: Baker Books, 1977, 1998.

Fyre, Northrop. *The Great Code: The Bible and Literature.* New York: Harcourt Brace Jovanovitch, 1983.

Gregg, Steve, ed. *Revelation: Four Views: A Parallel Commentary.* Nashville: Nelson, 1997.

Grenz, Stanley J. *The Millenial Maze: Sorting Out Evangelical Options.* Downers Grove: InterVarsity Press, 1992.

Gundry, Robert H. *The Church and the Tribulation.* Grand Rapids: Zondervan, 1973.

Guthrie, Donald. *The Relevance of John's Apocalypse.* Grand Rapids: Eerdmans, 1987.

Hanson, Paul. *The Dawn of the Apocalyptic.* Philadelphia: Fortress Press, 1979.

Hendrickson, William. *More Than Conquerors: An Interpretation of the Book of Revelation.* Grand Rapids: Baker, 1944.

Hobbs, Herschel. *The Cosmic Drama.* Waco: Word Books, 1971.

Ice, Thomas, and Timothy Demy. *The Truth About the Signs of the Times.* Eugene: Harvest House, 1997.

Ironside, H.A. *Lectures on the Revelation.* Neptune: Loizeaux Brothers, 1920.

Ladd, George. *The Blessed Hope.* Grand Rapids: Eerdmans, 1956.

LaHaye, Tim, and Jerry Jenkins. *Are We Living in the End Times?* Wheaton: Tyndale, 1999.

Lenski, R.C.H. *The Interpretation of St. John's Revelation.* Minneapolis: Augsburg, 1943.

Lindsey, Hal. *The Late Great Planet Earth.* New York: Bantam Books, 1973.

———. *There's a New World Coming: A Prophetic Odyssey.* Eugene: Harvest House, 1973.

Luther, Martin. *Works 35.* Philadelphia: Muhlenberg Press, 1960.

McGinn, Bernard. *Antichrist: Two Thousand Years of the Human Fascination with Evil.* San Francisco: Harper, 1994.

Meeks, M. Douglas. *Origins of the Theology of Hope.* Philadelphia: Fortress, 1974.

Milne, Bruce. *What the Bible Teaches About the End of the World.* Wheaton: Tyndale, 1979.

Morris, L. *The Revelation of St. John: Tyndale New Testament Commentaries.* Wheaton: Tyndale, 1969.

Mounce, R.H. *The Book of Revelation.* Grand Rapids: Eerdmans, 1977.

Palmer, Frederic. *The Drama of the Apocalypse.* New York: Macmillan, 1903.

Pate, C. Marvin, and Calvin Haines. *Doomsday Delusions: What's Wrong with Predictions About the End of the World.* Downers Grove: InterVarsity Press, 1995.

Pate, C. Marvin, Editor. *Four Views of the Book of Revelation.* Grand Rapids: Zondervan, 1998.

Pieters, Albertus. *The Lamb, the Woman, and the Dragon.* Grand Rapids: Zondervan, 1937.

Plantinga, Cornelius. *Not the Way It's Supposed to Be: A Breviary of Sin.* Grand Rapids: Eerdmans, 1995.

Ramsey, William. *The Letters to the Seven Churches.* Grand Rapids: Baker Book House, 1963.

Robinson, Douglas. *American Apocalypses.* Baltimore: The Johns Hopkins University Press, 1985.

Ryrie, Charles. *Dispensationalism Today.* Chicago: Moody Press, 1965.

———. *Revelation.* Chicago: Moody Press, 1968.

Smith, F.G. *The Revelation Explained.* Guthrie: Faith Publishing House, 1943, 1973.

Stedman, Ray. *God's Final Word: Understanding Revelation.* Grand Rapids: Discovery House, 1991.

269

Stringfellow, William. *An Ethic for Christians and Other Aliens in a Strange Land.* Waco: Word, 1973.

Swedenborg, Emanuel. *The Revelation Revealed* (3 vols.). Boston: Houghton, Mifflin and Company, 1907.

Swete, Henry Barclay. *The Apocalypse of St. John.* Grand Rapids: Eerdmans, n.d.

Tenney, Merrill C. *Interpreting Revelation.* Grand Rapids: Eerdmans, 1957.

Tichi, Cecelia. *New World, New Earth.* New Haven: Yale University Press, 1979.

Travis, Stephen. *Christian Hope and the Future.* Downers Grove: InterVarsity Press, 1980.

———. *The Jesus Hope.* Downers Grove: InterVarsity Press, 1974.

Wainewright, Arthur W. *Mysterious Apocalypse: Interpreting the Book of Revelation.* Nashville: Abingdon Press, 1993.

Walvoord, John. *Armageddon and the Middle East Oil Crisis.* Grand Rapids: Zondervan, 1990.

———. *The Millennial Kingdom.* Findlay: Dunham, 1963.

———. *The Revelation of Jesus Christ.* Chicago: Moody Press, 1966.

Weber, Eugene. *Apocalypses: Prophecies, Cults, and Millenial Beliefs Through the Ages.* Cambridge: Harvard University Press, 1999.

Wilcock, Michael. *I Saw Heaven Opened: The Message of Revelation.* Downers Grove: InterVarsity Press, 1975.

A Few Web Links for Exploring

Caution: We do not endorse *any* of these sites. They are offered as a convenience to allow you to explore a bit of what's available on the Web. Some are better than others. A few are a bit weird. As with any material on the Internet, filtering the information through a screen of discernment and a wee bit of skepticism is not a bad thing.

Apocalypse
www.geocities.com/historicist
An historicist interpretation, using a verse-by-verse analysis.

Be-Ready
www.be-ready.org
Bread Upon The Waters Ministry offers a four part, Bible-based message, focusing on preparedness for the end times.

Berean Eternal Life Ministries
www.bereanlife.com
Dumitri Duduman's prophecies on the coming destruction of America; prophecies that the Messiah has already come.

Bible Insight
www.bibleinsight.com
Sundry Christian prophecies and chronology studies.

Bible Prophecy News
www.bibleprophecynews.com
World news as it pertains to the Bible prophecies, with newsletter, resources, articles, and free courses.

Blessed Hope Ministries International
www.bhm.dircon.co.uk
A basic study of Bible prophecy with a particular emphasis on the second coming of Jesus Christ.

Collision with Prophecy
collisionwithprophecy.org
Online seminar presenting the biblical facts about the mark of the beast.

Countdown to Armageddon
www.countdown.org
Information on Armageddon, mark of the beast, 666, and the antichrist.

Daniel's 70 Weeks
www.sentex.net/~tcc/dan70.html
Daniel's Bible prophecies, explained in detail.

e-Historicist.com
www.e-historicist.com
Collection of historicist articles and essays.

End of the World and the Second Coming of Christ
secondcoming.freeservers.com
Aims to show how recent Middle East fulfillment of Bible prophecy show that the present generation will see the second coming of Christ.

End Times Prophecy: A Catholic Perspective
www.conventhill.com/endtimes
Collection of Catholic resources.

Endtime

www.endtime.com

Examining world events from a biblical perspective; details of the radio show "Politics and Religion" and magazine.

Endtimes Now

www.endtimesnow.com/index.html

Analysis of world events with end-times significance, articles, and chat.

Focus on Jerusalem

focusonjerusalem.com

Bible prophecy newsletter, links, contacts, and history surrounding Jerusalem's prophetic past, present, and future.

The Harpazo Network

www.harpazo.net

News and articles on various aspects of biblical prophecy.

HisTomorrow

www.historicism.com

Takes a pre-millennial historicism approach to Bible prophecy, with online books, articles, news, and essays.

The Historical Alternative

www.historicist.com

Seeks to refute the futurist interpretation of the signs leading up to the Second Coming.

Lambert Dolphin's Resource Library

www.ldolphin.org

Large collection of books, articles, and links to topics of interest in the fields of Christianity, science, and prophecy.

Last Days in the News

lastdays.fattony.net

Videos, news, and audio clips aiming to show how Bible prophecy is being fulfilled today.

Predictive End-Times Diary
www.bibletime.com/pr/prophesies/index.shtml
A day-accurate predictive outline of the events at the end of the age; based on a simple theme of a repeating chronology, one modern day for each ancient year.

The Preterist Homepage
www.preteristhomepage.com
Bible prophecy from a Preterist (past fulfillment) perspective.

A Prophecy Bible Study Site
cityoflight.net/prophecy
A variety of prophetic Bible study articles by Max Swan.

The Prophecy Site
www.prophecy2.co.uk
A Bible-based prophecy site offering commentary and news, with a message board and links.

ProphecyUSA.com
www.prophecyusa.com
A look at the United States of America in Bible prophecy; also additional Bible study and commentary.

Prophetic Roundtable Ministries
www.propheticroundtable.org
A ministry Web site by Don Franklin devoted to preserving the prophetic word of the Lord through prophecy, visions, parables, and songs.

Red White Blue & Brimstone
www.lib.virginia.edu/exhibits/brimstone
Online exhibit from the University of Virginia Library examines the role and impact of the Book of Revelation and millenarian thought on American culture.

Revelation Ministry
www.pioneer-net.com/~revmin
Provides biblical explanation of Daniel and Revelation, gives historical data confirming fulfilled Bible prophecy, and presents God's final warning to the world.

SeekersTrove.com Bible Prophecy Studies
www.seekerstrove.com/Prophecies/prophecystudies.html
Faith-filled prophecy studies from the Bible; timelines and multiple-choice quizzes.

Weekend
www.upway.com/weekend
News, discussion groups, and articles of interest to students of biblical prophecy.

Index

Numbers

1994, 251
2001: On the Edge of Eternity, 251
666 ("mark of the beast"), thirteenth Revelation, 107
88 Reasons Why the Rapture Could Be in 1988, 250

A

Abyss, fifth trumpet judgment, 79-80
additional reading, 267-270
amillennial interpretation
  comments, 259
  defining characteristics, 259
  pro and cons, 259
amillennialism approach to the return of Jesus, 229
angels
  choir of angels, 57-58
  golden censer, 75
  messages of the angels (fourteenth Revelation), 114-116
    first angel, 115
    second angel, 116
    third angel, 116
  Michael, war in heaven (twelfth Revelation), 100

mighty angel with a scroll
  description, 86-87
  eating of the scroll by John, 87-89
seven angels with the seven last plagues, 125-134
  fifth bowl of wrath, 129-130
  first bowl of wrath, 129
  fourth bowl of wrath, 129
  second bowl of wrath, 129
  seventh bowl of wrath, 132-134
  sixth bowl of wrath, 130-132
  third bowl of wrath, 129
trumpet judgments
  fifth angel, 78-80
  first angel, 76-77
  fourth angel, 78
  second angel, 77
  seventh angel, 96-97
  sixth angel, 81-82
  third angel, 77
Antichrist. *See also* Satan
interpretation, 191
  futuristic interpretation, 223
  preterist interpretation, 200-201

punishment of (nineteenth Revelation), 157
thirteenth Revelation, 102-104
Apocalypse, Four Horsemen of, 62-64
apocalyptic literature
  characteristics of, 6-7
    division into historical chapters, 7
    expectation of better things, 7
    future expectations, 7
    pseudonyms, 7
    symbolism, 7
  controversial issues, 8
  purpose of, 9
  uncovering hidden secrets, 9-10
  writing styles, 5-6
apodictic, 8
Apostles
John
  exile of John, 16
  identification of John as the author (first Revelation), 24-25
  vision of Jesus (first Revelation), 25-27
persecution of the Apostles, 15
Applewhite, Marshall, 246
archangel, Michael, 100
Are You Ready?, 251

ark of the covenant, 97

Armageddon (sixth bowl judgment), 130-132

army of horsemen (sixth trumpet judgment), 82

Artemis, 33

author, identification of John as the author (first Revelation), 24-25

B

Babylon, 115-116
- fall of Babylon (eigtheenth Revelation)
  - earthly perspective, 144-145
  - final destruction, 146-147
  - heavenly perspective, 142-143
- identified as the great prostitute, 138-139

Balaam, 37

Battle Hymn of the Republic, 120-121

Be-Ready Web site, 271

beasts
- Antichrist
  - first beast, 102-104
  - punishment of (nineteenth Revelation), 157
- second beast (false prophet), 105-107
  - "mark of the beast," 107
  - primary functions, 106
  - punishment of (nineteenth Revelation), 157
- symbolism, 99

benefits of reading, 28

Berean Eternal Life Ministries Web site, 271

Bible Insight Web site, 272

Bible Prophecy News Web site, 272

biblical warnings of Satan, 101

blaming of God for bad things that happen, 124-125

Blessed Hope Ministries International Web site, 272

books, listing of additional reading, 267-270

boulders, final destruction of Babylon, 146-147

C

Camping, Harold, end-time predictions, 251

censer (golden censer), 75

characteristics of apocalyptic literature, 6-7
- division into historical chapters, 7
- expectation of better things, 7
- future expectations, 7
- pseudonyms, 7
- symbolism, 7

charts, end-time predictions, 252-253

child, birth of male child (twelfth Revelation), 97-100

choir of angels, John's visions of heaven, 57-58

Christianity, misunderstandings, 16-17

churches
- first-century churches, 17-18
- greetings to the seven churches (first Revelation), 22-24
- historicist interpretation, 209
- letters to the seven churches
  - Ephesus, 33
  - Laodicea, 43-45
  - performance standards, 32
  - Pergamum, 36-38
  - Philadelphia, 41-43
  - reasons for choosing specific churches, 45-46
  - Sardis, 40-41
  - Smyrna, 35
  - Thyatira, 38-40

Clark, Doug, end-time predictions, 249-250

Collision with Prophecy Web site, 272

comments
- amillennial interpretation, 259
- dispensationalism view, 263
- midtribulation view, 265
- postmillennial interpretation, 260-261
- posttribulation view, 265
- premillennial interpretation, 262
- pretribulation view, 264

conflicting issues
- apocalyptic literature, 8
- good and evil conflict, 235-236

historicist interpretation, 210-211

idealist interpretations, 212

preterist interpretation, 203

ConventHill Web site, 272

Countdown to Armageddon Web site, 272

creatures, John's visions of heaven, 53-55

criticisms
   historicist interpretation, 210-211
   idealist interpretation, 212

cults
   Heaven's Gate
      death of followers, 247-248
      Do and Ti, 247
      spaceships, 247
      teachings, 246-247
   Peoples Temple
      death of followers, 245-246
      shared values of members, 245
      teachings, 245

curse, lifting of the curse of Adam and Eve, 172-173
   twenty-second Revelation, 181-182

D

Daniel's 70 Weeks Web site, 272

day of the locusts (fifth trumpet judgment), 80

death
   great white throne judgments (twentieth Revelation), 162-164
   second death, 163

defining characteristics
   amillennial interpretation, 259
   dispensationalism view, 262
   futuristic interpretation, 257
   historicist interpretation, 257
   idealist interpretation, 258
   midtribulation view, 265
   postmillennial interpretation, 259
   posttribulation view, 264
   premillennial interpretation, 261
   preterist interpretation, 258
   pretribulation view, 263

destruction of the Jewish temple, preterist interpretation, 198-199

dispensational futurism, 220-221

dispensationalism view
   comments, 263
   defining characteristics, 262
   pros and cons, 262-263

Do (Bonnie Lu Nettles), 247

doctrines, validity of prophetic teachings, 254-255

dragons, red dragon versus pregnant woman (twelfth Revelation), 97-101

dramatic interpretation, 213, 258

E

e-Historicist Web site, 272

earth
   harvest of the earth (fourteenth Revelation), 116-119
   new earth (twenty-first Revelation), 167-168

eating of the scroll by John, 87, 89

eighteenth Revelation
   fall of Babylon
      earthly perspective, 144-145
      final destruction, 146-147
      heavenly perspective, 142-143
      verses, 142, 144, 146

eighth Revelation
   opening of seventh seal
      golden censer, 75
      silence in heaven, 74-75
      trumpet judgments
         first angel, 76-77
         fourth angel, 78
         second angel, 77
         third angel, 77
      verses, 74, 76

elders, twenty-four elders in heaven, 53-55

eleventh Revelation
    power of two witnesses
        death of witnesses, 92-93
        three and a half year prophecy, 90
    seventh trumpet judgment, 96-97
    task of measuring the temple, 89-90
    verses, 89-90, 92, 96
end-time predictions
    Camping, Harold, 251
    charts, 252-253
    Clark, Doug, 249-250
    interpretations, 192-193
    Lindsey, Hal, 252
    popularity of the Book of Revelation, 234-235
    Van Impe, Jack, 251
    Whisenant, Edgar 250-251
Endtime Web site, 273
Ephesus (letters to the seven churches), 33
eternal life insurance, 14
Euphrates River, 130
exile of John, 16

F

fall of Babylon (eighteenth Revelation)
    earthly perspective, 144-145
    final destruction, 146-147
    heavenly perspective, 142-143
fallen star (fifth trumpet judgment), 79-80
false prophets
    punishment of (nineteenth Revelation), 157

thirteenth Revelation, 105-107
    "mark of the beast," 107
    primary functions, 106
twelfth Revelation, 106
fanaticism, 244
fear of future events, 13
fifteenth Revelation
    seven angels with the seven last plagues, 125-128
    verses, 126
fifth Revelation
    John's visions of heaven
        choir of angels, 57-58
        sealed scroll, 55-56
        slain Lamb, 56
    verses, 56-57
fifth seal, 65
fifth trumpet judgment, 78-80
    day of the locusts, 80
    fallen star headed for the Abyss, 79-80
final destruction of Babylon, 146-147
first-century churches, 17-18
first Revelation
    greetings to the seven churches, 22-24
    identification of John as the author, 24-25
    John's vision of Jesus, 25-27
    testimony of Jesus Christ, 22
    verses, 22-23, 25-26
first seal, 62
first trumpet judgment, 76-77
Focus on Jerusalem Web site, 273

Four Horsemen of the Apocalypse, 62-64
four living creatures, John's visions of heaven, 53-55
fourteenth Revelation
    harvest of the earth, 116-119
    messages of the angels, 114-116
        first angel, 115
        second angel, 116
        third angel, 116
    return of the Lamb and the protected group of people, 112-114
    verses, 112, 114-117
fourth Revelation
    John's visions of heaven
        descriptions of heaven, 53
        four living creatures, 53-55
        throne of God, 52-53
        twenty-four elders, 53-55
    verses, 52-54
fourth seal, 64
fourth trumpet judgment, 78
future events
    end-time predictions
        Camping, Harold, 251
        charts, 252-253
        Clark, Doug, 249-250
        Lindsey, Hal, 252
        popularity of the Book of Revelation, 234-235
        Van Impe, Jack, 251
        Whisenant, Edgar 250-251
    fascination with future predictions, 12

motivational factors for wanting to know the future
eternal life insurance, 14
fear, 13
hope, 14-15
preparedness, 190
Revelation as a book of the future, 18-19
futuristic interpretation, 218
Antichrist, 223
defining characteristics, 257
dispensational futurism, 220-221
fulfillment of God's promises to the Jews, 225-226
great tribulation, 223-225
pros and cons, 257
rapture of the church, 222
resurrection of the dead, 230-231
return of Jesus and the millennium, 227-229
amillennialism approach, 229
postmillennialism approach, 228
premillennial approach, 228
variations to interpretations, 229

G

God
blaming of God for bad things that happen, 124-125

great supper of God (nineteenth Revelation), 156-157
heavenly praises to God (nineteenth Revelation), 152-154
John's visions, 52-53
messages of God to all people, 237-238
patience of, 237
wrath of God
Battle Hymn of the Republic, 120-121
God as heavenly judge, 119
harvest of the earth (fourteenth Revelation), 116-119
seven bowl judgments, 128-134
golden censer (eighth Revelation), 75
good and evil conflicts (spiritual lessons), 235-236
great prostitute (seventeenth Revelation), 136-141
angel's explanation to John, 139-141
descriptions, 137-138
references to Babylon, 138-139
great supper of God (nineteenth Revelation), 156-157
great tribulation interpretation, 190
dispensationalism, 262-263
futuristic interpretation, 223-225
midtribulation, 265
partial-rapture view, 265
posttribulation view, 264-265

preterist view, 199
pretribulation view, 263-264
great white throne
interpretation, 191
judgments (twentieth Revelation), 162-164
Greek goddess Artemis, 33
greetings to the seven churches (first Revelation), 22-24

H

hail (seventh bowl judgment), 132-134
Hallelu Yah, 153
Harpazo Network Web site, 273
harvest of the earth (fourteenth Revelation), 116-119
heaven
hopes of heaven, 165-166
John's visions
choir of angels, 57-58
descriptions of, 53
four living creatures, 53-55
sealed scroll, 55-56
slain Lamb, 56
throne of God, 52-53
twenty-four elders, 53-55
mysteries of, 174
new heaven (twenty-first Revelation), 167-168
silence noted when opening seventh seal, 74-75
war in heaven (twelfth Revelation), 100

281

Heaven's Gate
    death of followers,
        247-248
    Do and Ti, 247
    spaceships, 247
    teachings, 246-247
hidden secrets of apocalyp-
    tic literature, 9-10
historians, preterist inter-
    pretation
    Flavius Josephus, 202
    Tacitus, 202
Historicism Web site, 273
historicist interpretations
    church history, 209
    comparisons to historic
        events, 208-209
    criticisms of, 210-211
    pros and cons, 257
hopes
    heaven, 165-166
    in future events, 14-15
horsemen
    army of horsemen (sixth
        trumpet judgment), 82
    Four Horsemen of the
        Apocalypse, 62-64
    rider on a white horse
        (nineteenth Revela-
        tion), 155-156

I

idealist interpretation
    criticisms of, 212
    nonliteral approach, 211
    pros and cons, 258
interpretations, 190
    authors' disclaimers, 231
    dramatic approach, 213,
        258

effects of technological
    advancements on, 195
Four Horsemen of the
    Apocalypse, 64
four primary interpreta-
    tion groups, 214
futuristic view, 218
    Antichrist, 223
    defining characteris-
        tics, 257
    dispensational futur-
        ism, 220-221
    fulfillment of God's
        promises to the
        Jews, 225-226
    great tribulation,
        223-225
    pros and cons, 257
    rapture of the church,
        222
    resurrection of the
        dead, 230-231
    return of Jesus and
        the millennium,
        227-229
great tribulation, 190
    dispensationalism,
        262-263
    midtribulation view,
        265
    partial-rapture view,
        265
    posttribulation view,
        264-265
    pretribulation view,
        263-264
historicist view
    church history, 209
    comparisons to his-
        toric events, 208-209
    criticisms of, 210-211

defining character-
    istics, 257
pros and cons, 257
idealist view
    criticisms of, 212
    defining characteris-
        tics, 258
    nonliteral approach,
        211
    pros and cons, 258
Jesus' predictions about
    the end of the age,
    192-193
judgment before the
    great white throne, 191
literary-analytical
    approach, 214, 258
millennium (thousand-
    year reign of Christ)
    amillennial view, 259
    postmillennial view,
        259-261
    premillennial view,
        261-262
multiple layers, 195
necessity of, 189
New Testament prom-
    ises, 193
Old Testament proph-
    ecies, 193
preparing for the future,
    190
preterist view
    Antichrist, 200-201
    conflicting issues, 203
    dating of the writing
        of the Book of
        Revelation, 204
    defining characteris-
        tics, 258
    destruction of the
        Jewish temple,
        198-199

great tribulation, 199

historians, 202

pros and cons, 258

return of Jesus, 201-202

rapture, 191

resurrection of the dead, 191

rise of the Antichrist, 191

second coming of Jesus, 191

seventh Revelation, 67-69

Y2K, 189-190

invitation (twenty-second Revelation), 181-182

J–K

Jerusalem

fall of the holy city, preterist interpretation, 199

new Jerusalem (twenty-first Revelation), 169-171

Jesus Christ

final messages of Jesus (twenty-second Revelation), 179-182

John's vision of Jesus (first Revelation), 25-27

millennium (thousand-year reign of Christ), 259-262

reign of Christ (twentieth Revelation), 158-159

second coming of Jesus

futuristic interpretation, 227-229

interpretations, 191-193

preterist interpretation, 201-202

twenty-second Revelation, 178-182

testimony of Jesus Christ (first Revelation), 22

wedding of the Lamb (nineteenth Revelation), 154-155

Jewish temple, preterist interpretation, 198-199

Jews, fulfillment of God's promise to the Jews, 225-226

John the Apostle

eating of the scroll, 87-89

exile of John, 16

identification of John as the author (first Revelation), 24-25

letters to the seven churches

Laodicea, 43-45

Pergamum, 36-38

Philadelphia, 41-43

reasons for choosing specific churches, 45-46

Sardis, 40-41

Smyrna, 35

Thyatira, 38-40

task of measuring the temple, 89-90

vision of Jesus (first Revelation), 25-27

visions of heaven

choir of angels, 57-58

descriptions of heaven, 53

four living creatures, 53-55

sealed scroll, 55-56

slain Lamb, 56

throne of God, 52-53

twenty four elders, 53-55

Jones, Jim (Peoples Temple), 244-246

death of followers, 245-246

Jonestown, 245

shared values of members, 245

teachings, 245

Josephus, Flavius (Jewish historian), 202

Judah (Lion of the tribe of Judah), 56

judgments

Battle Hymn of the Republic, 120-121

God as heavenly judge, 119

great white throne judgments (twentieth Revelation), 162-164, 191

seven bowl judgments, 128-134

fifth bowl of wrath, 129-130

first bowl of wrath, 129

fourth bowl of wrath, 129

second bowl of wrath, 129

seventh bowl of wrath, 132-134

sixth bowl of wrath, 130-132

third bowl of wrath, 129

Jupiter Effect, 249-250

The Complete Idiot's Guide to the Book of Revelation

L

Lamb
- John's visions of heaven, 56
- return of the Lamb (fourteenth Revelation), 112-114
- wedding of the Lamb (nineteenth Revelation), 154-155

Lambert Dolphin's Resource Library Web site, 273

Laodicea (letters to the seven churches), 43-45

Last Days in the News Web site, 273

Late Great Planet Earth, The, 252

layers of interpretation, 195

Lennon, John, "Imagine," 165

lessons (spiritual lessons)
- everyday choices have results, 236
- God is patient, 237
- good and evil conflict, 235-236
- messages of God to all people, 237-238
- people have choices, 236

letters to the seven churches
- Ephesus, 33
- Laodicea, 43-45
- Pergamum, 36-38
- Philadelphia, 41-43
- reasons for choosing specific churches, 45-46
- Sardis, 40-41
- Smyrna, 35
- Thyatira, 38-40

lifting of the curse of Adam and Eve (twenty-second Revelation), 172

Lindsey, Hal, end-time predictions, 252

Lion of the tribe of Judah, 56

literary-analytical interpretation, 214, 258

literature (apocalyptic literature)
- characteristics of, 6-7
  - division into historical chapters, 7
  - expectation of better things, 7
  - future expectations, 7
  - pseudonyms, 7
  - symbolism, 7
- controversial issues, 8
- purpose of, 9
- uncovering hidden secrets, 9-10
- writing styles, 5-6

locusts (fifth trumpet judgment), 80

M

male child, birth of (twelfth Revelation), 97-100

mania verses phobias, 238-239

"mark of the beast" (thirteenth Revelation), 107

measuring the temple (eleventh Revelation), 89-90

messages from the angels (fourteenth Revelation), 114-116
- first angel, 115
- second angel, 116
- third angel, 116

Michael, war in heaven (twelfth Revelation), 100

midtribulation view
- comments, 265
- defining characteristics, 265

mighty angel with a scroll
- description, 86-87
- eating of the scroll by John, 87-89

millennium (thousand-year reign of Christ), interpretation
- amillennial view, 259
- futuristic interpretation, 227-229
- postmillennial view, 259-261
- premillennial view, 261-262

motivational factors for wanting to know the future
- eternal life insurance, 14
- fear, 13
- hope, 14-15

Mount Megiddo, 131

multiple layers of interpretation, 195

mysteries of heaven, 174

N

natural disasters, sixth seal, 66

necessity of interpretation, 189

Nero, Emperor, preterist interpretation of Antichrist, 200-201

Nettles, Bonnie Lu, 246

new earth (twenty-first Revelation), 167-168

new heaven (twenty-first Revelation), 167-171

new Jerusalem (twenty-first Revelation), 169-171

New Testament promises, interpretation, 193

nineteenth Revelation
   death of Antichrist and false prophet, 157
   great supper of God, 156-157
   heavenly praises to God, 152-154
   rider on a white horse, 155-156
   verses, 152, 155-156
   wedding of the Lamb, 154-155

ninth Revelation
   trumpet judgments
      fifth, 78-80
      sixth, 81-82
      verses, 81

nonliteral approach of idealist interpretations, 211

number assignments, validity of prophetic teachings, 255

O

oceans, turning water into blood, 129

Old Testament prophecies, interpretation, 193

On Borrowed Time, 250

P–Q

partial-rapture view, 265

Peoples Temple, 244-246
   death of followers, 245-246
   shared values of members, 245
   teachings, 245

Pergamum (letters to the seven churches), 36-38

persecution
   of the Apostles, 15
   responses of first-century churches, 17-18

Philadelphia (letters to the seven churches), 41-43

phobias verses mania, 238-239

plagues (seven angels with the seven last plagues), 125-134
   fifth bowl of wrath, 129-130
   first bowl of wrath, 129
   fourth bowl of wrath, 129
   second bowl of wrath, 129
   seventh bowl of wrath, 132-134
   sixth bowl of wrath, 130-132
   third bowl of wrath, 129

popularity of the Book of Revelation, 234-235

postmillennial interpretation
   comments, 260-261
   defining characteristics, 259
   pros and cons, 260
   return of Jesus, 228

posttribulation view
   comments, 265
   defining characteristics, 264
   pros and cons, 264-265

praises to God (nineteenth Revelation), 152-154

predictions (end-time predictions)
   Camping, Harold, 251
   charts, 252-253
   Clark, Doug, 249-250
   interpretations, 192-193
   Lindsey, Hal, 252
   popularity of the Book of Revelation, 234-235
   Van Impe, Jack, 251
   Whisenant, Edgar 250-251

Predictive End-Times Diary Web site, 274

pregnant woman versus red dragon (twelfth Revelation), 97-101

premillennial interpretation
   comments, 262
   defining characteristics, 261
   pros and cons, 261-262
   return of Jesus, 228

preparing for the future, 190

Preterist Homepage Web site, 274

preterist interpretation
   Antichrist, 200-201
   conflicting issues, 203
   dating of the writing of the Book of Revelation, 204
   destruction of the Jewish temple, 198-199

great tribulation, 199
historians
    Flavius Josephus, 202
    Tacitus, 202
    pros and cons, 258
    return of Jesus, 201-202
pretribulation view
    comments, 264
    defining characteristics, 263
    pros and cons, 263-264
promises
    God's promises to the Jews (futuristic interpretation), 225-226
    New Testament promises, 193
Prophecy Bible Study Web site, 274
ProphecyUSA Web site, 274
prophetic predictions
    Camping, Harold, 251
    charts, 252-253
    checking validity of, 253-255
        character and reputation of individual, 254
        doctrines, 254-255
        number assignments, 255
        remain open to truth, 255
        sources, 254
    Clark, Doug, 249-250
    Lindsey, Hal, 252
    Van Impe, Jack, 251
    Whisenant, Edgar, 250-251
Prophetic Roundtable Ministries Web site, 274

prophets (false)
    punishment of (nineteenth Revelation), 157
    thirteenth Revelation, 105-107
    twelfth Revelation, 106
pros and cons
    amillennial interpretation, 259
    dispensationalism view, 262-263
    futuristic interpretation, 257
    historicist interpretation, 257
    idealist interpretation, 258
    postmillennial interpretation, 260
    posttribulation view, 264-265
    premillennial interpretation, 261-262
    preterist interpretation, 258
    pretribulation view, 263-264
prostitute (great prostitute), seventeenth Revelation, 136-141
    angel's explanation to John, 139-141
    descriptions, 137-138
    references to Babylon, 138-139
protected group of people
    return of (fourteenth Revelation), 112-114
    seventh Revelation, 67-70
pseudonyms, characteristics of apocalyptic literature, 7

punishments
    Antichrist (nineteenth Revelation), 157
    false prophet (nineteenth Revelation), 157
    release and punishments of Satan (twentieth Revelation), 159-161

R

rapture
    futuristic interpretation, 222
    interpretation, 191
    partial-rapture view, 265
reading, listing of additional reading, 267-270
red dragon versus pregnant woman (twelfth Revelation), 97-101
reign of Christ (twentieth Revelation), 158-159. *See also* second coming of Jesus
resources
    listing of additional reading, 267-270
    Web sites, 271-275
responses to Revelation, 239-240
resurrection of the dead
    futuristic interpretation, 230-231
    interpretations, 191
Revelation Ministry Web site, 274
Revelation
    as a book of the future, 18-19
    benefits of reading, 28
    eighteenth
        fall of Babylon, 142-147
        verses, 142, 144, 146

eighth
  opening of seventh seal, 74-75
  seventh seal, 74
  trumpet judgments, 76-78
  verses, 74, 76
eleventh
  power of two witnesses, 90-93
  seventh trumpet judgment, 96-97
  task of measuring the temple, 89-90
  verses, 89-90, 92, 96
fifteenth
  seven angels with the seven last plagues, 125-128
  verses, 126
fifth
  John's visions of heaven, 55-58
  verses, 56-57
first
  greetings to the seven churches, 22-24
  identification of John as the author, 24-25
  John's vision of Jesus, 25-27
  testimony of Jesus Christ, 22
  verses, 22-23, 25-26
fourteenth
  harvest of the earth, 116-119
  messages of the angels, 114-116
  return of the Lamb and the protected group of people, 112-114
  verses, 112, 114-117

fourth
  John's visions of heaven, 52-55
  twenty-four elders, 53-55
  verses, 52-54
interpretations. *See* interpretations
mania versus phobias, 238-239
nineteenth
  great supper of God, 156-157
  heavenly praises to God, 152-154
  punishment of Antichrist and false prophet, 157
  rider on a white horse, 155-156
  verses, 152, 155-156
  wedding of the Lamb, 154-155
ninth
  trumpet judgments, 78-82
  verses, 81
responses to, 239-240
second
  letters to the seven churches, 33-40
  verses, 33, 35-39
seventeenth
  great prostitute, 136-141
  verses, 137, 139-140
seventh
  interpretation, 67-69
  protected group of people, 67-70
  verses, 67-70
sixteenth
  seven bowl judgments, 128-134
  verses, 128-131

sixth
  fifth seal, 65
  first seal, 62
  fourth seal, 64
  second seal, 64
  sixth seal, 66
  third seal, 64
  verses, 62, 65-66
tenth
  mighty angel with a scroll, 86-89
  verses, 86-87
third Revelation
  letters to the seven churches, 40-45
  verses, 40-44
thirteenth
  first beast (Antichrist), 102-104
  second beast (false prophet), 105-107
  verses, 102-103, 105-106
time period and setting when written
  Christianity, misunderstanding, 16
  exile of John, 16
  persecution of the Apostles, 15
twelfth
  pregnant woman versus red dragon, 97-101
  second beast (false prophet), 106
  verses, 97-98, 100-102
  war in heaven, 100
twentieth
  binding of Satan, 158-159
  great white throne judgments, 162-164

reign of Christ,
158-159
release and punish-
ments of Satan,
159-161
verses, 158-159, 162
twenty-first
new heaven and
earth, 167-168
new Jerusalem, 169,
171
verses, 167, 169
twenty-second
an invitation and a
warning, 181-182
coming of Jesus
Christ, 178-179
final messages of
Jesus, 179-181
lifting of the curse of
Adam and Eve, 172
river of life, 171-172
tree of life, 171-172
verses, 171, 178,
180-181
rider on a white horse
(nineteenth Revelation),
155-156
river of life (twenty-second
Revelation), 171-172

S

Sardis (letters to the seven
churches), 40-41
Satan. *See also* Antichrist
biblical warnings, 101
binding of Satan (twen-
tieth Revelation),
158-159
release and punishments
of Satan (twentieth
Revelation), 159-161
*Satan Is Alive and Well on
Planet Earth*, 252

scrolls
John's visions of
heaven, 55-56
mighty angel with a
scroll
description, 86-87
eating of the scroll by
John, 87-89
seals. *See* seals
seals
fifth seal, 65
first seal, 62
fourth seal, 64
protected group of
people, 67-70
second seal, 64
seventh seal
golden censer, 75
silence in heaven,
74-75
trumpet judgments,
76-82
sixth seal, 66
symbolic uses, 68
third seal, 64
second coming of Jesus.
See also reign of Christ
futuristic interpretation,
227-229
amillennialism
approach, 229
postmillennialism
approach, 228
premillennial
approach, 228
variations to inter-
pretations, 229
interpretation, 191
twenty-second
Revelation, 178-182
second death, 163
second Revelation
letters to the seven
churches

Ephesus, 33
Pergamum, 36-38
Smyrna, 35
Thyatira, 38-40
verses, 33, 35-39
second seal, 64
second trumpet judgment,
77
secrets, uncovering hidden
secrets in apocalyptic
literature, 9-10
SeekersTrove Web site, 275
seven angels with the
seven last plagues,
125-134
fifth bowl of wrath,
129-130
first bowl of wrath, 129
fourth bowl of wrath,
129
second bowl of wrath,
129
seventh bowl of wrath,
132-134
sixth bowl of wrath,
130-132
third bowl of wrath, 129
seven churches
greetings to the seven
churches (first
Revelation), 22-24
letters to the seven
churches. *See* letters to
the seven churches
seventeenth Revelation
great prostitute, 136-141
angel's explanation to
John, 139-141
descriptions, 137-138
references to Babylon,
138-139
verses, 137, 139-140
seventh Revelation
interpretation, 67-69

protected group of people, 67-70
verses, 67-70
seventh seal
golden censer, 75
silence in heaven, 74-75
seventh trumpet judgment, 96-97
silence in heaven (eighth Revelation), 74-75
sixteenth Revelation
seven bowl judgments, 128-134
fifth, 129-130
first, 129
fourth, 129
second, 129
seventh, 132-134
sixth, 130-132
third, 129
verses, 128-131
sixth Revelation
fifth seal, 65
first seal, 62
fourth seal, 64
second seal, 64
sixth seal, 66
third seal, 64
verses, 62, 65-66
sixth seal, 66
sixth trumpet judgment
army of horsemen, 82
release of four bound angels, 81
slain Lamb, John's visions of heaven, 56
Smyrna (letters to the seven churches), 35
sources, validity of prophetic teachings, 254

spiritual lessons
everyday choices have results, 236
God is patient, 237
good and evil conflicts, 235-236
messages of God to all people, 237-238
people have choices, 236
star, fallen star (fifth trumpet judgment), 79-80
sun, fourth bowl judgment, 129
symbolism
beasts, 99
characteristics of apocalyptic literature, 7
seals, 68
smoke, 128

T

Tacitus (Roman historian), 202
task of measuring the temple (eleventh Revelation), 89-90
teachings
Heaven's Gate, 246-247
Peoples Temple, 245
prophetic teachings, 253-255
temples (Jewish temple), 198-199
tenth Revelation
mighty angel with a scroll
description, 86-87
eating of the scroll by John, 87, 89
verses, 86-87

testimony of Jesus Christ (first Revelation), 22
third Revelation
letters to the seven churches
Laodicea, 43-45
Philadelphia, 41-43
Sardis, 40-41
verses, 40-44
third seal, 64
third trumpet judgment, 77
thirteenth Revelation
first beast (Antichrist), 102-104
second beast (false prophet), 105-107
"mark of the beast," 107
primary functions, 106
verses, 102-103, 105-106
Thyatira (letters to the seven churches), 38-40
Ti (Marshall Applewhite), 247
tree of life (twenty-second Revelation), 171-172
tribulation interpretation, 190
dispensationalism, 262-263
futuristic interpretation, 223-225
midtribulation, 265
partial-rapture view, 265
posttribulation view, 264-265
preterist view, 199
pretribulation view, 263-264

trumpet judgments
  fifth angel, 78-80
    day of the locusts, 80
    fallen star headed for the Abyss, 79-80
  first angel, 76-77
  fourth angel, 78
  second angel, 77
  seventh angel, 96-97
  sixth angel
    army of horsemen, 82
    release of four bound angels, 81
  third angel, 77
twelfth Revelation
  pregnant woman versus red dragon, 97-101
  second beast (false prophet), 106
  verses, 97-98, 100-102
  war in heaven, 100
twentieth Revelation
  binding of Satan, 158-159
  great white throne judgments, 162-164
  reign of Christ, 158-159
  release and punishments of Satan, 159-161
  verses, 158-159, 162
twenty-four elders, 53-55
twenty-first Revelation
  new heaven and earth, 167-168
  new Jerusalem, 169, 171
  verses, 167, 169
twenty-second Revelation
  an invitation and a warning, 181-182
  coming of Jesus Christ, 178-179
  final messages of Jesus, 179-181
  lifting of the curse of Adam and Eve, 172
  river of life, 171-172
  tree of life, 171-172
  verses, 171, 178, 180-181
two witnesses (eleventh Revelation)
  death of witnesses, 92-93
  three and a half year prophecy, 90

U-V

validity of prophetic teachings, 253-255
  character and reputation of individual, 254
  doctrines, 254-255
  number assignments, 255
  remain open to truth, 255
  sources, 254
Van Impe, Jack, end-time predictions, 251
verses
  eighteenth Revelation, 142, 144, 146
  eighth Revelation, 74, 76
  eleventh Revelation, 89-90, 92, 96
  fifteenth Revelation, 126
  fifth Revelation, 56-57
  first Revelation, 22-23, 25-26
  fourteenth Revelation, 112, 114-117
  fourth Revelation, 52-54
  nineteenth Revelation, 152, 155-156
  second Revelation, 33, 35-39
  seventeenth Revelation, 137, 139-140
  seventh Revelation, 67-70
  sixteenth Revelation, 128-131
  sixth Revelation, 62, 65-66
  tenth Revelation, 86-87
  third Revelation, 40-44
  thirteenth Revelation, 102-103, 105-106
  twelfth Revelation, 97-98, 100-102
  twentieth Revelation, 158-159, 162
  twenty-first Revelation, 167, 169
  twenty-second Revelation, 171, 178, 180-181
visions of John the Apostle
  heaven
    choir of angels, 57-58
    descriptions of heaven, 53
    four living creatures, 53-55
    sealed scroll, 55-56
    slain Lamb, 56
    throne of God, 52-53
    twenty four elders, 53-55
  Jesus (first Revelation), 25-27

W–X–Y–Z

war in heaven (twelfth Revelation), 100

warnings
  against Satan, 101
  messages of the angels, 114-116
  twenty-second Revelation, 181-182

water, third bowl judgment, 129

Web sites
  Be-Ready, 271
  Berean Eternal Life Ministries, 271
  Bible Insight, 272
  Bible Prophecy News, 272
  Blessed Hope Ministries International, 272
  Collision with Prophecy, 272
  ConventHill, 272
  Countdown to Armageddon, 272
  Daniel's 70 Weeks, 272
  e-Historicist, 272
  Endtime, 273
  Focus on Jerusalem, 273
  Harpazo Network, 273
  Historicism, 273
  Lambert Dolphin's Resource Library, 273
  Last Days in the News, 273
  Predictive End-Times Diary, 274
  Preterist Homepage, 274
  Prophecy Bible Study Site, 274
  ProphecyUSA, 274
  Prophetic Roundtable Ministries, 274
  Revelation Ministry, 274
  SeekersTrove, 275
  Weekend, 275

wedding of the Lamb (nineteenth Revelation), 154-155

Weekend Web site, 275

Whisenant, Edgar, end-time predictions, 250-251

witnesses (eleventh Revelation)
  death of witnesses, 92-93
  three and a half year prophecy, 90

woman, pregnant woman versus red dragon (twelfth Revelation), 97-101

wrath of God
  Battle Hymn of the Republic, 120-121
  God as heavenly judge, 119
  harvest of the earth (fourteenth Revelation), 116-119
  seven bowl judgments, 128-134
    fifth bowl of wrath, 129-130
    first bowl of wrath, 129
    fourth bowl of wrath, 129
    second bowl of wrath, 129
    seventh bowl of wrath, 132-134
    sixth bowl of wrath, 130-132
    third bowl of wrath, 129

writing of Revelation
  preterist interpretation, 204
  time period and setting
    Christianity, misunderstanding of, 16
    exile of John, 16
    persecution of the Apostles, 15

writing styles, apocalyptic literature, 5-6

Y2K interpretations, 189-190

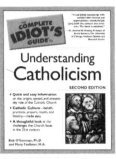
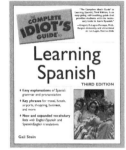
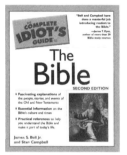

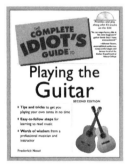